Contents

The Contributors

RICHARD BROWN
is Senior Lecturer in Sociology at the University of Durham.
He previously lectured at Leicester University. He is a joint
author of *The Sociology of Industry*, and of papers in industrial
sociology. He is currently completing a research project on
shipbuilding on Tyneside.

JOHN CHILD
is Senior Research Officer at the London Graduate School of
Business Studies. He has worked in the engineering industry
and at the University of Aston in Birmingham. He is author of
*British Management Thought, The Business Enterprise in Modern
Industrial Society and* joint author of *The Sociology of Industry*.

W. W. DANIEL
is Senior Research Associate at P.E.P. (Political and Economic
Planning) where he is carrying out studies in plant industrial
relations, redundancy and redeployment. His publications
include *Racial Discrimination in England, Beyond the Wage-
Work Bargain, Strategies for Displaced Employees,* and
Business Education at 18 plus.

J. E. T. ELDRIDGE
is Professor of Sociology at the University of Glasgow. He is
the author of *Industrial Disputes, Sociology and Industrial
Life,* and editor of *Max Weber: the Interpretation of Social
Reality.*

COLIN FLETCHER
is a Fellow of University College, Swansea, where he is carrying
out sociological studies into the concepts of health and illness.
He forsook gang leadership for a life of study, first at Liverpool
University then at the University of Aston, where he researched
into organizational sociology and alienation among junior
managers. He has published papers on a wide range of subjects.

ALAN FOX
is Lecturer in Industrial Sociology at the University of Oxford.
He left school at 14 and later in life studied at Ruskin, Exeter
and Nuffield Colleges, Oxford. He is author of *A History of
the National Union of Boot and Shoe Operatives, Industrial*

Sociology and Industrial Relations, and *A Sociology of Work in Industry*.

JILL JONES
researches at the University of London Goldsmiths' College. She graduated in sociology at the University of Essex. Until 1971 she was Sociology Research Officer for the N.E. Metropolitan Regional Hospital Board, doing research into consultant/G.P. relationships.

ROGER MANSFIELD
is Senior Research Officer at the London Graduate School of Business Studies. He was a Teaching Fellow at the University of Cambridge and a Visiting Faculty Member at Yale University. He has published papers on the subject of occupational choice and careers.

DAVID SILVERMAN
is Senior Lecturer in Sociology at the University of London Goldsmiths' College. He has taught at the London School of Economics and the University of California, Los Angeles. He is researching within a large local government authority and is a prominent contributor to current developments in sociological research methodology. He is author of *The Theory of Organizations*.

Introduction

Industrial sociologists have frequently been criticized by their colleagues for failing to make a sufficient contribution either to the development of sociological theory and method, or to the awareness of policy problems within modern industrial societies. Many industrial sociologists have indeed been prepared to work within a conservative theoretical tradition which leans heavily towards a structuralist frame of analysis and towards a positivistic mode of explanation. Equally, the contribution of some sociologists, working in the fields of work and organization, to elucidating the availability of social policy options has been restricted through their normative or *de facto* identification with the definition of problems by managerial or institutional sponsors.

An awareness of such problems has informed many of the contributions to the British Sociological Association's Industrial Sociology Section and much of the discussion at its meetings. The purpose of this new series of published volumes is to make available to a wider audience, of students and interested members of the public in addition to academic professionals, the recent research and analysis of those who have contributed to the Section. All the authors contained within this first volume have recently presented papers to the Section, and most of the content of the book comprises a further development of those original contributions.

One intention of this series is to make available to the reader work of wide interest which, however, would not otherwise enter into the general circulation of sociological publication for some while. Another criterion for inviting contributions has been the inclusion of material which represents a presently active focus of interest. The title 'industrial studies' implies a broader definition of the field than does a traditional view of industrial sociology, and this reflects the policy followed by the Industrial Sociology Section. Substantively, the Section's activities have extended to organizational analysis, industrial development, the labour movement, social mobility, and ideology. There have been contributions from psychologists and economists as well as from sociologists. Theoretically, however, the issues raised have been central to the sociological tradition of Marx and Weber. They have brought members face to face with methodological problems which are, fundamentally, shared by all the social sciences—those concerning the meaning of human and social phenomena and their relevance to resolving questions of moment in industrial and industrializing societies.

Each termly programme of meetings held by the Section has been organized around one central theme. This has made it possible to envisage a periodic publication of collected papers which have a degree of thematic unity. The genesis of the present volume lay in a term of meetings on the subject of theoretical and methodological problems within the field of industrial and organizational studies.

All the papers in this book are concerned with the adequacy of currently available modes of explanation. Brown and Daniel both examine the concept of 'orientation to work' and the social action frame of reference in the analysis of industrial attitudes and behaviour. Referring to their own research and that of others, they raise important questions concerning the construction of the subjective reality of work-related phenomena. Silverman and Jones in their paper illustrate a methodology for distinguishing different constructions of reality offered by the participants in what might appear to be a relatively matter-of-fact social process. This is the selection of graduate entrants into careers within a large public authority. Mansfield examines available studies, including his own work, on careers within organizations. He analyses the pursuit of personal strategies aimed at fulfilling the individual's own priorities within an organizational structure of institutionalized requirements which may severely inhibit the attainment of personal objectives.

The conflict between the goals of individuals and groups working in organizations and the formalized purposes of organizational controllers has been a major focus of interest throughout the history of sociological study. This conflict and the manner in which it assumes a political and social significance beyond the confines of industry itself, lends the subject of this book its social relevance. The last four contributions are more explicitly concerned with this question, which fundamentally is one of the prevailing and alternative forms of social order. Fletcher, who has carried out intensive research into the world of managers within a large electronics organization, highlights the vulnerability of the middle manager both in terms of his present-day insecurity and of the long-term viability of his role. The end of management, at least as we know it, could be a process of major social consequence. Eldridge takes a broader look at conflict in industry and examines the paradigms which have been used by sociologists to explain the incidence and patterns of industrial conflict in its various forms. He identifies a major sociological problem as being to recognize different expressions of industrial conflict and to tease out their significance in respect of the social order which forms their context. Fox's paper is concerned with the ideological interpretations offered for industrial conflict and relations. In particular, he gives a critical appraisal of pluralist ideology which, he concludes, provides a misleading picture of the realities of social power and serves those who wish to strengthen our acceptance of the *status quo*. Child is also concerned with the way in which a conventional wisdom, in this case on the design of organization, may obscure our awareness of the possibilities for pursuing alternative modes of social organization. A move from the *status quo* may not resolve the problems emanating from conflict in industry and society, but it may demonstrate some ways in which conflicting interests may each be better served.

This volume is a collection of individual contributions and not a textbook. The contributors offer what they have written as scholars in their own right, and there has been a minimum of editorial intervention. We would all like to thank the British Sociological Association, and Professor Tom Bottomore in particular, for the encouragement they have given to what we hope may be a long-continuing venture. Perhaps most of all, we are indebted to the members of the BSA Industrial Sociology Section whose contributions to this volume are beyond estimation. The preparation of the book for publication owes a great deal to the secretarial efficiency of Mrs. Kay Schraer.

The Search for Explanation

1 Sources of Objectives in Work and Employment[1]

RICHARD BROWN

'There are, then, two sociologies: a sociology of social system and a sociology of social action. They are grounded in the diametrically opposed concerns with two central problems, those of order and control. And, at every level, they are in conflict. They posit antithetical views of human nature, of society and of the relationship between the social and the individual. The first asserts the paramount necessity, for societal and individual well-being, of external constraint; hence the notion of a social system ontologically and methodologically prior to its participants. The key notion of the second is that of autonomous man, able to realize his full potential and to create a truly human social order only when freed from external constraint. Society is thus the creation of its members; the product of their construction of meaning, and of the action and relationships through which they attempt to impose that meaning on their historical situations.

In summary, one views action as the derivative of system, whilst the other views system as the derivative of action. And the contention here is that sociology has developed on the basis of the conflict between them.' (Alan Dawe, 1970)

Ten years ago the statement that there are two sociologies would probably have been taken to refer to 'functionalism' on the one hand and 'conflict theory' on the other. Ten years ago too a great deal of work in industrial sociology would have appeared unconcerned with such theoretical matters, dealing with apparently straightforward problems in an unproblematic

[1] An earlier version of this paper was presented to the Industrial Sociology Seminar at the University of Durham in October 1971. I am grateful to members of the Seminar for their comments.

way. Now, however, the social system/social action dichotomy – and some related and equally fundamental differences in approach – are on the centre of the stage in sociology generally; and the social action approach has been introduced into industrial sociology, at least in Britain, in a way which has made those in the field much more aware of the theoretical assumptions and presuppositions underlying their work. The revival of interest in this great tradition in sociology is to be welcomed, as is the increasing theoretical awareness of industrial sociologists.

THE ACTION APPROACH AND 'ORIENTATIONS TO WORK'

It is possible to argue that a good deal of earlier work in industrial sociology adopted, however implicitly, an action approach. Silverman (1968 and 1970), for example, imputes such an approach to Cunnison (1965) and Gouldner (1955). The most influential statement of it, however, was probably by Goldthorpe (1965 and 1966) in his account of the attitudes and behaviour of car assembly workers, repeated and elaborated in the first of *The Affluent Worker* volumes (Goldthorpe *et al.*, 1968). What was advocated here was that the starting point for analysis should be 'with the ordering of wants and expectations relative to work, and with the meaning thus given to work' and that a 'key explanatory notion' was 'the definition of work and of the work situation' of the workers studied (Goldthorpe 1966: p. 240). These workers' orientation to their work and employment was to be regarded as 'a crucial *independent* variable relative to what occurs in the work situation' so that to account for it involved investigating non-work aspects of the social lives of the workers concerned.

The introduction of the 'social action' perspective in these terms was seen as meeting two problems. On the one hand it enabled an explanation to be offered for the otherwise 'deviant' *empirical* findings made by Goldthorpe and his colleagues about the attitudes and behaviour of men on the assembly line. Such workers had previously been regarded as the classic case of the alienated worker, and a great many, mostly American, studies had documented their dissatisfactions and frustrations (e.g. Walker and Guest 1952, Chinoy 1955). The satisfaction

with their employer and employment situation, though not
with their tasks, shown by the Luton assemblers could only
be explained, it was argued, by taking into account these
workers' prior instrumental orientations to work. They were
prepared to accept the deprivations of their employment in
return for relatively high pay because this was their main
objective. More generally, the similarities of attitudes and
behaviour among the sample of affluent workers as a whole,
who were employed in three very different technological
environments, were seen as needing explanation in terms of
similar prior orientations to work. Such an approach was given
further support by the discovery that many of the differences
in attitudes and behaviour within the sample, where they did
exist, were not those which might have been predicted in the
light of a 'technological implications approach' (Goldthorpe
et al. 1968: pp. 52, 72–3, 180–6).

On the other hand, an 'action perspective' was seen as
overcoming the deficiencies inherent in existing *theoretical* viewpoints, especially the two most influential: the 'human relations
approach', and the 'technological implications approach'. The
former was criticized for stopping analytically 'at the factory
gates' and as increasingly defining the worker as merely reacting
to the supervisory styles and the general human relations
atmosphere of the enterprise. The latter was attacked as
essentially functionalist, seeing worker attitudes and behaviour
as role determined and the work role structure of an enterprise
as determined, or at least narrowly constrained, by its technology. In neither approach were the worker's own objectives
and definition of his situation regarded as important as independent variables. In both of them there was, explicit or
implicit, reference to basic 'human needs' in terms of which
workers could be expected to react to their work situation (see
Goldthorpe *et al.* 1968: pp. 178–80).

?ES OF ORIENTATION TO WORK

Advocates of an action approach suggest that analysis should
begin with the orientations to work of the actors concerned,
with the way in which workers order their wants and expectations relative to their employment, with the meaning work has
for them. Such orientations, wants, expectations, and meanings

are of importance because they are not to be seen as varying randomly from individual to individual but as being socially shared. It is possible therefore to develop 'ideal types' of orientations to work which can then be used to explain different patterns of job choice, job satisfaction, attachment to the employing organization and so on.

In *The Affluent Worker* study, three types of orientation to work are distinguished: instrumental, bureaucratic, and solidaristic; a fourth (professional) is mentioned, though it is stressed that all work activity in industrial society tends to have a basic instrumental component so that the other three might best be seen as deviations from this. Workers with an instrumental orientation (such as the Luton affluent workers) see work almost exclusively as a means of acquiring an income necessary to support a valued way of life, have a calculative relationship to the employing organization, are not involved in their jobs, and can be expected to divide work sharply from 'non-work'. A bureaucratic orientation involves service to an organization in return for a career, positive involvement in work and with the organization, and no sharp dichotomy of work and non-work. Workers with a solidaristic orientation are seen as experiencing work as a group activity which may lead to either identification with the firm, or with the work group as a source of power against the employer; social relationships and shared activities at work are found rewarding, and work relationships in some cases form the basis of occupational communities outside work (Goldthorpe *et al.* 1968: pp. 37–42).

Initially Ingham (1967) elaborated on one of these types. He used the term 'instrumental' in much the same way as Goldthorpe and his colleagues, but renamed the solidaristic orientation 'instrumental/expressive'. He then developed the distinction in the earlier account between a 'positive' orientation to the employing organization and 'moral' involvement in it ('instrumental/expressive (positive)'), and a 'negative' orientation to the employing organization and 'alienative' involvement in it ('instrumental/expressive (negative)'). (These three types were renamed by Silverman (1970: p. 179) 'Economic Man', 'Hawthorne Man', and 'Marxian Man'.) Subsequently Ingham (1970) has argued that a distinction can be made between orientations in terms of two variables – the importance attached to economic and to non-economic rewards – which give four basic types in terms of rewards expected: (i) high economic; high non-economic, (ii) high economic; low non-economic, (iii) low economic; low non-economic, and (iv) low economic; high non-economic. As available job opportunities tended to offer either economic rewards or non-economic rewards but not both, however, his own analysis concentrated on the contrast between type (ii) and type (iv), which he termed respectively 'economistic-instrumental' and 'non-economistic-expressive'. This was because he argued 'it is possible for economism – that is sensitivity to wage issues and the pursuit of high earnings – and instrumentalism to vary independently. For example, workers of the kind referred to by type (iii) above are non-economistic and instrumental. . . . In other words, instru-mentalism may be used to describe the definition of work as a means to an end but it does not necessarily imply anything about what these ends are' (Ingham 1970: p. 50).

The term 'economism' is derived from Touraine and Ragazzi's (1961) study of workers from agricultural backgrounds. These workers, who had definite 'projects' of achieving upward social mobility, tended to be interested predominantly in the economic rewards from their work and to interpret their social situation generally in such terms. The four-fold distinction made by Ingham may prove useful, even though it was not of direct relevance in his own research. Indeed, it is more likely to do so in so far as it cannot be assumed that available job oppor-tunities will not offer both economic and non-economic rewards. Thus in the conditions of the local labour market for manual workers on Tyneside, seeking employment as a skilled shipbuilding worker might well be the result of a realistic and realizable desire for both types of reward.

As might be expected, although Ingham's work represents a development of Goldthorpe and his colleagues' initial typology, it is compatible with it. Rather different distinctions have been made by others. In studying scientists, for example, Cotgrove and Box (1966 and 1970) (their work parallels research in the USA) have considered the extent to which scientists value autonomy, personal commitment, and disciplinary communism, and have formulated three types of orientation: the public scientist who values all three, the private scientist who is not concerned with the public world of science (disciplinary communism), and the instrumental or organizational scientist who merely uses his knowledge and skills for career purposes. These distinctions are themselves a welcome development of the familiar 'cosmopolitan-local' dichotomy, which has been widely applied and not only or primarily with reference to work and employment (e.g. Merton 1957).

Fox (1971) makes some further points. He distinguishes between 'substantive' orientations to work (desire for more money, or security, or more challenging work) and 'procedural' orientations (the desire to play some part in decision-making procedures in the organization). These latter may be either instrumental (as a means to better decisions for himself) or terminal (as a value in itself). It is certainly useful to draw attention to the importance of orientations to decision-making procedures, though there must be some doubt as to whether the substantive/procedural dichotomy (which is central to Flanders's analysis of industrial relations systems (1970: pp. 83–103 especially)) can always be usefully applied.

APPLICATIONS OF THE TYPOLOGIES

There are therefore a considerable variety of typologies of orientations to work in terms of which ideal typical patterns of ends and objectives in work can be expressed. The value of the approach, however, depends on how far it can be utilized to explain particular patterns of action. A number of relatively successful examples can be quoted.

With regard to job choice and attachment to the organization, for example, Goldthorpe and his colleagues were able to show, how, in many cases, the instrumentally oriented affluent workers had left employment in jobs which they preferred in terms of their tasks in order to take employment giving them the highest possible economic rewards. They were stable in such employment, despite its acknowledged tedium, because it met their expectations. Ingham similarly found that in Bradford instrumentally oriented workers (economistic-instrumental) choose to work in large bureaucratic high wage plants, but workers with a non-economistic-expressive orientation sought work in small plants which provided lower pay but both more satisfying social relations and more intrinsically rewarding jobs. In both cases labour stability was high, despite the large size of plant for the first group. Cotgrove and Box explained the job choices of scientists in terms of their orientations – the public (intrinsic) type seeking the opportunity to do basic research in university or government laboratories, rather than in industry.

Goldthorpe and his colleagues also used the instrumental orientation of the Luton affluent workers to account for their satisfaction with their employer, their attitude towards the trade union, and level and type of participation in its activities, and their lack of involvement in social relations with fellow workers outside work. Cotgrove and Box were able to show a relationship between scientists' orientations, their autonomy within the organization, and both their level of satisfaction and their productivity in terms of publications; public scientists were more likely to experience strains if the organization imposed constraints on their performance as scientists, and were the most likely to publish, especially if given a higher level of 'organizational' freedom (1970: pp. 110, 158–9). In a study of computer programmers, Sheldrake (1971) distinguished 'technical' and 'organizational' orientations to work and related these to differences in job performance and attitudes towards Bureau policy.

In earlier studies, without an explicit action perspective, variations in 'motivation', 'goals', or 'orientations' have been seen as more or less important in explaining attitudes and behaviour. In considering reactions to technical change (the introduction of computers), for example, Mumford and Banks (1967: pp. 202–6 especially) point to the need to take into account the extent to which clerks have work-centred goals, expecially the expectation of a career, which might be adversely affected. This was found to be more likely to be the case for men than women; differences in the 'motivations' of men and women, particularly married women, workers have been used to account for differences in attitudes and behaviour at work, for example unwillingness among married women to accept promotion to supervisory positions (Jephcott *et al.* 1962: pp. 78–83; Brown *et al.* 1964). In another study deviant reactions to incentive payment systems (i.e. willingness to 'rate bust') have been explained in terms of the different values of workers from rural and urban backgrounds (Collins *et al.* 1946). In a particularly careful attempt to relate levels of job satisfaction to the different characteristics of tasks and jobs, it was found necessary to explain variations in satisfaction in terms of the different expectations of town and big city workers (the former looking for intrinsically rewarding tasks, responsibility, and autonomy, whilst the latter preferred a favourable effort bargain on undemanding jobs) (Turner and Lawrence 1965). There is therefore no shortage, even in studies within different theoretical frameworks, of examples of the importance of considering the objectives of the actor in any explanation of social action and social relations.

SOURCES OF ORIENTATIONS TO WORK

The question of job choice is crucial for a further stage in the 'action approach' developed by Goldthorpe and his colleagues and by Ingham particularly; for they argue that orientations to work must be seen as a variable independent, at least in part, of the work situation. If it can be shown that workers choose employment in terms of their prior orientations, then the origin of such orientations must be sought outside the workplace. Both writers emphasize the importance of social and geographical mobility as likely to lead to an instrumental orientation to work, and in addition there is some evidence from *The Affluent Worker* study that that stage in the life cycle may also be of relevance. The homogeneity of orientations to work found in any category is seen, then, as due to choice of employment in terms of such externally determined objectives and priorities in a situation of relatively full employment (Goldthorpe 1965: p. 10). Though the mechanisms are different Cotgrove and Box's discussions (1970: pp. 57–62) of social marginality and social isolation as leading to a commitment to science provides an interesting parallel to the explanation of an instrumental orientation to work as a response to downward social mobility; in both cases problems of personal identity may be involved.

Others have suggested that both work and non-work factors may be relevant. Indeed Ingham (1970: p. 137) indicates that expectations with respect to non-economic rewards are likely to develop gradually and to vary with the type of industrial experience of the worker. Fox discusses the experience of work itself, board cultural values and ideologies, the values of sub-cultures and certain characteristics of modern industrial consumer-oriented society as determining 'work philosophies', and sees them as transmitted by family, community and work groups. Indeed with regard to sub-cultural influences on manual workers he writes: 'it is clear, then, that a substantial component of the subculture within which the individual is socialised is itself a product distilled from generations of experience in a particular type of work situation' (1971: p. 16).

The most comprehensive account available of the sources of orientations to work among manual workers is the implicit one in the discussion of variations in 'images of society', but it can be extracted, I think, without too much distortion of the argument. Bott (1957) and others have described the varied images of society to be found among different groups in society and have attempted to relate them to the immediate social milieu of the actors themselves. Lockwood (1966) developed this viewpoint and argued that we can distinguish three different types of workers and can infer that their different work and community relationships may generate very different forms of social consciousness.

Thus it is suggested that 'traditional proletarian' workers have a high degree of job involvement and strong attachments to primary work groups; they tend to be concentrated in relatively isolated solidary communities and to develop a dichotomous or two-valued power model of the class structure. By implication such workers would have an 'instrumental-expressive (negative)' orientation to work, and seek work giving them relatively high pay, intrinsically worthwhile jobs and the opportunity to develop and maintain strong ties with their fellow workers; their 'procedural' orientation might be one which challenged managerial legitimacy and favoured independent action in industrial relations (in the sense meant by the CIR Report on Shipbuilding and shiprepairing (1971: pp. 102–8)).

'Traditional deferential' workers on the other hand live in heterogeneous communities and work in smaller establishments where they have face-to-face relationships with paternalistic bosses; their class imagery can be expected to be a prestige or hierarchical model, and their orientation to work 'instrumental-expressive (positive)', with few claims to have any say in decision making at work.

In contrast the 'privatized' worker is seen as living on new housing estates where relationships are 'window-to-window', and as working in large modern industrial plants. Their model of the class structure is described as pecuniary, distinguishing individuals in terms of incomes and possessions, and seeing classes as categories rather than groups. Work is a necessary evil, a means to an end; their orientation to work is narrowly instrumental, with no emphasis on social relations or rewarding tasks, and the attitude to procedures is also calculative.

An outline of the position of the middle class (administrative, managerial, technical and professional employees) completes Lockwood's account. They are expected to hold a hierarchical model of society because of their own position in career hierarchies in work and of their residence in socially mixed communities with interactional status systems. Presumably such workers would have 'instrumental-expressive (positive)' orientations to work, but would differ from traditional deferential workers in placing more emphasis on a good career, on intrinsically rewarding and responsible work, and on some say in decision making in the organization as an end in itself.

THE NOTION OF 'ORIENTATION TO WORK'

A critique of this increasingly influential approach to industrial sociological problems can be directed either to the concept of an orientation to work as such, when used as an 'independent' or 'intervening' variable in analysis, and/or to the sources of such differing orientations, and consequently their significance. I would like to comment on each set of problems in turn.

In the first place, it is generally admitted, by proponents and critics of an 'action approach' alike, that it is difficult to determine a worker's or a workforce's orientations to work, their aims and objectives in employment. Especially in so far as orientations to work are constructs of the investigator it is crucial to know how closely they reflect the actual definitions of the situation of the actors. Most investigations have relied on written questionnaire and/or interview data (in some cases supplemented by participant observation). Though each of these means can provide some indication of goals and priorities, they all have limitations.

Apart from the question of research techniques, which it would be inappropriate to discuss in more detail here, there are perhaps more fundamental problems. How far does any worker's expression of his objectives in work merely reflect the meanings culturally available to him and considered appropriate as a reply to questions, for example about priorities in choosing a job? That such considerations have some influence was indicated by the writer's experience interviewing married women workers in the investigation referred to above: initial reactions were generally that 'of course' the respondent came to work 'for the money'; in the course of fairly unstructured interviews it often became apparent that a job was desired not only for the financial rewards, but also for a variety of other reasons, some of which were felt to be less culturally acceptable, or indeed had not necessarily been clearly articulated before. We can agree with proponents of an 'action approach' that the meaning of work for these workers could only be understood in terms of their total, work and non-work, situation; but for married women especially this situation is one of conflicting values and expectations in which those who work are likely to consider that only certain sorts of 'reasons' will be accepted as legitimating their action. As a result other objectives may be lost sight of, even perhaps by the actors themselves.

Similarly, except in certain contexts, asking about an actor's orientation to work implies that he makes a fairly continuous and conscious evaluation of priorities. This may be presumed to take place as a result of major events, in domestic or work life, such as marriage or the threat of redundancy; for example, such a change in the meaning of work can be inferred from Millward's discussion of 'going on board' among young women workers (1968); but can it be assumed to be the case at all times? Does any such evaluation necessarily result in a rational and coherent set of objectives? Or is there likely to be some inconsistency, for example, between limited short-term goals and a longer term strategy? How far do workers have clear sets of objectives – in their lives as a whole (the 'projects' Goldthorpe and colleagues refer to (1968: p. 116)) – or in their approach to work and employment?

Those who have made most use of the notion of 'orientations to work' do give fairly positive answers to these sorts of questions. Indeed, in contrast to some writers, they have emphasized that their respondents' behaviour in the labour market should be seen as the result of rational and reasonably well informed choices to achieve clear objectives (e.g. Ingham 1970:

27

pp. 88–97), though this is seen as dependent on the existence of full employment (Goldthorpe 1972).

This is important because the explanatory value of the notion of 'orientations to work' depends at least in part on their clarity and stability. In *The Affluent Worker* study, for example, it is suggested that such objectives and priorities could be determined relatively unambiguously among their sample of Luton workers, and I do not wish here to question their data or the interpretation of them (for such discussion, see Westergaard 1970). It does seem to me, however, that in this respect as in others, which will be considered below, workers with a narrowly instrumental orientation are atypical, and to generalize the explanatory model appropriate for them to other industrial situations may be very misleading. The crucial point about a 'single-stranded' instrumental orientation to work is that it is clear; no problems arise of priorities, or of incompatible objectives. For workers with more complex orientations to work, who are seeking not only economic rewards, such as high wages or security, but also various intrinsic or social rewards such as interesting work, autonomy on the job, or good workmates the question of priorities is bound to arise. In assessing a possible job or expressing one's satisfaction or dissatisfaction in an existing job a variety of incommensurable factors have to be combined and evaluated in making a choice or response. For those who want a number of things out of their employment it may not be entirely clear, even to the actors themselves, to which they attach the greatest importance. They may want what are likely to prove empirically to be incompatible ends – interesting work, or high pay, for example, without responsibility.

If this is so then the question of the *context* of choice or of action becomes crucial. This I take to be one of the main points made by Daniel in his criticism of Goldthorpe, where he states 'all research on occupational motivation requires that very sharp distinctions be drawn between the three areas of job choice, intrinsic job satisfaction, and job quitting' (1969a: p. 367). An example of the importance of context can be taken from Daniel's own work on productivity bargaining and automation (see Chapter 2 below and Daniel 1969b and 1971). In the bargaining situation the emphasis was all on pay and similar factors, which are seen as legitimate topics for negotiation; in the work situation subsequently, characteristics of the

job itself are what influenced workers' satisfaction or dissatisfaction, while levels of pay were accepted, more or less, as
a given.

Goldthorpe has argued, however, that this sort of evidence
does not really represent a criticism of the use of the concept
of orientation to work. Workers who are strongly instrumentally
oriented are not *'ipso facto* entirely desensitized to all deprivations or satisfactions in work that are of an intrinsic kind',
but are likely to be actively interested in 'all matters relating
to the effort bargain and to the conditions of work within the
particular shops and plants in which they are employed'.
What would be needed would be evidence of changes in workers'
order of priorities in work as a result of work experience
(Goldthorpe 1972). This is a point we consider below.

Our own work in shipbuilding, with workers who appeared
not to have a purely instrumental orientation to work, would
support the argument for the importance of context of choice
or action. When asked what factors they would consider important in choosing a job, shipbuilding workers emphasized
'good wages' and 'security', and to a lesser extent 'being near
home', 'good conditions', and 'interesting work'; when asked
what they most liked about working in a shipyard the most
frequently mentioned response was a reference to good sociable
relations with workmates, with intrinsically rewarding tasks as
second most frequent mention (Brown *et al.* 1972). The point
here is not that workers' objectives in the work situation have
been shown to be unimportant in explaining their attitudes
and behaviour, but that different objectives may receive
different priority in different circumstances.

As Fox (1971: pp. 22–3) argues, consideration must be given
to the priorities among workers' objectives and aspirations, and
to the way the order of priorities may be influenced by practical
possibilities of realizing them, or what could be termed the
conditions of action as perceived by the actors themselves.
Workers who would like to have interesting jobs with high pay
may give low priority to the former objective because they
realize that they are unlikely to find both; but this order of
priorities may change over the long, or even the short, term.

This brings us to the question of the stability of orientations
to work. Goldthorpe and his colleagues link orientations to
factors like stage in the life cycle, and social and/or geographical

mobility, which means that they will presumably change with changes in these 'determinants'. Further, in the case of a worker with a more complex set of objectives than the ideal typical instrumentally oriented worker, his orientation to work, or his order of priorities among his objectives, is likely to be less stable than that of an instrumental worker, just because it is more complex.

In addition, if the context is important in explaining which objectives come to the surface, changes in context at work as well as in the community, even quite sudden changes, may lead to marked changes in expressed objectives (see Fox 1971: p. 23). Such an argument might be relevant to the vexed question of the Vauxhall strike of 1967, and to the general question of the possibility of 'explosions of consciousness' in such situations. The changed context of a strike situation may lead workers to redefine what are practical possibilities and thus lead them to place emphasis on aspirations to which they had previously given very low priority indeed.

The recent occurrence of 'work-ins' in response to the threat of redundancy may be interpreted as supporting this line of argument. It is unlikely that such action would have been part of the 'procedural' orientation of any substantial number of workers until recently, even as a possible objective in certain circumstances. The relative success of the UCS 'work-in' and the publicity given to it by the mass media, have changed the context for other workers facing a redundancy they see as unnecessary or illegitimate. With reference to the point made earlier these cases also suggest that the media, as well as employees' sub-cultures, are important in contributing to the available stock of meanings of work.

THE SIGNIFICANCE OF 'ORIENTATIONS TO WORK'

The point of the discussions so far has been to suggest that the notion of orientation to work is problematic in some respects and cannot therefore be incorporated in a simple way into any explanatory model of attitudes and action in industry. I want to go on to argue that even if these problems can be overcome its place in any explanatory model must also be questioned.

Here again the clearest position is that adopted by Goldthorpe and his colleagues, though even this is hedged about with reservations which do allow of alternative interpretations (see, for example, the discussion by Silverman 1970: pp. 184–5). As I understand it the argument is that orientations to work are 'at least in part' (but by implication the part is very considerable) determined by the worker's non-work situation, particularly class, community, and family/life-cycle situation. In the case of the instrumentally oriented workers in Luton, and of both kinds of workers in Bradford, homogeneity of orientation in any particular workplace or work group, it is argued, comes about primarily by means of self-selection; in a situation of full employment workers are seen as able to move about rationally seeking a job which best fits their objectives. A similar suggestion is made by Cotgrove and Box, with the reservation that insufficient places in universities and similar settings for all public (intrinsic) scientists means that some will have to take jobs in industry, where further socialization may change needs and values. In these cases of self-selection the direction of the causation is clear, even if it is not seen as totally one way:

social situation⟶orientation to work⟶choice of job, etc.

This sort of 'model' seems to me to be too simple and, even if applicable in the Luton case, no basis for generalization. Indeed Lockwood's discussion of working class images of society does not give such a clear picture. Even with regard to the 'images', in which the sources of variations are being explained, the argument is not clearcut; one is presented with what might be termed 'configurations' of factors (some 'objective' like large plants or socially isolated communities, some 'subjective' like a high degree of job involvement or feelings of fraternity and comradeship) in terms of which certain images of society make sense, but to make sense of which certain images of society may in turn be necessary. The orientations to work which can be derived from the discussion of the three or four types of employee are even more firmly embedded in these configurations, influenced by community *and* work situations but at the same time influencing them (Lockwood 1966).

Here again it seems to me that the example of the worker with an instrumental orientation to work is very atypical and in a way misleading. It is precisely such workers and only such workers who are likely to be uninfluenced by the experience of work; work for them is not a central life interest, is not of significance, and therefore their objectives in employment are unlikely to be changed by the experience of employment. For workers with more complex objectives, with even a limited affective involvement in work, the experience of work is likely to be of significance and it becomes less possible to regard their orientation to work as even largely independent of the work situation. What is more likely is some sort of interactive relationship between objectives and expectations, and the experience of employment. This point appears to be accepted by Goldthorpe and his colleagues and by Ingham for a worker's past experience, but not so readily incorporated into their discussion of attitudes and action in the current job.

There is admittedly little clear evidence of the relative importance of prior orientation to work and socialization at work in determining subsequent attitudes and expectations, though there are a number of considerations of this issue. Some process of secondary socialization, for example, is essential to Baldamus's discussion of the emergence of common effort values (1961: pp. 81–101). In Turner's whole discussion of industry as sub-culture with shared systems of meaning the socialization of the newcomer has an important place (1971: pp. 47–53 especially). As we have seen, in Fox's discussion the experience of work itself is a major determinant of work philosophies. In considering the values and frames of a reference of propertied and non-propertied directors Nichols (1969: p. 119) suggests that 'the process of socialization undergone *within* the corporation is an equally, if not more important factor in the development of the director's value orientation' than pre-corporate socialization. Finally, the orientations of the computer programmers studied by Sheldrake (1971) were seen as resulting partly from differences in careers and work experiences, though in part also from prior differences in education and qualifications.

Some empirical support for the importance of socialization as an influence on orientations to work can be gained from our study of shipbuilding apprentices. Two cohorts of apprentices were asked to complete written questionnaires on three occasions over two and a half years during their training. Although the techniques used (the only ones possible in the circumstances) limited the sort of data which could be obtained, there do appear to be significant changes in attitudes towards work. For example, in one cohort, replies to an open-ended question

Table 1 JOB PRIORITIES

'*What kind of thing do you look for in a good job?*'

Types of factor mentioned:	Years in apprenticeship		
	One	Two	Three and a half
	(Per cent of all mentions – No. of respondents: 38)		
Financial rewards	33	33	25
Interesting work	20	20	34
Good prospects	16	16	3
Security	15	16	12
Good working conditions	11	11	13
Friendly workmates	5	4	8
Good employer	1	1	3
Other factors	—	—	2
	101	101	100
No. of factors mentioned	94	114	103

about the things looked for in a good job showed a shift towards an emphasis on the intrinsic qualities of the job itself and away from factors like pay, security and good prospects (see Table 1). There were changes, too, in attitudes towards promotion. The proportion of the same group who thought they would like a foreman's job fell (see Table 2), perhaps partly because the chances of getting one came to be seen as smaller than at first thought. A less marked decline occurred over the same period in the proportion wanting a manager's job, though in this case very few thought they had any chance of such a job at any stage.

In some contrast to the diminished importance of financial rewards as characteristics of a good job, choices by the same apprentices from a set of statements designed to summarize possible orientations to work tended to change over a one-and-a-half-year period towards stressing the importance of earnings (see Table 3). This choice was one of a number each apprentice was asked to make on each occasion the questionnaire was completed. The choices on other questions suggested that

C

attitudes became more hostile to the firm and its management, and more favourable to the trade unions, during the two and a half years between the first and third questionnaires. Two of

Table 2 APPRENTICES ATTITUDES TO PROMOTION

	Years in apprenticeship		
	One	*Two*	*Three and a half*
	(Per cent of respondents – N: 38)		
'*Would you like to become a foreman?*'			
Very much	17 } 48	28 } 41	18 } 29
Quite a lot	31	13	11
Not much	36 } 50	40 } 59	42 } 71
Not at all	13	19	29
No answer	2	0	0
	———	———	———
	100	100	100
'*What chance do you think you have of becoming a foreman?*'			
Very good chance	2 } 47	2 } 25	3 } 19
Good chance	45	23	16
Not much chance	48 } 53	53 } 68	45 } 79
No chance at all	5	15	34
No answer, don't know	0	6	3
	———	———	———
	100	99	101

the statements which received an increased proportion of choices over this period called for greater worker and union participation in decision making in the firm, which could be taken to reflect a change in these apprentices' procedural orientation. The data for the second cohort, who were questioned a year earlier in their training in each case, show similar though not identical trends.

These are preliminary findings and too much significance cannot be attached to them. They are, however, consistent with the view that orientations to work are influenced by socialization at work, and further that such socialization may be an important influence on the degree of homogeneity of expectations and objectives to be found among the workers in the same organization. Indeed it does seem necessary to consider the relationship between orientation to work and attitudes and behaviour at work as two-way not one-way.

Even if this were not so, however, for many workers their non-work situation is shaped and influenced in many ways by

Table 3 STATEMENTS ABOUT WORK

Statement agreed with *most (one out of three)*	*Years in apprenticeship*	
	Two	*Three and a half*
	(Per cent of respondents – *N:* 38)	
'Having an interesting job and good workmates are the most important things about work'	47	42
'The amount of money you earn is the most important thing about a job'	28	50
'Good bosses and a satisfying job are the most important things about work'	21	8
No answer	4	
	100	100

the industry they work in (again see Fox's discussion). This may not be true for the privatized worker on the new housing estate but in older and/or more mixed areas industry and 'community' are closely related. This is seen most clearly in traditional working class localities with one or two dominant industries, for example mining villages, shipbuilding towns, ports, and so on. In the case of shipbuilding, for example, the majority of the industry's labour force, including new entrants, come from localities where shipbuilding has been a dominant industry for generations. Knowledge and experience of shipbuilding, and of the tasks, conditions, and social relations of shipbuilding workers are widespread in these 'communities'. Work and non-work are not clearly separate 'worlds'. Even if orientations to work were to be treated as derived from family and community situation, that situation has in many ways been shaped and influenced by the work situation (Brown and Brannen 1970). One cannot therefore treat 'the subjective dispositions of the actors' as 'independent variables relative to the work situation'.

In addition to these points about the sources of orientations to work, there is the question of the source of the homogeneity of orientations to work in a particular population already referred to above. In this case too, as Goldthorpe (1972) has also argued, the mechanism of self-selection which applied in Luton cannot be generalized unreservedly. Homogeneity of orientation among any group of shipbuilding workers, for example, in so far as it did not come about by means of socialization in the work situation, should probably be attributed to socialization in the 'community'; the social origins of such workers are in important respects more homogeneous, and their opportunities for job choice much more restricted, than in the case of the Luton affluent workers. This is presumably the case in many traditional industries.

CONCLUSION

It has not been my intention to criticize the use of a 'social action approach' as such in industrial (or any other sort of) sociology, nor to suggest that 'orientations to work' are unimportant. I do consider, however, that some of the emphasis which has been placed on workers' objectives and priorities in entering employment as determinants of attitudes and behaviour has been misplaced. This emphasis has been possible because the notion itself has been regarded as relatively unproblematic and it has been incorporated in a fairly simple explanatory model. Once the notion itself is questioned, and its relationship to other factors seen as reciprocal rather than one-way, the sources of variations in orientations to work, and the significance of such variations, become more difficult to determine.

What is now needed is not an abandonment of the 'action approach', but a development of it. This should retain the emphasis on the importance of the actors' own definitions of the situation, but be prepared to explore the complex problems involved in investigating systems of meaning, and the ways in which they are created, sustained and changed. Both Silverman (1970) and Turner (1971) have indicated some of the directions necessary and research problems involved. Investigations of actors' 'orientations' may be usefully complemented perhaps by consideration of their 'identities', overlapping and/or conflicting, in work and non-work contexts.

Whatever the directions taken, it is to be hoped that research will not at the same time lose sight of the distributions of resources, of power and authority, and of the physical and technological conditions in industry, which form some of the more intractable 'conditions of action' for those pursuing their individual and/or shared objectives in work. Our discussion has also indicated that the industrial sociologist's frame of reference must be a wide one, broad enough for example to include consideration of the ways in which most employees' objectives in work come to be ones which are not too disruptive of the existing industrial order.

REFERENCES

BALDAMUS, W. 1961. *Efficiency and effort*, London: Tavistock.

BOTT, E. 1957. *Family and social network*, London: Tavistock.

BROWN, R. and BRANNEN, P. 1970 'Social relations and social perspectives amongst shipbuilding workers – a preliminary statement', *Sociology*, 4, 71–84, 197–211.

BROWN, R., BRANNEN, P., COUSINS, J. M., SAMPHIER, M. L. 1972. 'The contours of solidarity – social stratification and industrial relations in shipbuilding', *British Journal of Industrial Relations*, 10, 12-41.

BROWN, R. K., KIRBY, J. M., TAYLOR, K. F. 1964. 'The employment of married women and the supervisory role', *British Journal of Industrial Relations*, 2, 23–41.

CHINOY, E. 1955. *Automobile workers and the American Dream*, New York: Random House.

COLLINS, O., DALTON, M., ROY, D. 1946. 'Restriction of output and social cleavage in industry', *Applied Anthropology*, 5, 1–14.

COMMISSION ON INDUSTRIAL RELATIONS, 1971. *Shipbuilding and ship-repairing*, Report no. 22, Cmnd. 4756, London: HMSO.

COTGROVE, S. and BOX, S. 1966. 'Scientific identity, occupational selection and role strain', *British Journal of Sociology*, 17, 20-8.

COTGROVE, S. and BOX, S. 1970. *Science, industry and society*, London: Allen and Unwin.

CUNNISON, S. 1965. *Wages and work allocation*, London: Tavistock.

DANIEL, W. W. 1969a. 'Industrial behaviour and orientation to work – a critique,' *Journal of Management Studies*, 6, 366–75.

DANIEL, W. W. 1969b. 'Automation and the quality of work', *New Society*, 29th May, 833–6.

DANIEL, W. W. 1971. 'Productivity bargaining and orientation to work – a rejoinder to Goldthorpe', *Journal of Management Studies*, 8, 329–35.

DAWE, A. 1970. 'The two sociologies', *British Journal of Sociology*, 21, 207–18.

FLANDERS, A. 1970. *Management and Unions*, London: Faber and Faber.

FOX, A. 1971. *A sociology of work in industry*, London: Collier-Macmillan.

GOLDTHORPE, J. H. 1965. 'Orientation to work and industrial behaviour among assembly line operatives: a contribution towards an action approach in industrial sociology', unpublished paper to Teachers' Section, British Sociological Association.

GOLDTHORPE, J. H. 1966. 'Attitudes and behaviour of car assembly workers: a deviant case and a theoretical critique', *British Journal of Sociology*, 17, 227–44.

GOLDTHORPE, J. H., LOCKWOOD, D., BECHHOFER, F., PLATT, J. 1968. *The affluent worker: industrial attitudes and behaviour*, London: Cambridge University Press.

GOLDTHORPE, J. H. 1970. 'The social action approach to industrial sociology: a reply to Daniel', *Journal of Management Studies*, 7, 199–208.

GOLDTHORPE, J. H. 1972. 'Daniel on orientations to work – a final comment', *Journal of Management Studies*, 9.

GOULDNER, A. W. 1955. *Wildcat strike*, London: Routledge and Kegan Paul.

INGHAM, G. K. 1967. 'Organizational size, orientation to work and industrial behaviour', *Sociology*, 1, 239–58.

INGHAM, G. K. 1970. *Size of industrial organization and worker behaviour*, London: Cambridge University Press.

JEPHCOTT, P., SEEAR, N., SMITH, J. H. 1962. *Married women working*, London: Allen and Unwin.

LOCKWOOD, D. 1966. 'Sources of variation in working class images of society', *Sociological Review*, 14, 249–67.

MERTON, R. K. 1957. 'Patterns of influence: local and cosmopolitan influentials', *Social Theory and Social Structure*, Glencoe, Ill.: Free Press.

MILLWARD, N. 1968. 'Family status and behaviour at work', *Sociological Review*, 16, 149-64.

MUMFORD, E. and BANKS, O. 1967. *The computer and the clerk*, London: Routledge and Kegan Paul.

NICHOLS, T. 1969. *Ownership, control and ideology*, London: Allen and Unwin.

SHELDRAKE, P. F. 1971. 'Orientations towards work among computer programmers', *Sociology*, 5, 209–24.

SILVERMAN, D. 1968. 'Formal organizations or industrial sociology: towards a social action analysis of organizations', *Sociology*, 2, 221–38.

SILVERMAN, D. 1970. *The theory of organizations*, London: Heinemann.

TOURAINE, A. and RAGAZZI, O. 1961. *Ouvriers d'origine agricole*, Paris: Editions du Seuil.

TURNER, A. N. and LAWRENCE, P. R. 1965. *Industrial jobs and the worker*, Cambridge, Mass.: Harvard University Press.

TURNER, B. A. 1971. *Exploring the industrial sub-culture*, London: Macmillan.

WALKER, C. R. and GUEST, R. H. 1952. *Man on the assembly line*, Cambridge, Mass.: Harvard University Press.

WESTERGAARD, J. H. 1970. 'The rediscovery of the cash nexus', *Socialist Register*, London: Merlin.

2 Understanding Employee Behaviour in its Context: Illustrations from Productivity Bargaining

W. W. DANIEL

In this chapter I propose to challenge two distinct and apparently contradictory models of the relationship between the worker and the industrial enterprise. In doing so I shall present certain findings of my own which I suggest provide a framework that not only goes some way to reconciling these two different approaches but also points the way to a more satisfactory model for understanding and explaining industrial behaviour.

The two earlier approaches on explanation of the worker's responses to the organization that I want initially to examine are first the 'psychologically universalistic' or more loosely the 'human relations' theory, and secondly 'action theory' or the approach via 'orientation to work'.

By the 'psychological universalistic' approach I mean that adopted by American social psychologists or psychologists such as Argyris, Likert, Blake, McGregor, and Herzberg. For the purpose of this chapter some of the basic assumptions of this school can best be illustrated by a brief resumé of the essential conclusions of McGregor and Herzberg.

Fundamentally McGregor's answer to an understanding of the worker's response to the work situation is derived from Maslow's familiar theory of the need hierarchy (McGregor 1960, Maslow 1954). This postulates that man is a wanting animal with an ascending order of needs. As one is satisfied so it ceases to operate as a need and his demands rise a scale higher. At the bottom of the hierarchy are the physiological needs; the need for food, security, and shelter. Then follow the social needs; the need for group acceptance, membership, and belonging. Ultimately come the ego needs; the need for self expression, the need to use and develop one's abilities, and to create, as Argyris puts it, the need for 'self-actualization', to find and express oneself. In McGregor's popularization of this theory in relation to modern industrial society he argues that business organizations have largely satisfied all the lower order needs. Industrial man now has all the food, shelter, and security he needs. His social needs are largely satisfied too. Being satiated these now cease to motivate but the hunger that remains unsatisfied is the hunger for self-expression and creativity. This is what the worker is now really interested in and this is what industry should be giving him if it wants him to be motivated and involved. Moreover the beauty of the ego needs are that unlike their lower order fellows they are never satisfied. The finding and expression of self, the development of abilities, the meeting and conquering of challenge are all a lifelong task. For the manager or the managerial ideologist, then, the satisfaction of the ego needs provides a powerful means of integrating the individual with the enterprise.

Herzberg reaches much the same conclusion via a different route (Herzberg *et al.* 1959, Herzberg 1968). His starting point was how to explain variations in the motivation to work and how to increase the motivation to work. His basic assumption was that motivation is generated by the opportunity to satisfy needs in work and that if you want to know what the worker's needs in work are then look at the types of satisfaction he gets out of work. He therefore asked workers to recount to him incidents, events, and occasions in their jobs when they experienced a feeling of satisfaction, when they 'felt good'. And it is this question which is the key to an understanding of all his work.

The answers Herzberg received from his questioning, answers that have been widely replicated by his followers across a wide range and level of worker, suggested that events that give rise to a feeling of satisfaction were of five main types. The first referred to occasions when they had been able to complete some task that represented a personal achievement, they had attained some goal in which they could take pride and satisfaction. The second included occasions when their performance or achievements had been praised, complimented, rewarded, and recognized. The third chief source of gratification occurred when a special degree of trust or responsibility had been vested in them. Occasions when they had been promoted or moved to fresh demands and challenges provided the fourth category. And then there were the occasions when the tasks they were doing were intrinsically interesting and engrossing in themselves. Thus Herzberg concludes that what the worker wants from his job is opportunities for achievement, advancement, responsibility, recognition, and intrinsic interest. These are what provide him with positive satisfaction in the job, and the level of a worker's motivation to work will be closely related to the degree to which the job is rich in such rewards.

Herzberg and McGregor then illustrate the main characteristics of the psychological universalistic approach. They are psychological in that they analyse occupational behaviour in terms of needs, satisfactions, and motivations. They are universalistic in the sense that they suggest that there are certain needs shared by workers of all types and levels and their response to the work situation can be explained in terms of the extent to which these needs are satisfied. If the higher order needs are satisfied then they will be motivated, involved, committed, integrated. If they are not satisfied then all sorts of pathological consequences, from a managerial point of view, will follow, either in terms of active hostility to management, resistance to change, and overt conflict, or in terms of an apathetic opting out reflected in absenteeism, lateness, sickness, and turnover rates.

The second major type of approach, that via 'orientation to work', certainly avoids two of the major weaknesses of this analysis. First it allows for the possibility of variations between different types and levels of worker and more importantly for the possibility of intrinsic conflict between the goals of workers and the enterprise. Its starting point is that industrial behaviour and the response of the worker to the work situation can be understood only in relation to the expectations that the worker brings to the enterprise as a result of his social experience and relationships outside work. They key then to an understanding of the worker's relationship to the organization is his orientation to work. This approach has been brought to prominence in Britain by the studies of John Goldthorpe and his colleagues in Luton (Goldthorpe *et al.* 1968). The study was chiefly concerned with explaining the behaviour of motor car assembly line workers at the Vauxhall plant. Here is a job whose characteristics are perhaps better and more generally known than any in the labour market. It epitomizes the dehumanization of work through fragmentation and mechanization at the same time as having the reputation of providing very high earnings for semi-skilled workers.

Goldthorpe found that his assemblers had sought the job voluntarily, even eagerly. They had often given up work richer in interest, status, responsibility, and the opportunity to use their skills and abilities in order to take the job. Equally they were often aware of alternative jobs richer in intrinsic rewards that were available to them but they preferred to stay where they were. And the reason why they had sought the job, the reason why they had given up more interesting and satisfying jobs to take it, the reason why they stayed when they could easily find a more interesting and satisfying job, was that they attached an overwhelmingly high order of priority to money. What they sought chiefly from a job was high earnings. They defined their place of work as primarily a source of income and they were prepared to forgo all other types of rewards in order to maximize earnings. They were prepared to endure the deprivation, the pressure, the mindless repetitiveness of the assembly line for the high earnings. They were prepared to give a very high rating of satisfaction with the job and their employer, despite the quality of the work they did, because the job and their employer gave them what they wanted: high earnings. Vauxhall's (at that time) record of comparative industrial peace could be explained by this congruence between what they wanted from a job and what it gave. Their social experience and social circumstances were such that they had an 'instrumental orientation to work': they defined work as a means to an end, a source of rewards to be enjoyed outside work, rather than an end in itself, a source of interest, satisfaction, and intrinsic rewards in its own right. Thus they did not want to be encouraged, praised, or treated with respect, as an individual, by their supervisors. They were quite happy as long as he left them alone. They did not want the acceptance, and membership of work groups and approval of workmates, and they certainly did not want anything to do with workmates

42

outside work. Their instrumental orientation to work pervaded their response to all aspects of the work situation: the content of the work, relationships with supervisors, relationships with workmates, and evaluation of the firm and union.

Thus Goldthorpe's application of the action framework consists of establishing the priorities that the worker brings to the organization as a result of his socialization outside work. The assumption he works upon is that these priorities are best determined by looking at what the worker does when it comes to the crunch – when he has to decide between one job and another. He would suggest that if you do you will find that there is plenty happening in the consumer society to keep Maslow's lower order needs fully operative.

Thus these two different approaches provide quite different explanations of the relationship between the worker and the organization. The difference can be dramatized by highlighting the different conclusions that they reach with regard to what it is that the industrial worker is primarily seeking from his job in advanced industrial societies. On the one hand there is the suggestion that the relative affluence of industrial workers has created a situation where they are no longer concerned about increasing their material wealth and have become more concerned with reducing the impoverishment of the work they do, with increasing the opportunity for creativity activity in work, or, in other words, with maximizing intrinsic rather than extrinsic rewards. On the other hand there is the conclusion that the advertising, consumer society upon which the wealth of the advanced industrial societies is based creates an increasing demand for consumer goods which in turn ensures that the economic motive in work remains paramount for a large, and by implication growing, proportion of industrial workers, and that it will remain paramount for the foreseeable future. At the same time, while offering very different diagnoses of the relationship between the worker and the enterprise, these distinct approaches do have two important assumptions in common. The first of these is that the worker does have one overall, ordered, consistent set of needs of priorities in what he wants from a job and that this set of priorities is manifested in all aspects of his occupational behaviour and choices. The second is that an increase in demands along one dimension must be at the expense of those along another.

It is these common assumptions, particularly the idea that there is within each worker or group of workers one single, generalized set of priorities against which all occupational experience is measured, that I want to challenge here. Through an analysis of variations over time in two particular groups of workers' attitudes to a specific kind of organizational change I want to suggest first that there are different sets of priorities that relate to different situations and contexts at work, and secondly that increasing demands among workers along one dimension, such as the demand for increased intrinsic rewards, by no means necessarily means that demands for increased extrinsic rewards will become less. This analysis will further suggest that both the different approaches I have summarized in a very brief and simple way have an element of validity but that they are partial because they derive their account of priorities from just one context. The basis for these conclusions is provided by our findings on workers' evaluations of productivity agreements to which they had been party published in *Beyond the wage-work bargain* (Daniel 1970).[1]

The first agreement that we looked at was a classical productivity deal completed in 1968, of the type pioneered at Fawley by Esso which has subsequently been improved upon and become very common in continuous process plants like oil refining and heavy chemical production (Flanders 1964). As far as the men were concerned the agreement sought a reduction in manning (to be achieved through natural wastage, the management proposals carrying an absolute guarantee of 'no redundancy'); more flexibility among operators so that they would carry out a wider range and level of tasks over a broader span of the process and including some simple maintenance tasks; a simplification of the grading system by substituting five basic grades for the nineteen different rates of pay previously operating; a slight reduction in the seniority rules; and a stable

[1] This was an interim report of a programme of research on collective bargaining for change being undertaken at PEP and financed by the Leverhulme Trust. In this we report two case studies of workers' evaluations of productivity agreements in which they were involved and summaries of the findings are included in this chapter. Details of the nature of the surveys from which they are derived appear on pp. 43, 52, and 68. In our account of the second case, that referring to the ICI nylon spinners WSA application, we were grateful for advance access to the findings of interviews carried out by Clive Vamplew at the works. Subsequently his own account, together with that of his co-authors, has been published in full (Cotgrove *et al.* 1971).

40-hour week with no overtime or additional payments. The men's share of the savings thus brought about included increases in pay ranging from £4 to £6 a week, which represented proportions ranging from 15 to 30 per cent, and conditions of employment more akin to those of staff employees, which included a guaranteed annual salary paid weekly, full pay when sick, and an end to clocking in.

Our interviewing confirmed that relationships in the plant between management and men and between supervisors and men were excellent (Daniel 1969a), reflecting the mutual respect and reciprocity characteristic of those under continuous process technology (Blauner, 1964). Indeed continuous process operators find themselves in perhaps a uniquely favourable work situation for semi-skilled industrial workers. They have a relatively high level of opportunity to develop and use their abilities in learning and operating a sophisticated, integrated, chemical engineering complex. The unique knowledge they develop of the plant and its working gives them a high degree of personal and work group autonomy, and both management and supervision are highly dependent upon this specific and personal knowledge. There is no great pressure under normal working but there is always scope for improvement and refinement and the possibility of the unexpected to provide scope for sustained interest, and moreover this is enhanced by the learning and training process which is a continuous one. Operators feel a high level of responsibility in operating a large, impressive, complex, and potentially explosive plant.

If some of the more naive versions of 'human relations' or job enrichment theories of management were to be believed then one might have expected that the changes would have been welcomed. These theories tend to suggest that creating rewarding, supportive relationships between managers and workers, or enriching jobs with interest, responsibility, and scope for achievement, will make workers more pliable, more receptive to management demands for change and will wean them away from attachments to ideas of collective advancement and defence and consequently away from trade unionism (Nelson Jones 1971). Here was a group of workers already having both good relationships and a relatively very high level of intrinsic job interest, job satisfaction, and feelings of responsibility. The changes sought by the agreement promised, and

45

in the event delivered, even greater intrinsic rewards. And yet they were fiercely resisted, and were pushed through eventually only on the basis of tough bargaining over the men's share of the savings in terms of increases in earnings and fringe benefits in relation to the new skills they would have to learn and the new responsibilities they would have to carry. Even then it would have been more difficult had it not been for the incomes policy operating at the time which ensured that it was only within the framework of the acceptance of changes leading to greater labour productivity that they would have been able to achieve a substantial increase that year.

We interviewed the men nine months after the agreement had been accepted. Specific questioning on the agreement was confined to a very general, 'How do you find this new agreement is working out?' followed up by a series of 'probes' of the type, 'what makes you say that?' (for further details see Daniel 1970: pp. 43 and 52). Answers to these questions revealed that at this point there had been a complete change. The large majority of men now favoured the agreement and, more surprising than this reversal of their general attitude towards it, were the reasons that they now gave for approving it, shown in Table 1.

Table 1. REASONS FOR FAVOURING AGREEMENT

Base: all informants

	%	No.	
Greater job interest/satisfaction (intrinsic rewards)	68	33	
(More opportunities to use ability/do wider range of jobs		(33)	(16)
(Work generally more interesting)		(20)	(10)
(More opportunity to learn different jobs)		(13)	(6)
(More responsibility)		(3)	(1)
More money	30	14	
Better conditions of employment	25	11	
(Promotion, seniority systems better)		(15)	(7)
(Wages secure – full pay when sick)		(5)	(2)
(Clocking in ended)		(5)	(2)
Other	9	4	
(Working team bigger)		(3)	(2)
(Social equity (incomes policy good for low paid workers))		(3)	(1)
(Company's competitive position)		(3)	(1)
	132	62	

As can be seen, the most frequently mentioned items related to the 'job enrichment' that the agreement had spontaneously and tangentially brought about. Thus the most widespread sources of satisfaction with the agreement were the way in which the changes in working practice defined by the agreement had made work on the plant more interesting and satisfying by giving operators more chance to use and develop their abilities through learning and carrying out a wide range and higher level of job – both simple maintenance tasks and operating jobs covering a broader span of the process. The following are typical comments:

'You got stuck on a unit. You got used to the job. It was just repetition. Your mind didn't have to work. You were in a rut. Since the new agreement you have got to keep thinking all the time. You have got more scope, more variety, more to do – there is more interest. You have got interest in three plants not just one.'

'The scheme itself is good – men will stagnate if left on one plant for years and years – it is good when you get a chance to do different jobs and to learn different jobs. If you are here for eight hours you might as well be working for eight hours as getting bored doing nothing half the time.'

'You are more flexible now – before you were confined to just one job – now nobody is indispensable – you are not stuck for ever on one job – the more people that know the job the easier the running, the safer the job, and the more interesting it is.'

Over two-thirds of the sample spontaneously mentioned this type of item. The second most frequently mentioned item (cited by 30 per cent of informants) was increased earnings. Third was better conditions of employment, including those who felt they had benefited personally under changes in the promotion, seniority or grading systems, those who emphasized the way in which earnings had been made more secure, and those who welcomed the end of clocking in. Other items mentioned, by one or two people only, were the way incomes policy and productivity bargaining helped the lower paid worker, the fact that they had become a member of a larger work team, and the way it had helped the company's competitive position.

Particularly interesting here is the way in which the changes in conditions of employment and fringe benefits, that were designed to represent a substantial move towards staff status for the men, hardly featured at all among their reasons for now approving the agreement.

But certainly the most striking aspect of these findings is the way in which factors related to job interest and satisfaction were those most frequently mentioned, and indeed were mentioned by 68 per cent of all respondents. The proportion is more than double those spontaneously mentioning 'more money', despite the fact that every man interviewed had received a pay increase of at least 15 per cent and most had received increases nearer 30 per cent. Indeed the proportion mentioning items related to job interest or satisfaction exceeds those mentioning all other items including the money.

Thus we have an apparent paradox. The agreement had been negotiated and implemented in the face of strong opposition, only after hard wage-work bargaining backed up by national incomes policy. Yet nine months after the agreement, the majority of the men favoured the changes the agreement had brought about more because these represented job enrichment and heightened interest and satisfaction in their work rather than because of increases in wages. Managers and even trade unionists who have been engaged in hard productivity bargaining will find it hard to believe that workers are in any sense interested in intrinsic job satisfaction rather than in increased wages.

The point, of course, is that in the negotiating context they were not more interested or perhaps even at all interested in job satisfaction. They were interested in making the best deal for themselves in the terms that the negotiating context defined: increased earnings in some currency in relation to the increased responsibilities and work load that they are taking on with clear reference to the social and cultural implications.

But once agreement had been reached and once the changes had been implemented, the formal benefits that it had furnished were taken for granted and what then became relevant or salient was the changes that had been generated in the content and meaning of their day-to-day activities and relationships at work. And in practice this meant that there was virtually a complete reversal in priorities when the reference point was the work context not the negotiating context.

This illustrates our starting point in questioning the idea of a fixed set of priorities relating to all contexts, whether that fixed set of priorities be an 'orientation to work' or a 'need hierarchy'. If we had looked at attitudes to the agreement only at the negotiating stage then it would have seemed that Goldthorpe's conclusions on the workers' priorities is justified. Then they were primarily interested in increased earnings and resisted the agreement until the offer was high enough. On the other hand, if we had looked at their assessment of the agreement only at the operating stage their answers would have appeared to confirm the psychological universalistic approach, for then they welcomed the agreement because it gave them greater intrinsic rewards. Clearly anything approaching a complete picture needs to include both contexts and a recognition that quite different sets of priorities relate to each distinct situation, for in this case the men were evaluating the self-same agreement involving the self-same set of changes but the direction of their evaluations and the reasons for their judgments not merely differed dramatically but were in fact reversed at different points in time and with different reference points.

Just as priorities in rewards sought from the job varied from context to context, so did attitudes to management, or images of the relationship between management and men. On the one hand there was strong evidence that the men saw themselves as working together with management in a common enterprise. They expressed overwhelming approval of the firm as an employer. They expressed a similarly high degree of satisfaction with their relationships with supervisors. No one felt that he was under pressure from management in carrying out his job. Indeed it was clear that working relationships on the job were characterized by shared information, mutual inter-dependence, reciprocity, and collaboration. Despite all these signs of harmony, however, these men expressed more awareness of a fundamental conflict between management and labour than did Goldthorpe's assembly line workers in an albeit quiescent part of one of the most strife-ridden sectors of British industry. Invited to indicate whether they thought management and workers were basically on the same side or on different sides, 67 per cent of the Luton manual worker sample embraced the teamwork concept. By contrast only 58 per cent of this sample took that view. More interesting, however, was the way in which they explained their answers. These explanations showed clearly that although on balance they were more inclined to a conflict model of the management/worker relationship, they generally tended to feel that the question posed unreal alternatives, for in practice relationships were characterized by conflict in some contexts but by teamwork in others. This was succinctly summed up in the comment, 'On the job we work as a team. When it comes to money we're on different sides. It's as simple as that.' Thus while as indicated the men did not feel under pressure from management in carrying out their work, without exception they took the view that the firm could afford to pay them more without harming its own prospects for the future.

In this way it can be seen that the men were able to sustain two quite distinct, indeed logically contradictory, images of the relationships between management and labour, the one becoming salient in the bargaining context and the other in the work context. This was important with regard to attitudes to the agreement, for as far as the negotiating stage was concerned the conflict image had been salient, and any attraction that the changes in working practice might have had in terms of the individual experience of work on the job very much took second place to what was strategically required for collective advancement in a context where the men's interests lay in maximizing earnings while those of management lay in minimizing costs.

The way in which individual motivations are modified by workers' definition of the socio-economic framework in which they are operating can be further illustrated by these men's attitudes to promotion and the criteria on which they felt that men should be promoted. Opportunities for advancement within the petro-chemical industry, up to and including foreman level, remain relatively good compared to the position of manual workers generally. There were in this case four grades of operator below the level of foreman, which provided a promotion structure up which the men could progress with knowledge and experience. The men generally welcomed movement up the seniority structure because it meant more interest, higher earnings, and increased status. Where such advancement had been linked to their own performance or achievements they found it a source of personal gratification, as was indicated by answers to Herzberg-type questioning. And yet in general they opposed the principle of promotion on the basis of 'merit' (or rather the idea that management should be allowed to select men for promotion on its definition of merit) and they supported the principle of promotion on the basis of seniority with certain built-in safeguards such as union/management agreement that the man was up to the job. They eschewed the opportunity of personal advancement that promotion on merit might give them because they perceived that ultimately their own betterment was linked more to collective advancement than to individual advancement, and that if they permitted promotion on a managerial definition of merit this would reduce their collective strength and their basis for collective advancement. They argued that if management was allowed to select men unilaterally for promotion it would favour 'yes men' and 'blue-eyed boys', and penalize militants. This would divide the men, discourage militancy, reduce solidarity, and weaken their bargaining strength with management in relation to areas of conflict. Thus their perception of conflicts of interest, and their awareness that ultimately their own advancement was linked inextricably to that of the groups of which they were members, led them to forgo opportunities for personal gratification in the interests of collective strength.

These findings point to one of the chief weaknesses of the Herzberg approach which completely fails to place the nature of job content into any social or economic framework. Thus while highlighting the way in which promotion is widely experienced by the worker as a symbol of ego achievement, he completely ignores first the way that it can be used by management to break up the solidarity of industrial work groups and reduce their collective strength to resist management initiatives, by devising quite artificial promotional structures and creating the illusion of opportunities for individual advancement, and secondly the way in which the introduction of promotional channels may be resisted by workers because they are seen to be directed to these ends.

Indeed it is worth at this point having a more detailed look at the relevance of our findings to the two different approaches we identified initially. First from Goldthorpe's work on orientation to work can be extracted the following four fundamental assumptions or propositions upon which the whole of his theory is built.

1. Workers have a consistent set of priorities in the qualities they seek from their jobs.
2. Their priorities are expressed and revealed by the critical occupational decisions they make, which involve the evaluation of the relative merits and demerits, for them, furnished by different jobs. These include, for example, the decision to take one particular job in preference to others, or none; the decision to stay in a particular job rather than leave it for another, or none; and the decision to leave a particular job for another or none. Thus, the worker's priorities are best measured by focusing on the choices that are made at these critical points, and the evidence on how choices were made provided by their behaviour and explanations of behaviour.
3. The patterns of priorities revealed by these choices and decisions represents their orientation to work. Their responses to, experience of, and evaluation of all occupational events and situations will be mediated through this orientation.
4. By determining orientation to work it is possible to predict industrial behaviour through establishing the needs that the worker will bring to different situations and experiences, and thus, how he will respond to the rewards and deprivations it offers.

This process of reasoning just does not stand empirical testing, particularly in regard to the central thesis that priorities revealed by job choice priorities are the priorities against which all work experience is measured. *A priori* all that can be predicted from job choice decisions and priorities is job choice behaviour. It is not legitimate to project priorities derived from one situation, for instance the decision to take a particular job, on to a quite different situation, for instance the response to events, changes, and stimuli in the workplace itself. To do so, I have suggested, is to be guilty of the same kind of fallacy as those who argue that to pay nurses or foster mothers more would attract people who would stand around doing nothing while children were starving or patients dying (Daniel 1969b). This reasoning is borne out by our findings in this case, as can be illustrated by the men's answers to questioning on three key areas of occupational motivation. These were first, what it was that had attracted them to the job initially; secondly, what satisfactions they experienced in the job; and thirdly, what reasons they had had, if any, for ever considering leaving the job. It was security, earnings, and physical working conditions that attracted them to the job, and kept them in it. It was the opportunity to use their abilities in learning and problem solving, and the intrinsic interest of the work itself that they found rewarding on the job. And it was the lack of opportunities for advancement up the seniority grades because of the low labour turnover that predisposed those few not firmly entrenched to leave. This evidence of wide variations in the qualities sought and valued in the job according to context only serves to reinforce the findings derived from their attitudes to the agreement indicating that in the work context it was the interest and satisfaction gained from using and developing their abilities through learning and operating a broader span of the process that was both salient and the basis of their reasons for approving the agreement, while it had been earnings and fringe benefits that had been salient in the bargaining context. It would have been impossible to predict responses in either context from the priorities revealed by their attitudes and behaviour in the other, and certainly not possible to do so from their job choice attitudes and behaviour.

But just as these findings expose the limitations of an approach via orientation to work, so, as we have already begun to indicate, they also reveal how partial is the Herzberg type of explanation. He demonstrates how workers value achievement, recognition, advancement, intrinsic interest, and responsibility in their work. This suggests that they will seek and welcome this kind of event and be favourably disposed to changes that make it more likely. Indeed as illustrated by our second case described below some managements have concluded from such findings that if only they could devise productivity agreements that would change work content to bring about job enrichment then men would be attracted to them for this reason. In doing so they have made exactly the same error in reverse as those managers who assume that because what men are concerned about in the negotiating context is gaining the highest remuneration possible in relation to workload, all that they are concerned in the work context is doing as little as possible for as much as possible. Our findings described above demonstrate the weaknesses of both these types of thinking. The changes did promise richer jobs and they did bring about a more interesting and rewarding job content and this was subsequently experienced as gratification, but it was only within the framework of collective bargaining, and the different priorities that are salient in that context, that it was introduced. Moreover, just because that agreement was subsequently welcomed and experienced favourably it by no means meant that further agreements were welcomed and enthusiastically embraced when first proposed. Indeed what were seen by management essentially as two tidying-up agreements were subject to the same hard negotiation as the first.

Similarly at the individual level it is not always true that a job that is richer in intrinsic rewards because it demands more use of abilities will be attractive from the outside. The prospect of such a job may even be threatening and worrying. For instance in this case many of the older men were far from attracted by the increased demands on their abilities that were going to be made, and the training they would need to fulfil these demands. They were worried whether they could cope with the training and whether they could meet the increased demands. All other things being equal they would have preferred to have continued in their own quiet way, doing tasks that were familiar to them, which, if they had become relatively unexciting and uninteresting, were also undemanding. And yet having been required to make the change, they found the fact that they had been able to cope very gratifying, and very often found the new method of working more interesting and rewarding.

Our general theme is very well illustrated again by the second case we looked at. This was the ICI MUPS (manpower utilization and payments system, subsequently WSA – weekly staff agreement) application at their Gloucester nylon spinning works and was a particularly impressive example of the management of change. But from the point of view of this argument the most interesting features of the case are first that the ICI management consciously set out to build into the change programme an element of job enrichment, and secondly that it organized an ambitious programme of shop floor discussion groups as the basis for designing and bringing about the changes. The groups were set up to tell the men about the formal national framework agreement of which this was a local application, to give them an opportunity to express their ideas about what changes could usefully be made, and to outline to them the benefits that management saw them getting out of the agreement, not only in terms of increased earnings and improved fringe benefits but also in terms of increased job satisfaction.

In view of the way that management first consciously set out to design changes in working practice which would inject more interest, responsibility, and scope for achievement into the job, secondly stressed in the discussion groups how they hoped that the changes would increase intrinsic rewards, and thirdly assumed that the promise of heightened intrinsic rewards would serve as an additional attraction of the agreement, it is interesting to look at the men's retrospective assessments of what it was that had attracted them about the agreement.

Operators were asked what if anything had attracted them about the agreement initially. Forty-two per cent mentioned increased earnings alone, 25 per cent increased earnings coupled with an item related to job interest, and 33 per cent said there was nothing in it that had attracted them. Thus despite all the beneficial effects of the involvement discussions and the way that job interest items were featured in these, it was the promise of higher earnings that was the chief if not the only attraction of the agreement. For only a quarter of the men was the promise of greater job interest salient at the negotiating stage and even for them it was very much a secondary item. Moreover, in so far as interviewing was carried out after the changes had been implemented and hence these explanations of what had initially attracted them about the agreement were made after they had experienced any enhanced job interest the changes brought about, it is reasonable to suppose that even this low level of expressed interest in increased intrinsic rewards exaggerates if anything the actual interest at that stage. Certainly it is clear that it was only on the basis of the renegotiation of the wage-work bargain in a way that offered increased earnings and improved benefits that the changes were made possible.

Once again, however, as in the first case, while the initial attraction of the agreement was confined to the promise of more money, after the changes had been implemented there was a marked change in attitudes to the agreement and in reasons for approving it.

Once again the agreement enjoyed a wider range of support and for a much wider range of reasons. At the time of interviewing 75 per cent of the men said they felt more satisfied with the job as a result of changes the agreement had brought about (the residual 25 per cent feeling no different about it). Of those having experienced increased satisfaction, 12 per cent felt this was only very marginal and referred only to the increase in earnings but the remaining 63 per cent felt that they had experienced more substantial benefits, including not only the increase in earnings but also greater job interests through having wider areas of activity and responsibility, more rewarding relationships with workmates through membership of groups working together, and more freedom from supervision.

Thus this case again confirms the pattern of quite different aspects of work being salient in the bargaining as opposed to the operating context and the way in which establishing the priorities that prevailed in one situation would on their own have provided no basis for predicting behaviour and attitudes in the other. Moreover their job choice priorities would have provided at best a partial basis for predicting their responses to just one of the situations. This again underlines the limited predictive and explanatory value of an approach via orientation to work, which can be further illustrated by the men's responses to the involvement discussion groups in relation to their orientations.

On the basis of their reasons for taking the job and their work histories the large majority of workers were categorized as having an instrumental orientation. Of those giving reasons for their job choice, 67 per cent mentioned 'the pay' alone, 9 per cent mentioned 'pay' with some other item, and 25 per cent mentioned security. Adopting Goldthorpe's definition and use of the term, the responses to the type of involvement discussion groups described that would be predicted of men with such a highly instrumental orientation to work, could only be one of two types:

(i) being interested in only the increased earnings, being so disinterested and uninvolved in the work itself they would be prepared to accept virtually any change in return for higher pay. In this event they would certainly have no interest in contribution to discussion groups concerned with designing the changes;

(ii) being primarily concerned with increased earnings they would have been concerned only to ensure the minimum amount of change and improvement for the maximum pay increase. In this case their sole concern in the group would have been to be obstructive and unresponsive.

In fact, involvement in the discussion groups was high, the level of response was good as was the quality of suggestions for change and improvement. On management's account, the large part of the changes, that actually permitted a reduction in manpower of 25 per cent and substantially increased job satisfaction, were generated by the shop floor discussion groups and would not have been possible without them. Nearly two-thirds of the men interviewed felt that the discussion groups had a 'large' (28 per cent)or 'fair' (34 per cent) amount of influence on the changes made, on a five point scale.

Once again there is evidence of the total predictive failure of an approach via orientation as Goldthorpe uses it. Here was a group of men, apparently, on his measures, defining work solely in terms of a source of extrinsic rewards and seeking no reward or involvement in work. Yet first, they became highly involved and constructive in group discussions concerned with reorganizing working practices. Secondly, when evaluating the changes after they had been implemented they attached very high importance to the changes in intrinsic rewards. If the starting point had been their expressed needs at work measured by their job priorities or reasons for taking the job, the only reasonable predictions would have been first that organizing the group discussion would be useless because they had no interest in the content of the work, and secondly that any changes designed to enrich their job content by increasing interest, responsibility, and work group autonomy and cooperation would have been of little value because they did not seek such rewards in work.

And it is not simply a matter of their having gained both types of improvement, intrinsic and extrinsic, for as shown so clearly in the first case there was a complete reversal of priorities when evaluating the self-same agreement in different contexts.

CONCLUSIONS

Each of our case studies of workers' evaluations of productivity agreements in which they had been involved reveal a similar pattern. The agreements were initially regarded with hostility or strong reservations and they were pushed through on the basis of only the promise of higher earnings in relation to workload backed up by a statutory national incomes policy. Subsequently, however, after implementation, they were regarded favourably and more because of the way the changes in working practice increased intrinsic rewards rather than because of the increases in earnings. Underlying these changes in attitude can be identified two distinct contexts in which quite different priorities in what was demanded of work, quite different implicit definitions of the nature even of work itself, and quite different definitions of the relationship between management and labour prevailed. On the one hand there was the bargaining context where what was important was their share of the wealth generated by the enterprise expressed in terms of earnings and fringe benefits. Implicit in this context was the idea that work and change represent disutility for the worker and that consequently taking on more work and accepting change have to be compensated for. More explicit here was the idea that management and workers are on opposite sides with conflicting aims and interests.

On the other hand there was the work context where what was important to workers was the quality of their job content, the scope it gave for interest and the use and development of abilities, and the quality of interpersonal contact with workmates and supervisors in day-to-day activities and relationships at work. Here the implicit definition of work was activity that could be rewarding in its own right so that taking on more work both qualitatively and quantitatively could be even more rewarding. Relationships with management were more characterized by a sense of common interests.

From these findings and their analysis we have highlighted the importance, in seeking to understand and explain industrial behaviour, of not confining study to just one of these contexts but rather of seeking to take both into account as well as the interaction between them. We have seen how partial two very influential models of the relationship between the worker and the enterprise have proved in their explanatory and predictive value because they have derived their conclusions on workers' priorities, attitudes, and motivations from a study of those prevailing in just one context and have fallaciously assumed that these represent an overall generalized set of priorities, attitudes, and motivations that operate in all situations.

Indeed there has been a tendency among all those who have sought to understand and explain industrial behaviour, and not just for those adopting the two approaches that we have discussed, to focus upon just one of these contexts to the neglect of the other. Thus not only the 'psychological universalistic' school but also most socio-psychological types of approach have tended to focus very much on the work context and upon attitudes, motivations, and satisfaction in the workplace, in day-to-day activities and relationships on the job. In terms of changing industrial behaviour such approaches have given us job enrichment, participative styles of supervision, more appropriate socio-technical organization, improved communications and consultation, as well as better physical conditions of work and amenities, as ways of improving employee effectiveness and relations. But by focusing on just one of the major contexts it has tended to neglect the importance of the differences in power enjoyed by management and labour, the potential conflicts of interest between the different parties to the enterprise and thus the importance of collective bargaining.

The alternative approaches however have tended to do the opposite. They have focused upon the economic basis of the relationship between the worker and the organization and the intrinsic conflict between management and labour that this ensures. One would categorize the action framework, or at least Goldthorpe's application of it, among these approaches although he focuses upon the job choice situation rather than the collective bargaining one. But the more important approaches in this category are those via institutional industrial relations and labour economics. They have focused very much on the negotiating context and ways of regulating or resolving the conflicts between management and labour, and means of linking and regulating the economic attachment of the employee to his work, to his performance. Thus, in contrast to the main socio-psychological schools, they have suggested, for the purposes of changing behaviour, improved procedures and institutions for collective bargaining and negotiation, comprehensive plant agreements, productivity agreements, creative bargaining for change, quicker, more effective grievance and arbitration procedures, and more rational, equitable system of payment less prone to generate disputes, as the means of regulating potential sources of overt conflict and improving employee relations.

But we would suggest it is only when attention is focused upon both the different contexts and the different priorities and attitudes that are characteristics of each and the interaction between them that we can begin to understand, explain, and change occupational behaviour. Of course the distinction between the bargaining context and the work context will not always be as clearcut as it was in our cases. Under different technologies, systems of payment, management styles, degrees of organizational success there may be a tendency for the qualities that we have identified as being characteristic of one context to intrude into the other. Moreover while arguing that variations in priorities and attitudes according to context are characteristic of most workers in most workplaces we do recognize that there is a spectrum. At the one end there may well be workers who attach exclusive importance to extrinsic rewards and at the other to intrinsic rewards. Equally there will be workplaces where attitudes to management are almost exclusively characterized by feelings of congruence of interest and at the other by continuous open and permanent warfare. Indeed those who have adopted the different types of approach that we have identified have tended not only to focus upon just one context in the workplaces they have studied but moreover to have been attracted to or able to gain access to the types of workplace where their approach is most appropriate. Thus ever since Hawthorne the 'human relations' or 'psychological universalistic' school has tended to focus on workplaces characterized by (1) a relatively low initial perception of conflict of interests between employer and employees, with a paternalistic management attaching high importance to responsibilities towards employees; (2) a non-unionized labour force content to leave management to manage as best it sees fit, not seeking to restrict managements' discretion or resist change in any organized or collective manner as opposed to such individual action as is indicated by turnover, absenteeism, and sickness rates or individual output; (3) a semi-rural environment with none of the history of mass unemployment, prolonged bitter battles with employers for union recognition and minimum rights, which tend to characterize industrial areas.

At the same time while accepting that there is a spectrum in terms of basic attitudes to management and overall orientations to work, what our findings demonstrate is that there are certain workers in the middle of that spectrum. They seek both extrinsic and intrinsic rewards from work, with the one becoming salient in one context and the other in another. Equally they see both areas of common and conflicting interests with management in different contexts. As far as the understanding of such workers' behaviour is concerned the variations in their priorities and attitudes according to context are more important than any overall or general orientation or set of priorities. For them the critical question is not, 'What are they really interested in?' or whether they are more interested in intrinsic than extrinsic rewards but, 'When, in what situations, under what circumstances, are they more interested in one and when in the other?' It is a matter for empirical investigation as to what proportion of industrial workers could be categorized as being of this type. But our impression is that it is large and growing as industrial workers become more conscious and demanding on all dimensions.

The final important distinction between the job choice situation and the work situation is that in the first workers may be forced to trade rewards on one dimension off against those on another. They may be forced to choose between high earnings coupled with unrewarding work or low earnings for more interesting work. In the work situation, however, through collective action workers can seek to maximize on all dimensions. They can demand and pressurize for higher earnings, for a greater sharing of power and control, and for a reorganization of work that makes for more interesting and rewarding work content. There are increasing signs that this is beginning to happen, thereby confirming the Maslovian prediction that the needs at the top of the hierarchy will become increasingly important. The aspect of the Maslow model that this does not confirm, however, is that the rise in the demand for greater intrinsic rewards is by no means accompanied by any abating in the demand for increased material rewards.

REFERENCES

BLAUNER, R. 1964. *Alienation and freedom: the manual worker in industry*, Chicago University Press.

COTGROVE, S., DUNHAM, J., VAMPLEW, C. 1971. *The nylon spinners*, London: Allen and Unwin.

DANIEL, W. W. 1969a. 'Automation and the quality of work', *New Society*, 29th May, 833-6.

DANIEL, W. W. 1969b. 'Industrial behaviour and orientation to work—a critique', *Journal of Management Studies*, 6, 366-75.

DANIEL, W. W. 1970. *Beyond the wage-work bargain*, London: PEP.

DANIEL, W. W. 1971. 'Productivity bargaining and orientation to work – a rejoinder to Goldthorpe', *Journal of Management Studies*, 8, 329-35.

FLANDERS, A. 1964. *The Fawley productivity agreements*, London: Faber and Faber.

GOLDTHORPE, J. H., LOCKWOOD, D., BECHHOFER, F., PLATT, J. 1969. *The affluent worker: industrial attitudes and behaviour*, London: Cambridge University Press.

GOLDTHORPE, J. H. 1970. 'The social action approach to industrial socio-logy: a reply to Daniel', *Journal of Management Studies*, 7, 199-208.

HERZBERG, F., MAUSNER, B., SNYDERMAN, B. B. 1959. *The motivation to work*, New York: Wiley.

HERZBERG, F. 1968. *Work and the nature of man*, London: Staples.

MASLOW, A. H. 1954. *Motivation and personality*, New York: Harper and Row.

MCGREGOR, D. 1960. *The human side of enterprise*, New York: McGraw-Hill.

NELSON JONES, J. 1971. *The wages of fear: a memorandum on inflation and incomes policy*, London: The Bow Group.

3 Getting In: the Managed Accomplishment of 'Correct' Selection Outcomes

DAVID SILVERMAN AND JILL JONES

This paper is a report on a study which is being carried out on the graduate recruitment activities of a large organization in the public sector.[1] One of the things that struck us while we gathered material was that, like participants, we were fashioning our accounts of selection interviews with reference to their predicted or known outcome. Since selection outcomes were rarely revealed during an interview, talking-about-selection seemed to be a separate activity from participating-in-selection, deriving its rationale from more than the conversational exchanges that occurred in the selection interview. Furthermore, it was only possible for us to interpret talk as rational talking-about-selection-talk or participating-in-selection-talk by relying on our tacit knowledge of selection-in-general (and of interviews-in-general) to fill in the gaps and etcetera clauses provided by the speakers. Any account of a 'selection process', then, is a managed accomplishment for it derives its sense from the employment of such practices.

The theoretical focus of this paper is that an account of any reality derives its rationality *not* from its direct correspondence with some objective world but from the ability of its hearers (readers) to make sense of the account in the context of the socially organized occasions of its use (and, thereby, *to treat*

---

[1] This paper is based on research which is part of a wider project supported by the Social Science Research Council. We are grateful for the help we have received from many people in the organization concerned.

it as corresponding to an objective world). As Garfinkel (1967: pp. 3–4) has noted:

> 'In short, *recognizable* sense, or fact, or methodic character, or impersonality, or objectivity of accounts are not independent of the socially organized occasions of their use. Their rational features *consist* of what members do with, what they "make of" the accounts in the socially organized occasions of their use . . .'

Our task, then, is to consider 'selection' as an example of the way in which accounts of some phenomenon and the everyday practices in which they are grounded routinely make available the features of a real, non-problematic world.

SELECTION AS A SOCIAL PROCESS

Most studies of selection seek to link certain background variables to the selection outcome – for instance, social class may be related to entry to State mental hospitals or certain kinds of educational institutions (cf. Hollingshead and Redlich 1958, Floud and Halsey 1957). Another type of study will seek to get a better grasp of the process as experienced by those involved. Thus participant-observation and various types of interview will be used and examples of talk referred to in order to support the generalizations that the researcher wishes to offer (cf. Kadushin 1958). While these varieties of respectively quantitative and qualitative methods are often depicted as involving rather different research strategies, we want to focus upon their common features. These include:

1. A reliance upon taken-for-granted knowledge of the understandings and practices that constitute 'routine' interviews, tests and other selection devices and allow both participants and researcher to make sense of a selection process and its outcome.

2. A *tacit* dependence upon the reader's sense of social structure in order to grasp that what is 'really happening' is in line with the researcher's description. (All social science research is dependent upon this type of knowledge; the tacit aspect of this dependence is the crucial issue here.) For instance, in being convinced that X is a variable that plausibly relates to selection, while Y is not worth con-

sidering, or in accepting fragments of talk as being plausibly the exchanges that were crucial in the selection interview.

3. A treatment of participants' accounts as reflections or snapshots of the scene which they report and an attempt to gauge the extent to which accounts are fair records of such scenes. This misses completely the point that talk does not serve to capture the necessarily context-bound features of a past scene but rather it makes available ways in which its outcomes can be read as in-accord-with-a-rule. Accounts, then, are artful displays of the good sense of what has transpired; in themselves they provide neither descriptions of a past scene nor explanations of its causes.

In the exchange below, the Chairman of the Selection Board is recalling a candidate who failed at an interview some months earlier:

Chairman:	Oh! By heavens! Have you read his tutor's report?
Researcher:	Yes (laughs).
Ch:	This is obviously why he went down.
R:	You didn't have that actually, I think, at the time.
Ch:	Oh, we must have done.
R:	Oh, you must . . .
Ch:	We must have done . . . yes. We wouldn't actually see him without a tutor's report/ [diagonal lines indicate overlapping comments]
R:	/that's right, that's right . . . yeh. That was not the tutor he gave actually.
Ch: (after a pause)	Oh! I remember this fellow, yes! He'd obviously go down on this tutor's report, I should say . . .

In this case, the reference which is discussed was not available to the Board at the time of the interview and had only just been noticed by the Chairman when reading the candidate's papers which had been given to him a moment before by the researcher. This comment is not intended as an irony. The point is not the rightness or wrongness of the account but that it makes sense as a rational account of selection proceedings in

E

which 'bad' references are taken as grounds for rejecting a candidate. The Chairman is providing an account of a selection outcome as in-accord-with-a-rule. Thus a retrospective account is not to be taken as instancing what 'actually' happened in an interview for it derives its rationale not from the selection interview but from the expected concerns of the present audience – including what they may be taken to expect about interviews in general.

Our study is an attempt to understand the practical reasoning used by applicants and selectors to bring off what they count as comprehensible interviews and to justify, after the fact, certain outcomes. We do not seek to remedy members' accounts, by substituting 'more accurate' descriptions of 'what really happened'. Instead, we are concerned with the accounting process itself in terms of the interpretative work involved in generating understandings of situations and making talk comprehensible. Such an approach necessarily focuses attention not on a real world or on the way things 'really are' but on the routine *production* of realities.

THE SETTING AND THE DATA

Material has been gathered in the course of the selection of graduate recruits for a large organization in the public sector. Potential candidates apply through their University Appointments Board in their final year and are interviewed locally by a representative of the employing organization (henceforth referred to as the Organization). After these first-stage interviews, known to interviewers as the 'milk-round', roughly 150, about one-fifth of the candidates presenting themselves, are called for the group selection process at the offices of the Organization. Selection is by means of two group discussions (one on a concrete administrative problem, the other a general discussion about an issue of the day selected by the candidates) which are observed by Board members, and by a twenty minute appearance before the Board in the afternoon. The Board is chaired by a senior member of the Central Staff Department and two other senior administrators sit on it. Eight candidates appear before each Board and, depending upon the requirements of the Organization and the flow of applications, roughly two or three candidates are selected.

Overall about 40 out of 150 candidates at the group selection are offered jobs.

In accordance with our recognition of the dependence of selection outcomes upon the contingencies of actual social scenes, the material we have gathered consists of tape-recordings of these scenes and of the papers (references, application forms, and mark-sheets) referred to by the selectors. In addition, we have on tape retrospective accounts offered by the participants on being asked, 'What happened?'. In some cases we also have accounts given by administrators on subsequently hearing the tapes themselves. This allows us to observe the construction of multiple accounts of apparently the same social scene, as participants, at different times, focus on or recall varying particulars from the infinite properties of any social interaction. This procedure follows Cicourel's concept of *indefinite triangulation*. He writes about this:

'I use the expression "indefinite triangulation" to suggest that every procedure that seems to "lock in" evidence (thus to claim a level of adequacy) can itself be subjected to the same sort of analysis that will in turn produce yet another indefinite arrangement of new particulars or a rearrangement of previously established particulars in "authoritative" "final", "formal" accounts. The indefinite triangulation notion attempts to make visible the practicality and inherent reflexivity of everyday accounts. The elaboration of circumstances and particulars of an occasion can be subjected to an indefinite re-elaboration of the "same" or "new" circumstances and particulars.' (Forthcoming: manuscript, p. 43.)

It is worth noting that the recognition of the possibility of an indefinite elaboration of accounts would effectively ruin everyday communication. Garfinkel (1967) has illustrated, for instance, how subjects asked to spell out 'what they really mean' ultimately become confused and angry. Talk routinely proceeds, then, by providing ways in which it can be read not as *any* account but as an authoritative version of what happened, i.e. an account which appears to correspond non-problematically to the reality it purports to describe. As an example of this, the latter part of this paper will focus on the practices employed by administrators (and by researchers) in producing authoritative versions of past interviews.

For the moment, however, our intentions are relatively descriptive. We seek an understanding of selection outcomes by reference to the practical reasoning of selectors and candidates. More specifically, we have been concerned with the attribution of motives and qualities to others on the basis of interactions which include verbal exchanges. For instance, what do interviewers make of a certain answer to a question, what are (for them) the 'crucial' questions, and how do they attend to the candidate's appearance and bearing? Similarly, in what ways do the candidates make sense of the questions asked of them, what types of answers do they feel the selectors respond to favourably, and how do they judge their own performance and the performance of others who will have participated with them in the group discussions? At this level we have tried to bring off a successful ethnography – in the sense of describing 'the way things are' from the point of view of the participants. Yet, as we discuss later, to decide what was happening both researchers and participants have inescapably relied upon a stock of knowledge and a method of reasoning which (for them) constitutes the selection game as real and allows both to find 'meanings' in action, talk, and paper records.

ACCOUNTS OF SELECTION

Selection is activity in accord with a plan; doing selection involves arranging interactions with purposes – locating the right number and the right kind of recruits – which are extrinsic to the interactions themselves. In selection, unlike casual conversation, the point is never taken to be the talk itself; only the product of the talk, the practical outcome it produces (selection or rejection), is at issue. However, since many activities are designed to produce practical outcomes extrinsic to the activity itself (for instance, to ask a stranger for the time will not usually be taken to imply an interest in talking to strangers for its own sake), we will need to specify more clearly the assumptions that provide for doing selection. These include the assumptions of qualities, populations, and matching (some of this discussion relies on Garfinkel 1967, Chapter 7).

To do selection is to assume that certain qualities are required in a selected person, that such qualities are intrinsic features of certain persons and that available materials (talk, paper records, personal appearances) can be treated as displays of such underlying qualities. For instance, selectors at the public service organization have mark-sheets which list qualities in terms of which candidates are to be assessed (appearance, acceptability, confidence, effort, and motivation). These provide rules for attending to a candidate's relevant features and avoiding others – 'intelligence' for instance is absent from the organization's mark-sheets; the common educational qualifications of candidates, it is felt, provide all that is needed in this direction (see the Chairman's comments on 'high-flyers', p. 83 below). In addition, such forms can be used by the selector to display the 'sensible' grounds of his decisions.

Selection also involves the assumption that qualities are differentially dispersed among a population. Selectors then attend to three sorts of population: an initial demand population (people who apply) and sub-populations of persons accepted and persons rejected. Acceptance is based on selection operations which attempt to match the qualities of the candidates to the qualities required in the available positions. Selectors recognize that their selection operations may produce biased views of candidates' 'true' qualities since some people do well at selections but such presumed qualities are often required by the selecting organization ('acceptability' is something which the public service organization's interviewers must attend to and striking up a rapport in the interview situation counts strongly in the case of Fortescue – discussed below).

We now provide materials on the selection interviews of three candidates whose applications had different outcomes.

1. *Chadwick*

'I didn't find him very impressive as an individual . . . er . . . not frightfully mature, in fact rather gauche altogether.' (Mr James, the interviewer from the Organization, commenting subsequently on the interview.)

Chadwick, a 21-year-old economics student at the university, was rejected as the result of his milk-round interview. The official record of the meeting that produced this outcome consists of the mark-sheet filled out at the time by James (see below). If we initially focus on the comment about acceptability

69

('non-existent, rather uncouth') James's subsequent account is informative.

Chadwick's mark-sheet

NAME: Chadwick

1. APPEARANCE
   Tall, slim, spotty faced, black hair, dirty grey suit.
2. ACCEPTABILITY
   Non-existent. Rather uncouth.
3. CONFIDENCE
   Awful. Not at all sure of himself.
4. EFFORT
   High.
5. MOTIVATION
   None really that counts.

ANY OTHER COMMENTS
   Reject.

J: I found that he was – um – not particularly confident. He seemed to me to be rather diffident altogether – um the sort of chap who was . . . the sort of chap who really, coming from the background he did . . . er . . . was about what you would have expected. That is to say, without, I mean it sounds terribly snobbish, but um, he was the sort of bloke who had got there by hard work and, and it seemed to me had got very little out of being at university, except perhaps a degree – which I suppose is all important!

In this context, getting very little out of University may be taken to imply a failure to learn the social skills necessary to create an impression of 'acceptability' rather than 'abrasiveness' – terms used repeatedly by senior staff in conversations with researchers.

James later recalls that Chadwick's parents were apparently not interested in his entry to university. This detail seems to have been conveyed in the following exchange, after a discussion of the area (a poor one) in which Chadwick lives:

C: . . . The majority of people who went to my school weren't, er, university-orientated; they didn't want to go to university to do a degree, they just wanted to go out and have a /

J: /Did you find this a struggle though to get here? I mean in the sense that if everybody else left school, was there not a great temptation for you to, indeed for /

C: /There, there was a struggle for me, er, I was . . . I wasn't going to fill in the UCCA form/

J: /Mmm.

C: I was dead against it . . . er . . . I – I wanted to earn some money. When you see all your friends going out/

J: /Yes.

C: . . . and spending money, I wanted to earn some money but . . . I think, looking back, there's/

J: /What are your parents' views on this? What view did they take? Did they want you to go on?

C: Um . . . well really I done it behind their backs eventually. [Untranscribable sequence.] My mother was dead against it at first, but gradually I think she changed . . . she realized that I wanted to go.

J: Yes.

C: She's not a woman to stand in my way and she let me go.

J: What about your father?

C: He didn't say much (both laugh heartily). He's glad to get rid of me (renewed laughter).

J: God, bless my soul!

James comments afterwards: 'He appeared also to have done very little at university aside from work; he didn't seem to have very many interests outside his immediate course.' Participation in student societies would apparently have given James the impression of a candidate with administrative potential and, in this case, a determination to break away from his home milieu. Yet on Chadwick's application form there is hardly a mention of any such participation and the interview gives James no grounds for altering such an impression. An attempt to make this accountable is offered by two senior members of the Organization, not themselves participants in the selection process, on hearing a tape of the interview:

A1: . . . And bear in mind, of course, that the chap, admittedly he comes from, he is slightly less well-mannered

> than the other people James has interviewed because of his background . . .

A2: I wouldn't say well-mannered necessarily. We've interviewed one or two Etonians whose manners have been absolutely dreadful. But, uh, you know (laughs) . . .

A1: Ah, no. But his background is, perhaps, a partial reason for having, for being less, you know, socially conscious. Not that this is confined to a background as you rightly say.

A2: I think there is obviously a lot in background probably here. That . . . the fact that he doesn't seem to have spread himself very much, that he's had to concentrate on a few things, that he's not entirely happy perhaps at University. In the Sixth Form he was a rather exceptional being, he worked hard and all the rest of it. It's difficult to judge people, it's difficult to project . . .

Verbal exchanges in interviews are viewed by selectors in the light of what they make of the candidate's appearance and of his manner during different stages of the interview. Remove this information, especially where the interviewee doesn't exactly conform to the expected pattern (in this case he has a cockney accent), and a fair amount of confusion is created. Consider the following remarks made by two non-participants before they see James's mark-sheet:

A2: I must say appearance in this particular case would have been more useful than the last case [Fortescue – the next candidate discussed below]. Because I must say that, although it was a very good interview and a lot came out of it, I got an almost neutral impression at the end of it. I felt I needed more information . . .

A3: Appearance we don't know but I agree it would be very useful to have. One has a slight sort of impression he might look a bit sort of wild and that kind of thing, I don't know. He probably wouldn't cultivate his appearance too much, but that's just a guess based on almost nothing . . .

A2: [after a series of conflicting comments about the interview] You know this form tells you practically nothing about this individual whereas Fortescue's form was extremely helpful and extremely descriptive and it really bore out the later evidence. This gives you an almost negative impression and you think, well, I shall have to wait until the interview because I don't really know anything about this chap now at all. And when the interview takes place, although he talks a lot and James talks very little, one still feels one doesn't know terribly much about this individual. And I think this is almost borne out in the variation in certain comments we've made about him. We just didn't know very much about him by the end of the interview.

James's comments on appearance (see above) and his later remark about a person who was 'rather gauche altogether' provide a missing link in accounting for the discrepancy between the uncertainty of those exposed to the tape and James's clearcut 'reject' decision. As one of them comments after seeing James's mark-sheet:

A2: I think there's a greater degree of subjectivity in James's assessment here almost borne out from his marks on appearance . . . In that he was not impressed, this bloke walked through the door, he had a look at him and he wasn't impressed. And from then onwards you know, things just enhanced the dismal first impression. Um, it's difficult of course because undoubtedly you do see people that you take an instinctive dislike to, I mean this is a natural occurrence. And this is a chap who had everything going against him on appearance, one would feel.

Still another member of the Organization reads into the mark-sheet grounds for altering an initially slightly favourable impression based on the taped interview alone:

A1: I think, I mean we're all influenced by appearances, um, I think I would have given the appearance, if the appearance is accurate as James has described it, I don't think I would have raised him to a 'Call 2', because I think I would have been influenced too in that direction . . . ['Call 2' means a second priority selection for a second interview].

Later, when hearing a tape of a subsequent interview between Chadwick and a researcher he comments:

73

A1: His uncouth type of speech is more apparent here [although A1 feels favourably disposed to him].

The initial confusion of the listeners to the tape and their failure to note the 'rapport' between interviewer and subject which they claim to observe on hearing other interviews conducted by James (most notably with Fortescue – see below) seems to reflect not just Chadwick's accent but also the less smooth unfolding of the interview – as evidenced in relatively longer pauses and the frequent apparent misunderstandings between James and Chadwick about what intent lies behind each other's utterances. Consider the following exchange in which James seems to assume one sort of intent behind a question, discovers another, and has to adjust his answer:

J: Any other points at all?
C: Well, as I said at the beginning of the interview, I didn't know anything about the Organization. Could you, er, enlighten me at all?
J: Well, exactly about what? What it does, what its functions are, or what?
C: Well, about promotion.
 (short pause)
J: *Oh! Within the inter . . . Yes of course!* [our emphasis]. Well . . . when you come to us you come to us as an Administrative Trainee, don't you? . . .

Indeed, the feeling of lack of rapport seems to be mutual: as Chadwick later remarks to a researcher, 'You don't really know what's going on in his head'. (This compares with the remark about a similar interview made by another candidate (Fortescue): 'It ran very smoothly, it wasn't sort of jerky at all; it sort of neatly flowed from one thing to another.')

Such perceived misunderstandings no doubt influenced James's marking on acceptability. After all, if recruited, Chadwick would have to create the right impression and strike up a rapport with other members of the Organization. Yet his command of the sort of social skills required (both to pass the interview and to 'make it' in the Organization) strikes James as very limited. In this context, the exchange below is interesting:

J: . . . Now, any other points?

C: Er . . . basically no. Interviews to me – this type of interview – I . . . I object to most strongly actually . . .

J: Why?

C: Oooh, it's um . . . I know you kind of, you separate the wood from the trees, or whatever you . . .

J: Wheat and chaff, I think, yeah.

C: But, er, but what do you end up with? (laughs)

J: What do you mean, what do you end up with?

C: Well you still don't know what you've got at the end to a certain degree. You still don't know whether a person is suitable for a position of administration, even after . . .

J: Well you tell me something, would you? You put this up as a point? What method would you use for selecting people/

C: /I . . . I/

J: /for jobs other than an interview?

C: I . . . although I condemn it, I . . . I must admit it is in theory a formal interview. It's er . . .

While one of the non-participant members of the Organization interpreted this (before hearing about the candidate's 'appearance') as 'coming back and arguing well in the interview' it comes over to James as an example of naive aggression, he even has to correct a wrong analogy used by Chadwick ('wood from the trees'). He notes about this sequence for instance that:

J: . . . we discussed interviewing as such, he made the point to me that he thought all these interviews were a bit of a farce. Perhaps you could suggest a better way in which people could be selected? But, no, he couldn't suggest a better way . . . Um, and I, although one must agree in some ways that interviewing is notoriously inaccurate, I was amused that he should put forward this guise without being able to argue it out in any way.

While James might accept Chadwick's appearance and accent as an unfortunate concomitant of his background ('the sort of chap who really, coming from the background he did . . . er . . . was about what you would have expected'), his attempt to take the interviewer's role strikes James as a wilful choice of a person who had other (and less abrasive) options open to him. It may well be, then, that selectors distinguish impressions

75

thought to be controlled by the candidate from impressions which are seen as an inevitable feature of his background.

To conclude: Chadwick's failure needs to be located in a misapprehension about the kind of self that would be success-fully received in such an interview and about the utterances that would be taken as exhibiting that self – in short, he failed because he didn't seem to understand the rules of the game that he was being asked to play, and, possibly, because he was anyway unable or unwilling to bring off successful participation in that kind of game.

Examples abound of Chadwick's misunderstandings of the situation as defined by James. For instance:

1. He cites a docker as a character referee on his application form. (Another informant in a senior position in the Organization has implied that a public service official is the right sort of choice; references will never, as far as we can see, be taken up – the point is to create the right impression.)
2. He did no reading beforehand about the Organization and says so in interview – 'That's a shocking admission', James says to him.
3. When asked by a researcher what he was trying to get across in the interview, he answers: 'That I wanted the job . . . that I want to go places' – hardly the sort of impression which, if conveyed, would by itself commend him to the representative of the Organization.

One final exchange is an illustration of these points. It occurs near the beginning of the interview, where James is talking about what it takes to be a successful administrator:

J: . . . Put it another way, what would you be looking for?
C: A logical mind.
J: That's the mental equipment. But what kind of bloke would you look for?

Here James treats Chadwick's reply as an answer which is not an answer – for Chadwick has failed to grasp the point of the question. 'Intelligence' as already noted does not even appear on James's mark-sheet; 'Acceptability' does!

2. *Fortescue*

'He, he struck me as being a reasonable sort of bloke – British and proud of it, you know, sort of stiff upper lip and all that . . . tended to play things down a bit. Um. However, one had to admit that one could see him fitting in extremely well in this sort of atmosphere . . . Quite an acceptable sort of chap, he was quite mature and quite pleasant.' (James commenting on the first interview.)

Fortescue, aged 21 and studying for an English degree, is assessed by James as follows on the mark-sheet after his first interview.

Fortescue's mark-sheet

NAME: Fortescue

1. APPEARANCE
   Tall, thin, straw coloured hair. Neat and tidy.
2. ACCEPTABILITY
   High. Pleasant, quite mature sensible man.
3. CONFIDENCE
   Very good. Not conceited but firm, put himself across very well.
4. EFFORT
   Excellent academic record.
5. ORGANIZATION
   Excellent, both at school and university.
6. MOTIVATION
   Keen on administration and very well informed on it. Has had considerable experience. Quite well informed about both Organization and its functions generally.

ANY OTHER COMMENTS
   Call 1, First rate.

As with Chadwick, the key to Fortescue's interview outcome is seen to lie in judgments about his 'acceptability'. The remarks of two of the non-participants from the Organization on listening to the interview between Fortescue and James indicate what this term means in practice:

A2: He seemed also to strike some rapport with James during the interview, but you know, that's all you can go on in fact for acceptability.

A1: Acceptability – he certainly appeared to be, um, respond very well to James here, and this business of rapport. I mean I thought he got this sort of rapport with the interviewer.

An exchange right at the start of the interview indicates that one basis for judging 'rapport' is the extent to which speakers provide evidence of shared backgrounds and activities:

J: Do sit down please . . . St Dominic's School. Now why does that ring a bell . . . Oh, I knew somebody that went to school there, that's right.

F: Oh yes, which one? There are masses.

J: That's right there are about 200 of them. A very tall bloke, now what was his name?

F: Pearson?

J: Pearson, that's right yes, yes you knew him did you?

F: Yes.

J: . . . Nice chap. Now what do you want to do if you come to us, Mr Fortescue?

Here Fortescue has already been located in an 'acceptable' background, a location which is apparently strengthened by a feature of his application form noted by A2:

A2: We often look for a background in the public service, so his father in fact is a civil servant and this sometimes is useful. He in fact puts this on his application form; we've very frequently found that it's the sort of business where there is this . . . where the background does help.

Fortescue's application form is in fact a veritable mine of information. He lists (alphabetically) ten leisure-time pursuits, and for example, under one of these – sport – puts in brackets 'I play Badminton, Croquet, Rugby, Squash and Tennis and have organized fun rugby matches for charity'. Fortescue has held many posts of responsibility – Head Boy at School, Senior Cadet with the School Corps, University Theatre Workshop President (producing a winning production in a competition), President of the Literary Society and several other committee posts.

When asked by James how he managed to fit in all these activities, Fortescue remarks:

F: English is . . . a flexible subject. This means that you can budget your time a little more flexibly than most people can, um . . . I like to be busy, I don't like sitting down doing nothing.

This provides grounds for James's comments 'tended to play things down a bit' and 'not conceited, but firm'.

James also asks:

J: Do you suffer fools gladly, Mr Fortescue?

F: Er, no, no I don't, but I, I don't wish to sort of lash out though, I prefer to – um – get it seen to quietly rather than make a noise about it.

J: What is your reaction to the sort of garrulous fool which one gets on most prominent committees? How do you stop him? You must have had these people in the past.

F: Er, . . . well if you have a well-organized agenda, um . . . on – with the subjects er very well limited, you keep the topic very closely to that.

These remarks by Fortescue provide grounds for reading the sense of James's comments (on the mark-sheet), 'Quite mature, sensible man . . . not conceited but firm . . . keen on administration and very well informed on it'. James's questions may be seen as intended tests of Fortescue's social skills and non-abrasive manner. 'Getting it seen to quietly' with the minimum of personal confrontation accords exactly with the interviewer's picture of a good administrator.

Fortescue gets off lightly in his first interview when asked about his knowledge of the organization for which he is applying. James is satisfied with Fortescue's word that he knows about it and pursues it no further. He appears already at this stage of the interview to have decided to send Fortescue up for the second selection process. (Another administrator later comments: A3: Half-way along you've made up your mind and are validating it.)

The Group Selection process consists of two parts – group discussions in the morning amongst eight people, and individual interviews before a panel of three people in the afternoon.

All three assessors mark Fortescue highly on the basis of his morning performance. Out of a total of 25 possible marks, he scores 20 with B1 (Chairman of the Board), 20 with B2, and 19 with B3.

Fortescue says, when asked what he felt the assessors were looking for during the discussion:

> F: Er, I think they were looking for constructive comment, um, gradually building up, taking other people's point, um, looking for people who worked well, built on other people's suggestions.

The following examples of Fortescue's contributions to the discussion demonstrate this. He holds a non-radical position throughout and comes over as neither an impracticable do-gooder, nor an impetuous extrovert.

> F: [on Women's Liberation] If this movement is going to get across, they're going to have to do something serious about, if you like, the sort of practical difficulties of getting a point across.
>
> [later] The very people who say 'what a lot of rot' . . . the bottom slot if you like who read these *Dr* Germaine Greer and the other woman who's got a Ph.D with her thesis. It's almost a 'them' and 'us', I would have thought.
>
> [later] Nevertheless, to be fair to them, it has been marked by emotional moments such as, I mean, Mrs Pankhurst's campaign, the throwing under the horse . . . There's no point to extremism in that it only alienates the people you're trying to get across to.

From comments made by the selection panel, for instance the Chairman's later remark 'a good solid type', Fortescue's presentation of a 'moderate' and 'practical' viewpoint is exactly what is needed to impress. Notice how he refers to the 'practical difficulties of getting a point across', attacks purely academic learning and suggests that 'there's no point to extremism'.

When he is being introduced in the group discussion, Fortescue is again immediately accepted by the Chairman of the Board in the following exchange, following a discussion on Fortescue's part in organizing charity rugby matches:

> B1: Jolly good yes – Have you ever read a book on coarse rugger?
>
> F: Yes.
>
> B1: Sounds awfully like coarse rugger to me . . . Well I don't know, these old people who dash about playing

games. They get me periodically to play cricket and I have to spend the next two days in bed . . . er . . . however, that's as may be. . .

Fortescue then goes up for his individual interview in the afternoon. He remarks afterwards:

F: I didn't seem to get the heavy pressure technique that some of the others did.

The second interviewer is supposed to adopt an argumentative role, according to the accounts of the interviewing process given us by the interviewing Board. The interviewee is supposed to withstand fierce questioning and to be self-confident, but in a manner which respects the accumulated wisdom and experience of the Board. The second interviewer asks Fortescue:

B2: Why did you go to university?
F: Because I wanted to.
B2: Because *you* wanted to?
F: Because I wanted to. Though I must admit at the school I went to, there was a sort of carrying forward process that you would go to university . . . Also my family background, both my parents went to university [once again the background].

Fortescue is also asked about the ways in which university failed to live up to his ideals. He says:

F: As I said during the first interview, a degree, as far as I can see, is merely an indication that one is able to learn rather than something . . . which qualifies one to do a job. When I first went I wasn't so conscious of the fact that if I came away from university I would have to start training for my particular discipline that I took up, and that my university education was broadening my mind and only teaching me how to learn rather than teaching me actually what I was learning.
B2: So what's the next step in your life, in your career?
F: Um, as I see it, to get a job which involves a certain disciplinary training.

Injecting our own understandings into the situation, we become aware that a successful interviewee will not overstress the importance of a university education. The assessors are

F

mainly non-graduates themselves, and prefer the candidate who defers to experience and allows himself to be talked down to, rather than the one who stresses logic and academic training. (The same interviewer says to another candidate: 'We don't live by logic do we? We'd become a lot of automatons if we lived alone by logic.') Fortescue both plays down his university education, and does not react abrasively when questioned as follows:

B2: [noticing that Fortescue has also applied for theatre management] Well, you know, can you think of anything more um terrific variation, more difference between an Organization Officer, 9 to 5 p.m., bowler hat, 5.21, you know, in the evening and, you know, theatre management – probably the most dicey profession in the world, isn't it?

F: No I disagree with you, I would say rather than look at the differences I'd look at the similarities.

B2: Well, ah, come on, *this is what I was leading up to*. What are the similarities? [Compare Fortescue's ability to convince the interviewer that he can follow the latter's train of thought with Chadwick's unexpected question about promotion – on p. 74 above.]

F: ... Essentially the management problems of the theatre as distinct from the social artistic ... 50 per cent of it is dealing with people ... it's a problem which, like any other management job, should be the correct marriage of techniques – well people, ideas and things really, and, in essence, it's really the same thing. [The non-participant administrators later agree that this was a particularly significant and good answer.]

After Fortescue's interview, the chief assessor remarks:

B1: A good run of the mill, without any particular flair of any description; you know, goes through life with their head buried in the sand, but jolly good types anyway, – I liked him.

J: He was quite a nice chap though really.

The chief interviewer later listens again to the interview with Fortescue, and remarks:

B1: But I wrote 'very well balanced chap without any

particular flair'. Um. He's a good run of the mill er chap ... You do appreciate that very largely high-flyers don't necessarily um commend themselves to us because high-flyers usually fly somewhere else. I like good solid types and it struck me as a good solid type. What's S. written? 'Good – good lad, enthusiastic; would work well at anything which interests him' ... Yes, he's um, he's just a pass, he's not a high-flyer by any means.

R: Yes, yes I see.

B1: Now, let's have Andreski.

Fortescue succeeds throughout by virtue of his knowledge of what is expected of him in the selection process and his ability to live up to his perceptions. He comes over as 'acceptable' in appearance, non-abrasiveness, and social background; he 'sells himself' without appearing to brag; he allows himself to be talked down to without taking offence; he takes others' views into account; he recognizes the value of experience and common sense over logic and university degrees; he seems to have reasonable motivation towards joining the Organization and organizational experience, and he is not a high-flyer who will 'fly somewhere else'. Fortescue thus successfully brings off in interview a display of the social skills which the members of the Organization take to be essential in administrative work.

3. *Andreski*

'Um ... an odd sort of chap this. I found him quite impressive. I found with this chap that he was extrovert, quite self-confident, not afraid to make his own point of view even when it obviously didn't agree with mine – this I think is a very good thing ... He seems to me to be just the sort of chap who had an extrovert personality, a good imagination, fresh ideas, just the sort of bloke that one would in fact be looking for.' (James commenting on the first interview)

Andreski, who is 23 and studying sociology, gets a favourable report as seen above on his milk-round interview, and is accordingly sent forward to the Group Selection process. Unlike the previous candidate, Fortescue, Andreski fails miserably at this second procedure, and by comparing some of the things said about him and by him with Fortescue, the reasoning and criteria used by the selectors can be more fully understood.

Andreski is asked to give an account of his first interview, from which the following quote is taken:

> A: I think it was the nicest interview I had, er . . . simply because I think I was asked intelligent questions, you know, questions where you had to think. I mean one doesn't feel that he was looking for little spots of mud on your shoes or, um, sort of a little piece of bristle on your face, or the length of your tie or something like that. He was just trying to find out what sort of person you were.

The form which James completed after the first interview on Andreski perhaps begins to show a few of the factors which become increasingly important for the second interview and group discussion, and on which Andreski at this stage does not get the highest marks possible. The comment 'extrovert, rather overconfident', in particular, is a reading of Andreski's manner which is to count against him later.

Andreski's mark-sheet

NAME: Andreski

1. APPEARANCE
   Medium height and build, droopy moustache. Quite neat and tidy.
2. ACCEPTABILITY
   Quite good. Improved as interview went on.
3. CONFIDENCE
   Extrovert, rather overconfident.
4. EFFORT
   Good.
5. ORGANIZATION
   Magazine editor, etc.
6. MOTIVATION
   Quite good, seemed keen on the Organization and adminis-tration. A good chap who has ideas.

ANY OTHER COMMENTS
Call 1.

When Andreski takes part in the group discussion he has a lot to say, and James who leads the group has several times to

stop him so that someone else can speak. The discussion is on
the topic of race relations (Andreski is of Polish origins).

> A: If you, if you are branded by an identity, if your
> name is George Edwards and you're black, no
> matter how much you try to identify your skin
> colour is going to brand you, your children and
> your grandchildren unless they can assimilate a
> certain amount of cream into the coffee/
>
> Miss X: /Where I think/
>
> A: /And, er, and huh merge into the general popula-
> tion/
>
> X: But do you think. . .
>
> A: (raised voice) But with the problem you were
> talking about. . .
>
> James: Hang on! Let Miss X have a go!

Later on in the discussion the Chairman of the Board joins in:

> B1: I've had experience of practically everybody. During the
> war I commanded both Muslim and Hindus . . . And
> to me they were all 'chaps', and until the Race Relations
> Act told me people were different I regarded everybody
> as chaps.

Andreski shouts his way in to the conversation again a few
seconds later: and, unlike the Chairman, insists on taking the
matter seriously and expressing a firm point of view:

> A: The point, THE POINT IS that when the sikh comes
> over he takes a job as a carpenter or a bricklayer.
> The West Indian is almost invariably a carpenter
> or an unskilled labourer . . . That is a fact.
>
> Miss Y: Er, but is this true . . . /
>
> A: /but, but they/
>
> B1: /or, or a fast bowler!
> General laughter.
> [Researcher present noticed that Andreski didn't
> laugh.]
>
> A: Or OR a fast bowler but that doesn't constitute a
> great proportion of the immigrant population/
>
> B1: /No, no, quite!
>
> A: But the point is that when . . . when they're in
> competition for the high, you know, higher jobs,

85

jobs that they couldn't do before – they were all right as long as they knew their place and were carpenters and bricklayers and so on. But when they, when they start competing with people, are they going to say 'Well they're all just chaps' and so on ...

On the morning discussion's marking sheets, Andreski fares badly on two of the three assessors' ratings. On the marking for 'taking others' views and feelings into account', he gets 1 out of 5 and 2 out of 5 from two of the assessors, the lowest mark they give anyone on any attribute.

Andreski is later asked by the researcher:

R: What struck you as the qualities they were looking for in the group discussion?

A: Er, eh-eh-eh ... Ability to express an opinion, ability to, um, when confronted with an unfamiliar problem to sift through it, sort out the relevant points and er push forward what you think are the relevant points ... Ability to influence.

Unlike Chadwick, Andreski feels fairly confident that he knows 'what is going on' in the selection process, but comparing his assessment with that of Fortescue shows a totally different conception of the rules of the game. Most notably, he fails to attend to Fortescue's recognition of the necessity of 'taking other people's point'.

Some examples of Andreski's performance in the afternoon interview may serve as illustrations of the different attitude he adopts towards varying types of questions, compared to the transcripts of Fortescue's interview already given.

A: Why the Organization? I like this town, I'm familiar with this town. Um, secondly, I hope I share, *I hope I share with you a certain aversion towards private industry/*

B1: /Yes?/

A: /which I do actually. Um. I would rather work for a group or a corporation or whatever you call it/

B1: /Yes, yes./

A: /in which I feel I am contributing more to people/

B1: /Yes./

A: /to a maximum number of people than to a minimum

number of wealthy people – I know this is – seems very idealistic/

B1: /But can't this apply to private industry as well? You're agin private industry you know, I feel, aren't you? *Some private industry is very good.*

A: Oh yes. I'm not deriding private industry flat out but I personally wouldn't feel satisfaction in working as a personnel manager for ICI or for er . . . This is a personal feeling. [A2 later comments about the Board: 'They want to avoid if possible, the, um, graduate do-gooder. You know the person who says, "I don't want to go into industry because I dislike the idea of profit, um, I dislike the idea of people who are concerned with making a thing work efficiently." ']

Unlike Fortescue, Andreski gives the impression of being prepared to express strong feelings about matters that are likely to be contentious. ('I hope I share with you a certain aversion towards private industry', he says. This misjudgment of the Board's attitude is reflected in B1's comment: 'Some private industry is very good.') After the Board's Chairman has asked his questions, the second interviewer's opening comments reveals that Andreski's remarks have been interpreted as abrasive:

B3: I get the impression, and pardon me for saying so, but I'm here to say what I think, I get the impression of somebody fairly aggressively feeling a fair large chip on the shoulder. Now, is this true?

A: That I feel a large chip on the shoulder?

B3: Aggressively. You're an aggressive person. If you've got a chip on your shoulder it's going to be a fairly large one.

A: I would say that I'm aggressive to the extent that if I feel that something ought to be done, you know, I sometimes get annoyed if I ask somebody to do a favour, you know. I wouldn't say that I'm naturally aggressive but I tend to get a bit impatient when I did certain things like the Rag Committee and things like that. Um and one just has to be aggressive to get anything done because one/

B3: /Your showing this morning left one certainly in no doubt that you've got a fairly thrustful nature.

A: I suppose that could be said.

Andreski ends up with very low marks overall and is inevitably rejected. Before he goes in for the interview the following exchange takes place between the selectors:

B1: We've got the real problem one last, haven't we?
B3: You'd like him wouldn't you? (jokingly)
James: He'd be a challenge wouldn't he?
B3: I don't go in for challenges.

After the interview:

B1: He was absolutely abysmal with me. He was much better with you two wasn't he?
B3: You were too generous [referring to the slightly higher marks B1 had given].
B1: James, I'm sorry but he was your man wasn't he?
James: Yes he was. I was saying earlier in defence, you know, that he was the sort of bloke one ought to see.
B1: Exactly . . . He was a good catalyst to have in the group.

The same three non-participants from the Organization later listen to the interview, without hearing the Board's comments or knowing their marks.

A2: A bit self-opinionated, unwilling to compromise.
A3: As a kind of selling job on himself he did a terrible job. He seemed to resent the whole process so much if that interview is any guide. There was no attempt really to be friendly or warm of forthcoming, or volunteer anything.

After hearing Andreski's account of the Group Selection process given afterwards to the researcher:

A2: He was highly suspicious. Where he was critical he wasn't constructively critical. He was destructively critical the whole time. A totally different impression. A sort of knocker you know. The chap who would knock the system without necessarily finding a better way, which we got a glimmer of in the interview.
A3: Yes, I would agree with that.

While James later repeats his view that people like Andreski
should be accepted, but he wants Andreski as a 'catalyst' and
in this way differs from the Board.

One of the selectors sums up the more general view:

B3: For what is a safe kind of service you need a safe kind
of servant.

In conclusion, it is perhaps worth adding that not all the
administrators whose accounts we have reported identify with
every quality which is at a premium in the selection process.
Chadwick, for instance, has been seen by some of them as a
personally pleasant sort of person with a great deal to contribute
who, unfortunately, would not fit in at the Organization. From
their point of view, pleasant people get into the Organization
by having the good sense to play according to the rules of the
game (whatever their own views). To do otherwise, for instance
by dressing in the wrong way or by expressing 'abrasive'
opinions, is not, as they see it, to be morally wrong; it is
simply to be socially maladroit. For such behaviour reveals a
lack of the basic social skills necessary to get by in most British
organizations: as one administrator put it: 'It's rather like
swearing in Church.'

SELECTION AND ACCOUNTING

Administrators are not alone in seeking to produce authoritative accounts of an event. Faced with tapes of selection
interviews, it is tempting for the researcher to set about producing
a list of candidate qualities which explain the known outcome
of their applications. With the data available in this present
study, it would also be possible to refer to the subsequent
accounts of members of the Board in order to support a
particular interpretation. It must be stressed, however, that
the explanations of both selectors and researchers resolve the
indefinite elaboration of accounts only by employing practices
designed to further practical outcomes. For bureaucracies and
scientific peer-groups require *authoritative* accounts of events;
a requirement which is satisfied by adopting various procedures
to 'close' the infinite features of any interaction – for instance,
by using such rules as 'let it pass', 'enough is enough', etc.
(see Garfinkel 1967, quoted on p. 64 above).

In the case of the Organization, the mark-sheets completed by the selectors provide such authoritative accounts. They stand as displays of the rational accountability of selection decisions by providing the 'grounds' of any decision. Since such grounds are presumably viewable by any person, the decision can be seen as generated by the intrinsic properties of the candidates rather than by the 'bias' or 'subjectivity' of the interviewer. Yet, for analytical purposes, such reported grounds must not be confused with the determination of the selection outcome. The point in time at which the selection decision is made and the grounds for making it (the appearance of a candidate as he gives an answer, the impression he makes as he enters the room) are irremovably linked to the context in which they occur. To 'discover' such grounds would imply a research design in which the selectors had to tape their thoughts during the unfolding of the interview. But even here one would be getting accountably rational 'reasons' for decisions rather than the thoughts (and hence the decisions) themselves. The mark-sheet used by the selectors, then, demonstrate that their activities are in-accord-with-a-rule; they do not report on the grounds of the decision *as it was made*.

We have argued that accounts of 'what happened', whether lay or sociological, in no way stand by themselves as simple snapshots of the events which they seek to depict. Any correspondence between an account and such events is negotiated, depending upon situated reconstructions of the past for its production and understanding. In terms of this paper, then, any attempt to offer a list of qualities 'important' in the selection process would necessarily rely upon, as a tacit resource, the interpretive work required by the researcher to encode a verbal exchange as a depiction of some quality and by the reader to decode a truncated list of qualities by employing his lay knowledge to 'visualize' the missing particulars. Rather than play that particular game, we have chosen to analyse the accounting activities on which such a game depends. In this final section, then, we eschew offering one more 'authoritative' account of 'what happened', in favour of an analysis of the production of authoritative accounts of selection interviews.

In order to make the world available to themselves and to others, members engage themselves, by means of their accounts, in the production and maintenance of certain assumed pro-

perties of a setting. In making events accountable, members'
talk also serves to confirm the existence of a 'real' world. Thus
an account provides for the assumed features of the setting
which it purports to describe – it is *reflexive* upon that setting.
Further, since the account necessarily must leave much unsaid
(for, indeed, there is much that cannot be said or better ex-
plicated without lapsing into absurdity), the hearer relies on
his tacit knowledge to fill in 'what is meant' by an utterance.
Talk, then, is treated by members, both lay and sociological,
as an *index* of certain properties of the world. As conversation
unfolds, so more things become clear and, in the process, the
participants discover (what will pass for the moment as) the
sense of what they are saying.

The classic discussion of the accounting process occurs in
an early passage of Garfinkel (1967: p. 3):

'(1) Whenever a member is required to demonstrate that an
account analyses an actual situation, he invariably makes
use of the practices of "et cetera", "unless", and "let it
pass" to demonstrate the rationality of his achievement.
(2) The definite and sensible character of the matter that is
being reported is settled by an assignment that reporter and
auditor make to each other that each will furnish whatever
unstated understandings are required. Much therefore of
what is actually reported is not mentioned.
(3) Over the time for their delivery accounts are apt to require
that "auditors" be willing to wait for what will have been
said in order that the present significance of what has been
said will have become clear.
(4) Like conversations, reputations, and careers, the particulars of accounts are built up step by step over the actual
uses of and references to them.
(5) An account's materials are apt to depend heavily for
sense upon their serial placement, upon their relevance to
the auditor's projects, or upon the developing course of the
organizational occasions of their use.'

Considerations of this nature raise the following questions
about the earlier parts of this paper:

1. What stock of knowledge is implied in reading talk as
   comprehensible 'interview talk'?

2. What particulars do members attend to in producing multiple accounts of ostensibly the same phenomenon? and

3. How do members retrospectively close the indefinite features of any social scene by offering authoritative accounts of its nature, i.e. what is involved in successful rewriting of history?

Each of these questions is considered below.

1. *Shared competences*

In this section we are concerned with the competences used by subjects and researchers in attending to scenes (as participants or by means of tape) as an undoubted example of an interview (which can go well or badly, smoothly or shakily) and in treating what passes as a display of motives, qualities, and personalities.

The following examples give some indication of the complexity of members' skills and knowledge:

    1. B1: [after hearing tape of part of the interview] I wasn't frightfully impressed with his answers, but on the other hand, I must make allowances for the fact that I'm the first person speaking/

Researcher: /That's right . . . yes.

        B1: So they're nervous to start with. Er, so the first two questions which I ask are always answered very hesitantly. He maybe got, er, better when B2 asked him questions . . .

        [later the Chairman says he was prepared to take him on the strength of his answers to B2's questions.]

    2. A1: [commenting on tape] His confidence was shaken by the Chairman but not by B2.

In these examples the non-participant administrator seems to have no difficulty in detecting in a tape recording the features of an interview in which acceptability and rapport can be displayed and observed. Taken with the Chairman's comments, his remark indicates the way in which talk is always decoded in terms not only of the presumed 'topic' of the talk but of the serial placement of an utterance, which may be taken to indicate acceptable nervousness at one stage and unacceptable lack of confidence if heard later on.

The explicitness with which the Chairman defines his strategies for making sense of utterances is a feature of the 'organized' occurrence of interactions like interviews compared with the chance nature of many encounters (cf. Turner's (1971) discussion of therapy talk). In the former situation, members may pay more *explicit* attention to the structuring of what goes on as well as to its presumed content. In the following example, the Chairman has started to talk to a researcher about the 'selection procedure':

> B1: I've already told you that the initial start to my questions on, er, do they know anything about the activities of the Organization is simply to find out if they're swanning around or not . . . Then the second person always has a go at them . . . to see whether they will stand up to someone being argumentative and rather unpleasant. And the third person just tidies up . . .

To some extent, then, while the organization of everyday conversations, exchanges of greetings, etc., are not made the subject of comment, unless something appears to go drastically wrong, in non-chance encounters members treat it as accountably rational to formulate a planned structure and to understand each other's talk in terms of such a structure. Moreover, such activities can appear visible to participants not involved in the planning stage. For instance, in offering an account of his appearance before the Board, Fortescue has some conception that the Board are not acting 'naturally':

> F: . . . Well, *obviously* they're adopting roles . . . as part of the interviewing technique, i.e. having one quite friendly, one less friendly and one who attacks you.

Perhaps, even more surprising, if one takes the stance of viewing accounts as anthropologically strange, is the ability of non-participants (researchers, other administrators) to attend to a tape-recording as a non-problematic example of 'interview-talk' and to produce off-the-cuff accounts of what was going on, what was intended, etc. In this connection, the following exchanges are interesting:

A3: [after hearing tape of milk-round interview] What an excellent interviewer James is!

A2: Yes I liked the way he squashed the attempt of the candidate to interview him at the end of the interview. He just killed it stone-dead really without being rude, which is terribly difficult to do in fact . . .

A3: And he got a tremendous amount of frankness out of the chap, the chap's real attitudes, in a very short time, which is what interviewing . . . what seems to be the chap's real attitudes as far as one can ever tell in that period of time . . .

[further talk about the qualities of the candidate]

A3: I would have made it slightly harder for him. James was some of the time, given the fact that it was a fairly short interview, making it very easy for him to say 'yes'. I mean I've written down a lot of James's questions and in fact they're not sufficient, he does point out the kind of answer he's looking for in the question on at least three or four occasions.

A2: He very rarely asks the tough, difficult question. He likes to get the person talking and, if you like, exposing the facets of his personality in fact. This is what he tries to do, simply that. And then all he does is to nod, to agree, to call for responses to come from the individual.

A3: Yes, that comes out of the transcript.

A2: And this comes out in this [presumably the tape].

Only a partial list of the competences presumed in these exchanges would include: (1) a knowledge of what constitutes a 'good' interviewer; (2) an ability to make out an attempt by an interviewee to take over the interviewer's role; (3) knowledge of what might be involved in 'killing' such attempts, with or without rudeness; (4) an understanding of what may be taken to be 'frankness'; (5) an ability to spot the kind of question which points out its own answer; and (6) knowledge of what passes as a non-tough interview. (See Silverman (forthcoming) for an examination of interview-talk in terms of such competences.) It is also necessary to bear in mind, however, that members attend to interview-talk with certain practical outcomes as their main concern. Formulating the structure of the interview is only a minor part of their interest and, indeed, may only be called for in so far as it is seen to relate to the display of the candidates' abilities, motives, and preferences which the interview is taken to offer, and the decision of acceptance or rejection which follows from witnessing this display. However, what, in the context of the unfolding of a certain social scene, will be viewed as the expression of a quality must remain problematic. As the following examples show, a candidate's answers are never taken at their face-value, i.e. stripped of their situational context:

1. B2: You ask questions for a reason – to find out what makes them tick, see how they react to criticism. It's not only the content of a reply, it's also their interests. You've got to sort out the good interviewee who simply mugs it up.

2. A1: [after a disagreement about what a tape reveals] This, this is a question, isn't it, of the clues you pick up, um, much more than the actual form of the interview . . . And I suppose, in a way, it's a question of, um, what, you know, a person gives you an answer in a certain manner. It may be the, the absolutely pat answer.

   A3: Yeah.

   A1: But I mean some people will think of the pat answer for themselves./

   A3: /A good point/

   A1: /And the thing that it's the pat answer is not the point but whether it's given as the pat answer/

   A3: /Quite so.

3. A1: [after commenting on a candidate's performance] This is a subjective evaluation of a remark. It isn't what he says so much.

These comments illustrate the way in which attempts by members (lay and sociological) to depict the meanings of social scenes (their supposed norms, the imagined character of an exchange) irremediably rely upon practices employed to cope with the inherent gaps and inconsistencies in talk and, thereby, to assemble, for all practical purposes, a particular reality. As Cicourel (forthcoming) suggests in the course of an analysis of the limitations, from a sociological point of view, of linguistic theories:

'If we hope to construct a theory of meaning that enables us to understand how we assign sense to our everyday worlds and establish reference, then we cannot assume that oral language syntax is the basic ingredient of a theory of meaning. The *interactional context*, as reflexively experienced over an exchange, or as imagined or invented when the scene is displaced or is known through a text, remains the heart of a general theory of meaning.' (manuscript, p. 71)

These practices include attempts to insert the missing particulars of an utterance (i.e. to remedy a gloss) and to treat part of a conversation as an occasion to describe that conversation (i.e. what may be termed 'formulating practices' (Garfinkel and Sacks 1970) provide a full discussion of these practices). They share in common the attempt to remedy the necessarily context-bound nature of an utterance.

Viewed in this light, lay and sociological attempts to produce authoritative accounts of selection outcomes seem more interesting as practical accomplishments than as descriptions of any reality. As Cicourel comments on the interpretive work that allows one to produce such accomplishments:

'The setting is not merely a passive vehicle for witnessing universals of language [or, in our case, of 'qualities']; the setting is constitutive of how properties of cognition as displays of practical reasoning render a scene sensible or socially meaningful . . . The discovery of constancies (comprehensible conversation, stable identity, etc.) reflects the normative organization of everyday experience by an inescapable reliance on memory and practical reasoning.' (forthcoming: manuscript, pp. 21–2)

2. *Multiple realities*

'The fact that it's not the organization, it's somebody in the organization that decides as an immediate outcome.' (administrator commenting on the selection process)

One of the central problematic questions for the social sciences is the availability of the social world for description and explanation. While the natural scientist can often make visible, if only by means of measuring devices, the existence of the properties which he claims to characterize an object or process, the sociologist is unable to demonstrate (at least in the same manner) that an interaction possesses the properties of roles, norms, and values. Furthermore, while all scientific explanations claim only to focus on some limited features of a vastly complex reality, the natural scientist can rightly claim that he alone is responsible for the selection activity. In the social world, however, the participants themselves select features to which they attend. Similarly, confronted with a predefined reality, the observer of social scenes can only begin his descriptive and explanatory work by relying upon taken-for-granted knowledge of the world gained as a participant himself.

The previous section discussed some of the competences involved in making out a sequence of utterances as a selection interview, in which personalities may be displayed and detected, i.e. made into observable-reportable events. In this section we want to examine the construction of multiple accounts from ostensibly the same social scene. For, while nobody seemed to doubt that what they were hearing was 'in fact' an interview and that what went on was relevant to selection outcomes, they often read different things into a speech exchange.

The first example is drawn from Chadwick's milk-round interview, the surface features of which were discussed earlier. In the sequence below, Chadwick is talking to a researcher about James after the selection interview:

C: Fortunately he lives in D. [an inner-city area], I don't know if, uh, uh, do you know that?
R: Mmm.
C: It's just down the road from you. And so, you know, he knew the type of life, the type of environment I'd been into; *this was no sort of stumbling block . . .*

Chadwick seems to have gained his information that James lived in the same part of town through the following interview exchange:

J: Um . . . from your school did you, most people go on to university or not?
C: Out of the Sixth Form only two went to university/
J: /Really?!
C: . . . It's a very poor educational school . . .

J: Well *you* did well enough out of it.

C: I may be called an exception. Um, I'll give you a typical example of . . . when I first . . . In my first year there were seven forms of thirty boys and by the Upper Sixth there was eleven people.

J: W-w-well, why do you think this is. . . I mean?

C: Er, well in as much as B. is a tougher area than D.

J: Come orf it! I live there (both laugh).

C: I – I just, I know, you, you *you're just like me, an exception* – you've got somewhere . . .

Both to the researcher and to James, Chadwick implies that selector and candidate have similar kinds of backgrounds, taking James's utterances to indicate that they move in the same social milieu. James's account of the same interview, however, conveys that he reads something very different into what transpired:

J: . . . [Chadwick was] the sort of chap who really, coming from the background he did . . . er . . . was about what you would have expected. That is to say, without, I mean it sounds terribly snobbish, but um, he was the sort of bloke who had got there by hard work . . . I didn't find him very impressive as an individual . . . er . . . not frightfully mature, in fact rather gauche altogether.

Focusing on Chadwick's cockney accent, which differed from his own, James treats the interview as an occasion which reveals Chadwick's lack of acceptability. Following on from the early clues offered by Chadwick's accent and appearance, he launches into an exchange (which satisfies him about the former's background) by means of a question, introduced as a new topic, which he does not ask of any other candidate: 'Um . . . from your school did you, most people go on to university or not?'

Competing accounts of interviews also arise among different administrators as the following discussion about the supposed qualities of Fortescue suggests:

A2: I would call him [for a second interview] . . . He seemed acceptable to his fellows and to James. He showed confidence – he wasn't shaken by questions and had occupied positions of authority.

A1: I would call him too . . . He seemed at ease in the interview situation . . . an acceptable person . . .

A3: He seemed to lack confidence when he changed his mind over a topic raised by James; . . . I would have thought you would have put him down as a hold . . . He seemed too keen to please, a 'yes-man'.

The displays of multiple realities illustrated by these examples confirm that members respond not to a sequence of words or actions in themselves but to the supposed meaning or logic that underlies them. To ascertain this logic they rely on situated constructions of past experiences and the unfolding cues (both visual and auditory) observed in any social scene. Under-standing, then, always derives from the ongoing discovery of a set of relevances. (See Schutz 1970 for an analysis of lay and scientific relevance structures; for a treatment of film in this way see Silverman 1972.)

It follows from this that there are no context-free rules by which the observer can maintain that any of these accounts are right or wrong. It is fruitless, therefore, to pursue the question of whether Fortescue really 'did' lack confidence. Such questions are only posed and answered for the purpose of settling practical outcomes. From the selector's point of view, decisions about events must be made and justified; as a consequence a specific reading of an interview will be offered as a 'final' account. In the context of selection, there is no possibility of questioning such accounts: if Fortescue is defined by a selector as being 'confident' that is indeed what, for all practical purposes, he will have to be. Observers, like A3, who have made the 'wrong' reading must then reformulate their accounts by attending to features of the interview that they had previously missed (see the next section for A3's reformula-tion).

If sociology is ultimately a 'folk' science, in so far as its discoveries about society are necessarily made from the 'inside', the discussion in this section carries the implication that the question, 'What (really) happened?' is irretrievably a lay member's question. To produce answers that justify a discipline that is not to be a wordy restatement of 'what everybody knows', sociologists must ask other questions. More specifically, the question, 'What happened?' could be replaced by the following: (1) What accounts do members offer of their realities? (2) What features they have to provide for in the world in order to offer such accounts? (3) What do listeners have to assume so as to comprehend them as rational accounts?

3. *Rewriting of history*

As has already been noted, the treatment of accounts as a *description* of a past series of events is part of the natural attitude. For accounts are always generated and understood by reference to the relevances of a present social scene; the context-bound properties of the past can never be reconstituted. It is the concern of the sociologist to analyse how accounts come to stand as representations of past events, i.e. it is his concern to examine how the past is constituted as an observable-reportable phenomenon, as sets of activities in-accord-with-a-rule.

In their accounting activities members address themselves to the task of displaying what will currently be understood as the rational grounds of past actions and as rational explanations of past social scenes: that is to say they attend to the production of authoritative accounts. Once again, however, it must be stressed that their accounts in no way stand for, report upon, or describe what were taken to be such rational grounds and explanations *at that past time*. In order to make visible this rewriting of history (*creation* of history might be a better term since history is only written when an account is offered of it), we have shown application forms and played tapes of interviews to members of the Organization's Selection Board several weeks after these interviews occurred. They were then asked to offer an account of the performance of different candidates. Only later did we provide them with the mark-sheets completed at the time and remind them (if they had forgotten) of the actual selection outcome. As more information was received by the auditor, so a new account would be offered in order to make what was currently known accountably rational.

The first example arose when the Chairman (B1) was played a tape of the part of the interview where he questioned Fortescue (he had already remembered that Fortescue had been accepted):

B1: Yes, I remember him.

R: And what do you think of his answers to your part?

B1: A bit shaky . . . er, I wouldn't have said that I would have marked him very highly; I should have said offhand er, er, Jill, that he'd have got through on the marking of Mr B. and Mr S. if they were the other people. . . .

R: Would you like to hear the comments of the others?/

B1: /Yes, yeah:

(the tape is played)

B1: His answer to me, er, though I didn't hear it very properly on the playback, on whether it would be a good idea to centralize education, I thought was quite good. Now, *having thought about it while S. was talking*, he would have been a borderline with me, with my marking. But I would have said that S. and probably myself listening to him standing up to S. would probably get him through.

R: Mmm.

B1: *So that's probably the answer* that, because he showed distinct guts in standing up to a necessarily abrasive type of questioning.

R: And that was what got him through?

B1: That's . . . *that I think was what got him through.* And you, you must admit he was speaking far more intelligently to S. than he was to me. . . .

In this example, the Chairman treats the tapes as providing materials which supply, if read properly, the sensible grounds of the Board's decision (e.g. 'So that's probably the answer').

The managed accomplishment of a 'correct' account of an outcome is equally apparent in the Chairman's remarks about Andreski, although in this case it is a rejection decision which must be justified:

R: What do you remember about him from the interview?

B1: A rather specious individual who probably, I think, interviewed pretty well . . .

(the tape of his part of the interview is played)

B1: This was a very poor interview . . . I got the impression that he was, er, just sort of swanning around, that he was, just trying us as a, as a last resort.

(the tape of most of the rest of the interview is played)

B1: Right!

R: Is that enough to remember or do you want to hear any more?/

B1: /I can see, yes, I can see why we didn't take that fellow ... we felt that it would have, he had some difficulty in fitting in to the Organization because we felt he was a somewhat aggressive personality.

The Chairman hears the tape of the researcher's interview with Andreski after Group Selection:

B1: He's got no depth, has he? He's got no depth, this fellow, at all – no/

R: /No.

B1: /depth of character. Er. I'm fascinated Jill when you said that we didn't get the [tutor's] report until after the interview.

R: Mmm. I think his tutor was on holiday, and a different tutor sent the report in

B1: H-how absolutely fascinating, because *it just shows that our procedure is pretty accurate*, because, look here, there's the report which we got after the interview.

Since paper records are rarely kept at the time of interactions, members are relatively free subsequently to make of them what they will to a third party – always within the bounds, of course, of what will stand as a rational description. In the case of bureaucracies, however, a special problem arises for members when an account is later apparently 'disproved' by reference to a record made of the events which the account purports to describe. Such a problem occurred in the following conversation between B3 (a member of the Board) and a researcher:

B3: [interrupting the playback of the taped interview with Andreski] I don't need to know the rest – I remember the man ... I did not like Andreski ... I think he was probably accepted.
(B3 is shown the mark-sheets which reveal that Andreski was rejected)

B3: I obviously did not overcome my prejudices ... We obviously came to the feeling that, though intelligent, he would be more of a nuisance than anything else ... I thought we had taken Andreski, but *very obviously the bad qualities outdid the good ones.*

(the researcher's interview with Andreski is played)

B3: ... His social something or other comes out, he wouldn't fit in ... I'm glad we turned him down ... he's got a cool, calculating manner, people ought to have a bit of a social conscience.

Notice how the 'sense' of what transpired is re-read in terms of the selection outcome ('very obviously the bad qualities outdid the good ones').

Selectors' accounts of past interviews provide, then, the rational grounds for seeing the appropriateness of a selection decision – they do not report on how the decision was made, but demonstrate that it was a decision in-accord-with-a-rule.

We will take as a final example of the rewriting of history in the light of official outcomes, the series of remarks made by an administrator on hearing tapes of Fortescue's passage through the selection process.

1. I certainly wouldn't recommend calling that guy for Group Selection, neither would you or James I imagine. [the first comment after hearing the interview]
2. I would have thought you would have put it down as a hold ... I would like to have seen the guy and see his reactions. [after hearing the other auditors' comments]
3. I reckon I must have got an anti feeling to this guy. [after hearing a tape of James's comments]
4. I got a slightly better impression of the guy. [after hearing the second interview]
5. I had missed his sense of humour. [after hearing the second interview]
6. He showed awareness of complexity. [after hearing the researchers' interview with the candidate]
7. My impression of him got steadily better ... I was very surprised about his ability to sum up what was wanted of him. It was quite out of keeping with my impression of him ... This is all frightfully confusing ... [on being asked by a researcher to summarize his reactions towards the candidate]

While even at time 7 he is prepared to restate his earlier impression of a candidate about whom he was not sure whether he doesn't fit in too much, is too smooth, the administrator by now is clearly prepared to accept a favourable interpretation of the candidate's performance.

CONCLUDING REMARKS

The main import of this paper lies in again drawing attention to the availability of the mundane world as a resource for studying normative structures. Both in everyday life and in the scientific attitude, members tacitly rely on this availability as an essential resource for carrying out practical actions and for finding normative structures in their analyses. In so doing, they conceal from themselves the activities through which the mundane world is constituted, provided for, and attended to. Only by means of scientific focus upon the taken-for-granted practices required to assemble the world can social scientists begin to claim to explicate that world. (Ultimately and para-doxically, however, they engage themselves in what must inevitably be a folk science – for their only clue to the nature of folk knowledge is their own folk knowledge. For further discussion of the nature of folk science see Pollner 1970 and Zimmerman and Pollner 1971.)

Our concern with the socially organized activities glossed as 'selection' has served to illustrate the dependence upon these practices of the explanatory work of both participants and researchers. In a sense, this work is never concluded. For the 'correctness' and 'rationality' of selection outcomes is a con-tinually managed accomplishment and must be demonstrated at all times but especially when a recruit is found to be inade-quate. In such a situation, staff members will attend to (and discover) certain features of the recruit's personality and life-history which may be taken to account for what now seems like a 'wrong' decision, or they may recall (or invent) certain reserva-tions they had at the time about the candidate's acceptance. Thus what will have been seen as 'correct' decisions *at the time*, will now be viewed as decisions based upon incomplete know-ledge but ones which do not cast doubt upon the rationality of a particular decision or upon the good sense of the selectors. Indeed such possible accounts are provided for before the suitability of a recruit becomes apparent; selectors have stressed to researchers the 'subjectivity' of the process and the problems involved in 'thumbnailing' a person. Note, however, that, rather than making nonsense of their decisions, such talk provides for them to be read as the'reasonable' products of 'sensible' persons. Moreover, researchers' attempts to reconstruct the features of a selection interview will, in the same way, seek to demonstrate the rational accountability of certain outcomes ('what had to be') by reading some rule into observed activities. If participants and observers are playing slightly different games (justifying-my-own-actions-in-everyday-language as opposed to accounting -for-others'-actions-in-scientific-language), it is difficult to deny that the production and understanding of their accounts as rational reflections of a world depends upon competences used to make out the features of some kind of game and to produce a comprehensible move.

Viewed in this light, analysis of the accounting process seeks to reveal the standards of adequacy used by participants and researchers to bring off 'rational' actions and to construct 'sensible' interpretations. Because they treat accounts (both lay and sociological) as non-problematic 'snapshots' of the world, conventional notions of methodology can thus be understood as sets of practices designed to preserve the mundaneity of the world by remedying the inherent indexicality and reflexivity of communication.[1]

1 For a critique of the positivist auspices of contemporary social science, see Filmer *et al.* 1972. It is ironic that the two disciplines where similar breakthroughs in the understanding of the world have already been made—philosophy and linguistics—are subjects about which social scientists tend to be least informed. We have in mind here Wittgenstein's contention that the meaning of a word is governed by the language-game in which it figures and Chomsky's concept of linguistic competence understood as the ability to generate 'coherent' sentences, 'appropriate' to situations; Chomsky (1968) gives a largely non-technical introduction to his work, while Hartnack 1965 is a useful introduction to Wittgenstein. This is not to imply, however, that such work leads in entirely the same direction as that described here. Indeed, it differs in many important ways—see Cicourel (forthcoming) for a discussion of transformational grammar (1971) and Turner's (1971) treatment of the work of J. L. Austin; Blum and McHugh (1971) apply Chomsky's notion of deep and surface structures to an analysis of 'motives'.

REFERENCES

BLUM, A. and MCHUGH, P. 1971. 'The social ascription of motives', *American Sociological Review*, 36, 98–109

CHOMSKY, N. 1968. *Language and mind*, Harcourt, N.Y.: Brace and World.

CICOUREL, A. Forthcoming. 'Ethnomethodology', in T. A. Sebeck (ed.), *Current trends in linguistics*, vol. 12, Geneva: Mouton.

FILMER, P., PHILLIPSON, M., SILVERMAN, D. and WALSH, D. 1972. *New directions in sociological theory*, London: Collier-Macmillan.

FLOUD, J. and HALSEY, A. 1957. 'Intelligence tests, social class and selection for secondary schools', *British Journal of Sociology*, 8, 33–9

GARFINKEL, H. 1967. *Studies in ethnomethodology*, Englewood Cliffs, N.J.: Prentice-Hall.

GARFINKEL, H. and SACKS, H. 1970. 'On the formal structures of practical actions', in J. McKinney and E. Tiryakian, *Theoretical sociology: perspectives and development*, New York: Appleton-Century-Crofts.

HARTNACK, J. 1965. *Wittgenstein and modern philosophy*, tr. M. Cranston, London: Methuen.

HOLLINGSHEAD, A. B. and REDLICH, F. C. 1958. *Social class and mental illness*, New York: Wiley.

KADUSHIN, C. 1958. 'Individual decisions to undertake psychotherapy', *Administrative Science Quarterly*, 3, 379–411

POLLNER, M. 1970. 'On the foundations of mundane reasoning', unpublished Ph.D. dissertation, University of California, Santa Barbara.

SCHUTZ, A. 1970. *Reflections on the problems of relevance*, tr. R. Zaner, New Haven and London: Yale University Press.

SILVERMAN, D. 1972. 'Introductory comments', in P. Filmer *et al.*, *op. cit.*

SILVERMAN, D. forthcoming. 'Interview talk: an ethnography of a research instrument'.

TURNER, R. 1971. 'Words, utterances and activities', in J. Douglas (ed.), *Understanding everyday life*, London: Routledge and Kegan Paul.

ZIMMERMAN, D. and POLLNER, M. 1971. 'The everyday world as a phenomenon', in J. Douglas (ed.), *Understanding everyday life*, London: Routledge and Kegan Paul.

4 Career and Individual Strategies

ROGER MANSFIELD

The concept of career draws attention to the processes of change and development. At the same time the idea of a career forces consideration of the individual and of the social systems through which he moves, and of the interaction between the individual and these social systems. A career is both a highly personal experience and a publicly observable phenomenon. As Hughes (1937) has suggested, career may usefully be viewed as a two-sided concept. One side refers to the succession of more or less institutionalized positions through which the individual passes during his working life. This side of a career is publicly observable and, at least in theory, is objectively measurable. This side of the concept will be referred to as the individual's *objective career*. The other side of the concept refers to the individual's personal assessment of himself, his job, and his career within the overall context of his working life. That is, it is career as experienced subjectively by the individual; and this is only accessible to investigation by inference from the individual's words and deeds. This second side of the concept of career will be referred to as the individual's *subjective career*.

This usage of the concept of career is somewhat broader than that advocated by many writers. For example, Wilensky (1960) argues that the concept loses utility when we speak of the 'career of the ditch-digger'. He goes on to suggest that 'a career viewed structurally, is a succession of related jobs, arranged in a hierarchy of prestige, through which persons move in an ordered predictable sequence'. He admits that the implication of this narrowing of the concept limits usage of the term to discussion of the lives of a minority of the population. This

107

sort of career is what Becker (1952) has termed a 'vertical career'. Becker argues, contrary to Wilensky's viewpoint, that there is also a need for research into 'horizontal careers' in which individuals pass through a succession of occupational statuses which are equal (or nearly so) with regard to prestige, influence, and income. He further suggests that there is a need for investigation into the interrelation between vertical and horizontal careers. Here, the wider concept of career is used to gain, it is hoped, a fuller understanding of the relationship between the individual and social structure.

From the notion of career suggested above, it follows that career development may be conceived as a process in which the objective and subjective sides of an individual's career interact to precipitate each successive stage. This interaction will be limited by the constraints imposed by the social systems within which the individual's career is worked out. Viewed in this way career development may be considered to be the result of three types of process. First, there is the process of socialization, by which the individual adapts to his social environment. Secondly, there is the process of career choice, in which the individual decides between the various alternatives he sees open to him at a given time. Thirdly, there is the process of environmental change, in which the individual's social environment alters. These alterations in the individual's environment may be divided broadly into two categories for the purposes of this analysis: (1) changes that occur in response to actions of the individual; and (2) changes that result from causes separate from the individual. At particular times in an individual's life, the processes making up career development are particularly obvious. Thus, just before a person leaves full-time education the process of career choice is normally clearly evident as he decides between the various options he perceives as open to him. Just after starting work for the first time, or after transferring to a radically different job, the socialization process is typically clearly visible.

Although the socialization process is not obvious at some stages of a person's career, it is generally acknowledged that the process continues throughout his life. If the process of career choice is taken to include all career-relevant decisions and not just occupational and organizational choices, then it may be assumed that this process also continues throughout a career.

Allowing the continuous nature of the processes involved in career development, then overall it may be viewed as an ongoing, cyclical process in which one part of the cycle corresponds to the socialization process, a second part corresponds to the career choice process, and the cycle is completed by the reactions of factors in the individual's social environment to his actions. In addition, inputs to this cycle coming from other changes in the individual's social environment will influence the nature of the cycle. A schematic representation of this model of career development is shown in Figure 1.

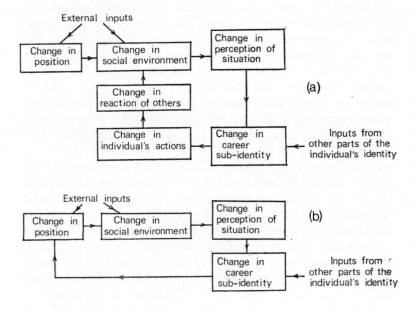

FIGURE 1

When an individual changes his position, this change will, by definition, change his social environment. The individual will tend to adapt to these changes in his social environment by changing his subjective assessment of himself in relation to his social environment. This subjective appreciation of self within the moving perspective of career would seem to correspond to what some authors (for example Hall 1971) have called the individual's *career sub-identity*. That is, that part of his identity vested in roles ensuing from career positions. The change in career sub-identity, following upon a change in position, may be in the direction of conformity, but it is not suggested that great conformity always follows a change of status. Rather, it is suggested that the individual must in some way take account of the changes in his environment. He must integrate his perceptions of them into his sense of personal identity.

The individual's career sub-identity may, in part, be regarded as his predisposition to choose certain courses of action rather than others, and to choose in predictable ways between alternative positional transitions. Thus, in situations where the individual's behaviour is not unduly constrained, changes in his career sub-identity will lead to changes in the career-relevant actions he performs. By changing the actions he performs, the individual will tend to change the ways in which others react to him, thus changing his social environment. Hence, the cycle is completed (Figure 1a). Alternatively, when the constraints of the social system allow, certain changes in a person's career sub-identity may lead the individual to choose a different position, thus completing the cycle in a different way (Figure 1b). These cycles suggest two sorts of career choice. One sort occurs when a choice of action is made while the individual remains in a given position. The other sort of choice involves the individual choosing to change his position in a particular way. It would seem likely that each cycle of the sort in Figure 1b will normally be followed by a number of cycles of the type shown in Figure 1a before the next cycle of the former type.

As has been mentioned above, changes in the individual's environment may also stem from separate causes. The two arrows at the top of Figures 1a and 1b indicate the most obvious ways in which other factors in the individual's environment may directly impinge upon and influence this cyclical process of individual career development. Also, other aspects of the individual's life will affect the process of career development through the interaction of his career sub-identity with other parts of his total identity.

Integral to this suggested model of career development is the idea that the individual views his job, or any other position, in the context of what he remembers he was, and what he wants and expects to be. Thus, each cycle in turn may, to some extent, be seen as the individual attempting to control the direction in which his career is developing. In these terms, each cycle may be considered as the individual's appraisal of his situation, followed by some decision guiding his action, followed by reactions of others to that action, and then the individual's reappraisal of the social situation. Thus, each cycle may be seen as one in which the individual makes choices to further his career, takes actions in accordance with these choices, then sees what results these actions bring, readjusts his ideas, and makes new choices. This way of viewing the cycles suggests that the individual is, in a rational, calculating, and self-conscious way, trying to control his destiny. In certain circumstances this may be true but it would seem likely that, more normally, the individual is likely to act in an intuitive manner, only thinking in detail about the processes at times of crises, perhaps not even then.

The main purpose of this model is to provide a framework within which consideration can be given to the various aspects of career development which have formed the subject of empirical studies and theoretical writings. As a way of organizing these various studies and theories, the career will be followed in essentially a developmental order, that is, consideration will first be given to occupational choice, then to processes of adaptation to work, then to studies of career stages and career development through middle age, and finally to the ends of careers and retirement. After this, consideration will be given to the ways in which variables relevant to career interact with variables relevant to a person's out-of-work activities and the way such interaction affects individual career development and the social forces acting upon organizations through individual careers.

INITIAL OCCUPATIONAL CHOICE

The first and often most decisive influence the individual exercises on his own career is in choosing an occupation in which to work. This particular career decision has been the focus of a considerable quantity of theoretical writing and empirical research from both sociologists and psychologists. A reading of the literature on occupational choice suggests that the process involved is not just a simple career decision in the sense outlined in the previous section. Occupational choice is the final outcome of a process which involves many cycles of the model suggested above. Blau *et al.* (1956) have suggested that occupational choice is the result of a series of decisions. In the extreme, Musgrave (1967) has argued that the first choice of an occupation is influenced by processes commencing at birth.

A wide variety of factors has been shown to have a systematic effect on individual occupational choice. For example, Blau and Duncan (1967) showed that the father's occupation was a good predictor of the socio-economic class of the occupation entered by the son. Other studies (for example Mansfield and Davies 1971) have shown that the father's occupation also, to some extent, predicts the type of occupation chosen. It has also been shown that each sex chooses differentially between different occupations (for example Davies 1961). These two predictors of choice (father's occupation and the individual's sex) clearly can begin to affect the individual's view of the world from birth, as they will both normally exert considerable influence on early socialization processes.

Most of the other predictive variables examined in the occupational choice literature are at least partly a result of the individual's development up to the time of choice. Thus, they can be seen to be a partial consequence of past development and a partial cause of future development for the individual. For example, occupationally related values have been shown to exercise considerable influence on occupational choice and to be influenced in turn by entry into a new occupation. Such a process would be predicted by the model suggested in the previous section. In particular, Rosenberg (1957) and Davis (1961) showed that certain values seemed to be especially salient to those choosing within certain groups of occupations. For example, Rosenberg showed that those choosing careers in social work or teaching typically rated working with people rather than things, or having opportunities to help others, as very important. Those choosing careers in engineering and science, on the other hand, would tend not to rate these values as particularly important. Those choosing careers in business tended to value status and pay, whilst those choosing careers in art, architecture, or journalism tended to value self-expression more than others. Broadly, Davis's later study confirmed the patterns Rosenberg had found and a British study (Mansfield and Davies 1971) also found similar relationships. Underhill's

(1966) longitudinal study showed fairly conclusively that value orientations were both a cause and consequence of occupational choice. In addition to values, Korman (1967a, 1967b) has shown that the individual's ethical judgments and his self-perceived abilities will affect his occupational choice. This set of findings may be summarized by saying that individuals tend to make occupational choices in such a way as to enter occupations which are seen as being consistent with their values, ethics, and self-perceived abilities.

These empirical findings fit within the framework of 'self-implementation' theory. This theory, argued by Super (1957), states that an individual makes an occupational choice in order to implement his concept of self. In broad developmental terms, Super suggests that the individual's self-concept is largely developed during adolescence and implemented in adult life. He sees the first occupational choice as the first attempt in a trial and error process culminating, if successful, in the individual entering an occupation which is largely consistent with his self-image. This theory fits easily into the cyclical model suggested earlier if it is allowed that the self-image relevant to a career (or career sub-identity) changes after adolescence to take account of the changing social reality that the individual confronts as his career begins to develop.

The empirical evidence supporting the 'self-implementation' theory of occupational choice is impressive (for example Englander 1960, Holland 1963). However, it has also been argued (Paterson 1962) and shown empirically (for example Sewell et al. 1969) that significant-others such as parents, wives, teachers, and friends, are likely to affect the career choices an individual makes. Within the cyclical model suggested, this need not provide any inconsistency, as the model would predict that the individual is constantly taking account of others (i.e. his social environment) in shaping his view of himself and of the world, and hence it follows that these others would influence the individual's occupational choice.

The cyclical nature of the model helps to remind one that occupational choice need not be a once and for all process. An individual may decide to change his occupation after entry for a number of reasons. These reasons may be summarized briefly under six headings.

H

1. *The naturally short career*

It is inherent in the nature of some occupations that careers in them will last for a shorter time period than an individual's normal working life. An obvious and dramatic example of such an occupation is that of professional sportsman. Careers in sport will typically reach their peak in early adulthood and in early middle-age, or before. As one star, major league base-ball player described his occupation – 'By its nature it is a brief, self-liquidating life. It is a temporary life, a period between the time of our youth and the beginning of a life-time career' (Koufax 1966: p. 14).

In this respect the sportsman is representative of a wider field of occupations which require physical strength or some other ability which typically decreases with age. With the normal retirement age now in the middle sixties, it may be that this problem is one which has to be faced by some members of most occupations, no matter how little such occupations may appear to depend on such qualities. For example, the executive may find few difficulties in keeping up with his work under pressure while he is in his forties, yet ten or fifteen years later the strains may be too great. In a society which tends to assume that careers should involve upward movement from starting work to retirement, ageing may present particularly acute problems. At the very least, people are expected to avoid downward mobility, yet this may be the only solution for some people who are no longer able to keep up with the day-to-day pressures of their jobs.

2. *Occupations as way-stations*

A second reason for changes of occupation in mid-career is that some people regard their first occupation as a means to some other end. For example, a person may become a lawyer because he feels that such action will provide him with openings for a career in politics or administration, as well as in law itself. In a study of graduates who had just entered industry in Britain, it was found that over 20 per cent were seriously considering changing to careers outside industry (Mansfield 1971). In addition, many felt that they would leave their early specialism for some form of general management, if the chance presented itself. In such cases as these, a person does not necessarily change his career line, he may merely pursue a career that crosses occupational boundaries.

3. *Changes in the occupational system*

As the normal length of a working career is upwards of forty years, it is to be expected that significant changes in society and, in particular, the occupational structure of society will occur during the course of an individual's career. Thus, some occupations become obsolescent as others are created. At the same time, other less dramatic changes occur, changing the skill requirements of an occupation or its prestige in society. Some occupations change from being skilled to semi-skilled as mechanization and automation are increased, while others become professionalized, often for similar reasons. As these changes take place, some people within an occupation will find it less appealing, whilst others outside may find it more appealing.

4. *Changes with seniority*

Even when the structure of an occupation does not change during an individual's career, there may be significant changes in what is expected of the individual as he becomes more senior. For example, scientists are often expected to take on increasing amounts of administrative work as they become more senior. Such changes may greatly affect the aptitudes required and the interest and challenge involved in a job. While some individuals may welcome such changes, others may feel disposed to change to an occupation more congruent with their view of themselves.

5. *Changes in the individual*

As was mentioned above, the individual is likely to change and develop during the course of his career. Although there is probably a tendency for the influence of peers and superiors to cause the individual to change in the direction of greater compatibility with his occupation, the reverse may also occur. This would seem to be particularly likely where the individual's

115

contact with other members of his occupation is slight, or where the individual is not very successful in his occupation.

6. *Changes in extra-occupational life*

During the course of the individual's occupational career, other aspects of his life may change. He may develop new interests and commitments and lose old ones. Thus, conflicts may be created between the different positions he occupies at a single time. For example, when a man gets married and has children he may feel inclined to change from an occupation which involves a great deal of travelling to one which allows him to stay in one place and thus spend more time with his family. (The reverse may also conceivably occur!) Different aspects of an individual's extra-work life may affect what he wants from his work. Thus, at some times money and security may be more important than at others.

With so many possible reasons for occupational change, one might wonder why more people do not make changes. One of the reasons is suggested above. That is, that individuals in an occupation are most likely to be socialized towards, rather than away from, the values and identity congruent to their occupation. Thus, it is necessary to consider the processes by which an individual adapts to his occupational setting.

ADAPTATION TO WORK

Strauss (1959) has suggested that 'the lives of men and women can – theoretically at least – be traced as a series of passages of status'. Some of these passages of status will be of great significance to the individual; indeed, they can be considered as 'turning-points' in the individual's career. Corwin (1961) has argued that the focus for the study of individual careers should be on these 'turning-points'. As he says, 'most transformations are so mundane they go unnoticed, but occasionally an incident of great conceptual and personal significance is encountered. At these turning-points, fundamental terminological and status shifts occur, reclassifying and re-assessing the job – indeed the self.' As Corwin suggests, it is at such times that the effects of the individual's objective career on his subjective career can be most clearly seen. For most persons one of the most significant transitions of status would seem likely to be the entry into the world of work; however, it would seem likely to vary by occupation as well as by individual. Dornbusch (1955) has described the relatively extreme circumstances faced by cadets in the American Coast Guard Academy, and suggests that the recruits are given 'a new personal and social identity'. 'The new role', he says, 'is a new social world.'

Brim (1966) has argued that 'role acquisition is probably the most important aspect of adult socialization'. However, adopting a role in the world of work does not mean becoming committed in any long-term sense to a particular occupation, or to a particular employer. It is, therefore, necessary to consider the conditions under which adaptation to a new occupational position leads a person to become committed to that occupation and that employing organization, rather than leading him to search for a different occupational position which he would perceive as more congruent with his career sub-identity.

Becker (1960) has argued that commitment to a line of activity depends on three things. First, the individual is in a position where his decisions with respect to a particular line of activity have implications for other interests and activities not necessarily related to it. For example, deciding to change jobs might force a person to interrupt his children's education. Secondly, the individual has put himself in the position by his own actions. And thirdly, the individual is aware of the implications. As Becker points out, an individual is likely to commit himself in this sense to a number of lines of action by the act of joining an organization. Further actions, or turns of the career development cycle, may increase or decrease the impact of this initial act of commitment, according to the principles Becker has laid out. McClelland (1967) has suggested that individuals working in organizations gradually increase their investment in a career line by spending time in it and narrowing the field of alternatives.

Becker and Carper's (1956a) study of graduate students led them to conclude that certain 'mechanisms' precipitate identification with an occupation. They found that the 'mechanism of development of interest and acquisition of skill' led to identification with the task. The 'mechanism of acquisition of ideology' operated to produce identification to the occupational title and was likely to come from informal groups. 'The internalization of motives, most effective in producing attachment to institutional positions associated with a given work identity, seems to operate primarily in clique and apprenticeship relations.' They also found that 'sponsorship' was likely to lead to a strengthening of ideology and identification with an occupational title as the sponsored person feels obliged to remain what he has become. In another paper, Becker and Carper (1956b) suggest that for an individual to identify with his task he must know what his task is, and it must not be too general in nature. It is arguable that in a work organization as opposed to a training organization such as a university, the acquisition of ideology may lead to identification with the organization as well with the occupational title. This would be because individuals normally join a work organization for an indefinite period, rather than for a fixed period to be trained for a position external to the organization, as is usually the case with post-graduate students.

Berger (1964) suggests that an individual's capacity to identify with his occupation will depend on his ability to create a stable profile of himself based on his occupation. This notion fits well with the ideas of Super (1957) that the first occupational choice is the beginning of a trial and error process which only ends when the individual feels able to implement his self-concept in his career.

In a study of medical students, Huntingdon (1957) found that individuals who felt that they handled patients' problems well were likely to identify with the occupational title and associated ideology, that is, they developed a professional self-image. Gebhard (1948) and Berlew and Hall (1966) also found that where the individual perceived outcomes of tasks he performed as successful, he was likely to develop more positive attitudes towards the job or task, Berlew and Hall found that this was particularly the case where this involved meeting demanding expectations of the individual's superiors. Bidwell (1961) found that identification was impeded where the individual felt powerless to control his job. This fits in with the idea advanced by many writers that feelings of powerlessness are likely to precipitate alienation.

These various factors affect the extent to which the individual identifies with and becomes committed to a particular career line. However, as Mansfield (1971) has pointed out, commitment to a career line does not necessarily imply continuance in a particular job in a particular organization. He suggests that a person will continue in a particular job if he is committed to the career line, considers the prospects there as good or better than elsewhere, and is reasonably satisfied overall with his position. In general, Mansfield provides evidence to support these contentions. However, he provides evidence that suggests that career commitment, at least in the first year at work, is likely to be fragile. He concludes: 'changes in the social system, in the nature of the job, or in obligations apart from work, may divert or break a career path'.

Up to this point the processes by which individuals choose occupations and adapt to positions in the world of work have been considered. Now attention is turned to the career as a whole, to examine the way careers in general seem likely to pattern, and the factors which seem likely to affect the patterning.

CAREER STAGES AND LINES OF DEVELOPMENT

The idea of life stages or career stages has been taken up both by psychologists and sociologists. Miller and Form (1951) suggest five work-related life stages. First, there is a preparatory period lasting approximately for the first fifteen years of life, during which the individual learns about work by doing jobs around the house, attending vocationally oriented lessons at school, and perhaps by doing casual jobs, although during this time he does not occupy any formal occupational position. The second period of development in Miller and Form's assessment lasts about three years and involves the individual's first introduction to a formal working position. For many, this introduction is only in the form of a holiday or Saturday morning job, whilst for others it involves a first full-time job. The third stage which they call 'the trial work period' can last until the middle thirties. During this period the individual will tend to change jobs frequently as he searches for a stable occupational position for the next stage, which they describe as the stable work period. This fourth stage lasts until the fifth stage of retirement is reached, typically in the sixties. This model is based on broad considerations of positions and mobility between them and tells little about the individual's subjective career.

Buehler's (1935) psychological model, however, attempts to distinguish broad stages in the development of the subjective side of careers. She suggests that the working career begins with an 'exploratory stage' lasting for something like the period from 17 to 28. This clearly corresponds closely to the 'trial work period' identified by Miller and Form, and is the time of life when the individual explores the various career possibilities. The second work stage Buehler calls the 'selective' stage, and is the period when the person selects a life-time career and begins to work and accomplish things within it. This, Buehler suggests, is followed by a five year 'testing stage' in the mid-forties, when the person looks both forward and backward at his career. This mid-career stage fits with a great deal of recent work of both a theoretical and empirical nature which suggests there is some period of crisis in middle age, in which the individual faces up to mortality and re-evaluates his career in terms of a limited span (for example Jaques 1965). This 'testing stage' is followed, Buehler says, by an 'indulgency stage' during which the individual tends to maximize self-gratification. The final period she calls the 'completion stage' in which the individual typically lives on memories of past satisfaction and achievements.

A third model has been put forward by Maslow (1968), who has suggested that the development of the healthy person is characterized by changes in the saliency of different types of needs, much like a series of life stages. Concern for physiological needs would characterize infancy, needs for security would become the most salient during childhood, and then social needs during adolescence. During the adult years, the ego needs for esteem and autonomy would be the most important during the early career years. Then in the middle and late career years, Maslow argues, the individual becomes chiefly concerned with the highest order needs of self-realization, that is, becoming whatever he is able to become.

Argyris (1957) concludes from his survey of the literature that healthy personality development for the adult as well as for the child, involves movement along a number of dimensions: (1) from passivity towards increasing activity; (2) from dependence on others to relative independence; (3) increasing the number of behaviour patterns in the individual's repertoire; (4) deepening of interests; (5) increasing one's time perspective; (6) from subordination to equality or supremacy; and (7) increasing awareness of self. Argyris suggests that an individual's degree of self-actualization may be regarded as his scores on each of the seven dimensions. Argyris, however, argues that the pressures on organizational members to utilize rational systems, which characterize formal organizations, may produce conditions which conflict with the growth needs of individual employees. In particular, he argues that the processes inherent in the concepts of task specialization, the chain of command, unity of direction, and span of control will cause individuals to experience frustration, psychological failure, short time perspective, and conflict. These effects, Argyris states, are symptomatic of the blocking of healthy psychological growth. He suggests that in response to this reduced esteem and blunted growth, the individual will come to place greater value on lower order needs (such as for security and material rewards), and lower value on higher order needs (such as self-realization). Data from a study of priests in an American diocese of the Roman Catholic Church, an organization of the bureaucratic type, confirm Argyris's predictions (Hall and Schneider 1969). Porter's (1962) study of nearly 2,000 managers, ranging from lower level management up to corporation presidents in the United States, also showed that the importance of the needs for security and social satisfactions increases with age, whilst the importance of needs for self-actualization decreases with age. In the U.S. Forest Service, however, an organization known for the relatively high integration of its members (Kaufman 1960), a decrease in the importance of growth needs was not found, although the importance of security did increase with age (Hall *et al.* 1970). These latter findings are similar to those from Macmillan's (1971) survey of a sample of members of the British Institute of Management. She found that security is more valued with increasing age, but found no systematic change with age in job values associated with higher order needs.

At first sight, evidence on research scientists (Glaser 1964), and on university teachers (Caplow and McGee 1958), suggests that for these categories of organizational employee, security is an early career concern. Further examination of the evidence, however, suggests that a very different notion of security is used by the writers in question, which may be more usefully thought of as the need to establish oneself as a professional. The evidence of these studies tends to suggest different directions of development from those outlined by Maslow. This may be taken as strong support for Argyris's theory of the debilitating effects of organizations on employees. This interpretation of the evidence is further supported by Porter's (1962) evidence that the increasing importance of lower order needs and decreasing importance of higher order needs with age is less noticeable amongst higher ranking managers than amongst lower ranking ones.

Glaser's (1964) study also showed that the major mid-career concern of the organizational scientist was with getting promotion to a supervisory rank. Obtaining promotion also appears to have been a major preoccupation with the managers and technical specialists in mid-career studied by Sofer (1970). This concern with obtaining promotion may be accentuated by the feeling that the mid-career years correspond to peak performance in this type of career, as Pelz and Andrews's (1966) data suggest. This peak may result in a sense of depression that the future may hold more decline than growth. The idea of being most concerned with becoming a supervisor at this career stage fits with the notion of generativity (Erikson 1968), as the individual tries to extend the meaning and content of his work by stimulating the development of his younger colleagues. It may also explain the increasing organizational involvement of older men found by Hall *et al.* (1970) in the Forest Service study. They found that organizational involvement and the need to identify with one's employing organization both increased with age in a sample of professionals employed in the U.S. Forest Service. The greater involvement of older men may be because they see their work being justified and carried on by their employing organization.

In considering processes of adaptation to occupational positions and the ways in which careers develop, implicit and explicit mention has been made of potential and actual conflicts between the needs of the individual and those of the organization. Mention has also been made of some of the ways in which organizations provide for the needs of individuals. In the next section attention is focused specifically on these issues.

ORGANIZATIONAL CONSTRAINTS AND OPPORTUNITIES

Organizations have become such a common and ubiquitous feature of life in industrialized societies that it makes the assessment of the specific impact of work organizations on careers difficult, if not impossible. The language of careers, at least in everyday terms, is couched partly in organizational terms. For example, what would the concept of promotion mean if organizations with their formal hierarchies did not exist? As Becker and Strauss (1956) have said, 'concepts like career carry the import of movement through structures'. In modern society, career means movement through organizational structures. Certainly not all persons involved in occupations are organizational employees, but virtually all work in some contact with work organizations. Organizations provide individuals with resources which they would not otherwise be able to use. For example, many modern research physicists require equipment costing millions of pounds which can be made available by organizations, but which could scarcely be acquired by individuals. The move from a subsistence economy to the present modern industrial system with its highly specialized division of labour seems to have equated entering an occupation with entering or moving into a close relationship with a work organization. Thus, when consideration is given to the functions of work, this is almost the same as considering the functions of working in an organizational setting. Slocum (1966) has suggested that work serves six basic functions in modern industrial society. First, work is a source of money, which in our economy may be exchanged to provide for various requirements of the individual. Secondly, work tends to regulate the individual's activities. By imposing more or less regular time-keeping commitments on the individual, it affects not only his activities on the job but also his non-work activities. Thirdly, work provides the individual with a number of social relationships. Fourthly, a substantial part of the individual's identity is anchored in his work. Fifthly, work provides experience which gives content and meaning to the individual's life. And sixthly, the work the individual does is a major factor in deciding the social standing accredited to him by himself and others. Thus, it can be said that working in an organization structures part of the individual's

123

environment and provides him with rewards, economic, social, and psychological.

However, working in an organization has costs for the individual as well as rewards. As long as the individual stays within an organization he gives up some degree of control of his own activities. As Argyris (1957) has suggested, the psychological costs of working in organizations are likely to be greatest at the bottom of the hierarchy. This fits with the evidence from Porter's (1963) study of all levels of management. He found that need satisfaction was highest at the top and lowest at the bottom.

One way in which individuals could gain greater satisfaction, then, would be to move up the hierarchy. However, in order to do this the individual will probably have to give up still more freedom in the short term, in order to perform in such a way as to be promoted. In many organizations, particularly large bureaucratic ones, the rules governing promotion, whether formally prescribed or not, may be widely known. Hence, at least to some extent, the individual can work at gaining promotion and thus exercise a measure of control over his own career. However, a recent study by Sofer and Tuchman (1970) has shown that there can be systematic failures to communicate between superior and subordinate in performance appraisal interviews. This finding leads to a suspicion that the ways and chances of gaining promotion may not be as well understood by organizational members as some social scientists tend to assume.

There would appear to be a further problem for the individual, at least in some organizations, about adopting strategies in order to obtain or speed promotion. Such strategies may involve behaviour which is not officially prescribed by the organization but rather involves some amount of political manoeuvring. Dalton (1959) found in his study of managers that cliques formed amongst persons at the same and at different levels in organizational hierarchies, and that these cliques were important in helping individuals to be successful in their jobs and to obtain promotion. Clearly, clique membership not only helps the individual be successful, but involves him in risks of failure as the clique may lose power or senior members of it may leave the organization, leaving those who stay in vulnerable positions.

Burns (1955) differentiates two sorts of groups which form in organizational settings and which serve to aid or defend the career interests of individuals. The first type (termed a 'cabal' by Burns) is typically comprised of younger men eager for organizational change and career advancement and is likely to adopt an aggressive strategy in organizational politics. The second type (termed a 'clique' by Burns) is mainly comprised of older men who feel threatened by change and by their younger colleagues, and is likely to manifest an orientation towards extra-occupational activities within the group whilst adopting largely defensive strategies in organizational politics.

However, apart from the difficulties which individuals may experience in understanding the way promotion is to be obtained, and the risks in political manoeuvring, the pyramidal shape of the hierarchy in most organizations means that only a minority can expect promotion up the hierarchy to provide them with greater satisfaction and meaning in their work and greater control over their own situation.

Another way in which the individual can gain some degree of control over his career is by inter-organizational mobility, particularly at times of economic boom, when such movement is relatively easy. It seems that people, particularly those in managerial and professional positions, are increasingly moving from organization to organization in search of better jobs and career prospects (Jennings 1967, Macmillan 1971). However, for most the change is presumably quantitative rather than qualitative, as they tend to move to similar jobs in similar organizations.

One possibility which offers a qualitative change in career is that of moving out from the position of organizational employee and setting up one's own business. However, as Chinoy (1955) has documented for automobile workers in one American factory, this possibility is unlikely to be more than a dream for many. Chinoy (1955: p. 110) describes the fate of these auto-workers' aspirations as follows: 'They do not aspire to the top levels of business and industry; they want to become skilled workers, to gain promotion to supervision, to engage in small-scale farming, to open a retail store or a small service establishment of some kind. Since even most of these alternatives entail serious difficulties, however, comparatively few workers persist in hope, remain strong in intention, or persevere in effort. But desire frequently survives.'

Despite the lack of satisfaction and meaning in many jobs and the difficulties in remedying this by promotion or mobility, it seems that the majority of people do not just work for money. Morse and Weiss (1955) found that 80 per cent of their American national sample of employed men said they would continue to work even if they inherited enough money to live on. However, the reasons given for this desire to continue working varied considerably with occupation. Typically, those in 'middle class' occupations tended to mention interest and opportunities for achievement in the job, whilst those in 'working class' occupations tended to mention the need for some directed activity to fill their time.

WORK AND NON-WORK

The individual's working career may be a critical part of his life, but it is certainly not all of it. One of the characteristics of modern society is the degree of differentiation between what an individual does at work and what he does outside. However, despite a high degree of differentiation between the working career and the rest of a person's life, there is a relationship between the two at all stages of a person's career. Dalton (1951) showed that social connections outside work and membership of particular community organizations can help a manager obtain career advancement. Davis and Olesen (1963) found that student nurses 'experience considerable identity stress because of the difficulty they have in psychologically integrating the student nurse role with a concurrently emerging identity of adult womanhood'. Carper and Becker (1957) found that the effect on members of extra-work role-sets for occupational identification depended on the specificity and saliency of their expectations for the individual. Dalton (1959), as a result of his study of managers in several firms, concluded that age, ability, and personal and community responsibilities all lead to 'differential identification'. These effects, important though they may be, are relatively subtle compared with the impact of the money earned at work, or of a geographic change of job on non-work activities. Clearly, a change of working location can lead a person to change his house, nearly all his social contacts and those of his family, and the places where his children are educated. This impact of work on extra-work activities can be a major source of marital conflict and can seriously affect career possibilities.

Sofer (1970) found that the managers and technical specialists that he studied either reported that work tended to dominate their lives or that they kept work and non-work activities separate. Of those who felt that work dominated their lives, nearly half reported that their wives objected to this. Where the respondents had attempted to keep work and non-work activities separate, they reported that their wives were happy with this arrangement. Pahl and Pahl's (1971) findings seem approximately congruent; as they say, 'these middle managers in British industry appear to be willing slaves to the system; only their wives complain and even they are not sure whether they ought to' (1971: pp. 258-9).

Potential conflicts would seem likely to be greater if both husband and wife are attempting to make successful careers at the same time. Rapoport and Rapoport (1971) suggest that where both marriage partners are making successful careers and raising a family considerable stresses are created within the family and between the different aspects of both the husband's life and the wife's life. However, the Rapoports found that the 'dual-career families' that they studied had chosen and accepted fairly high levels of stress as part of their way of life.

Despite the obvious interaction between work and non-work in people's lives, this is a surprisingly unresearched aspect of careers. Two major conflicting theories of the effect of work on the rest of a person's life have been extant in the social science literature for more than a hundred years. Wilensky (1960) calls these the 'spillover leisure hypothesis' and the 'compensatory leisure hypothesis'. The first hypothesis suggests that the person who has work which facilitates self-actualization will seek out self-actualizing activities out of work, whilst the person whose work leads to alienation at work will be alienated out of work. The second hypothesis tends to imply the reverse, in particular it suggests that the alienated worker uses his leisure hours to give him the rewards of which he is deprived while at work. Recently, one small study of a sample of managers (Mansfield 1972) provided some evidence to suggest that both these theories may be inadequate in general. Rather, his evidence suggested that both work and non-work may affect the individual; and that the rewards he seeks both in and out of work are the result of these effects. At least for this small sample the evidence suggested that the individual's conceptions of his experiences and motivations both at work and outside work were closely integrated. However, the evidence that some workers adopt a strongly instrumental orientation to work (Goldthorpe *et al.* 1968) suggests that the compensatory leisure hypothesis may be true for some other members of the workforce. Clearly, there is a need for more research in this area.

SOME CONCLUDING COMMENTS

In this chapter, both the concept and reality of individual careers have been explored. A rudimentary theory of career development has been suggested, and the way careers start and develop has been considered. In all this consideration, there has been an underlying assumption that the social system is largely fixed and that forces for change tend to act only from the social system to the individual. These assumptions are useful for purposes of analysis in that they allow attention to be focused on the development of both the objective and subjective sides of the individual's career without having to consider the way the careers of individuals change the social systems through which they pass. However, these assumptions are clearly incorrect and their utility in some sorts of analysis must not allow the underlying reality to be hidden. As individuals develop and change and move through organizational systems, they will generate social forces that will tend either to change the organizational system or to maintain the *status quo*.

In highly stable social systems such as the village communities of many preliterate tribes, the passage of individuals through positions in the social system is typically highly predictable and timetabled. In such a system the processes of socialization and anticipatory socialization are such that personal changes largely coincide with positional changes. Thus, the passage of generations rarely causes great imbalances in the system, rather it tends to reinforce the existing order.

In social systems where positional changes are less regularized and where the impact of other systems is both greater and more immediate, then it is to be expected that the values and abilities of those in particular grades in the system will change over time. These changes will be due to the changing age distribution across grades and to persons socialized in different ways moving up in grade. Changes in the distribution of values and abilities in the organizational system are likely to generate forces tending to change the system. In work organizations in industrial society members only enter the social system as adults or near-adults, and then normally continue to live much of their lives outside the direct influences of social forces from within their employing organization. In such systems, the potential for forces for change, being generated as persons who have been socialized differently move through the system, should be much greater than in the isolated village community. Some of this effect, however, will no doubt be reduced by the selection processes used by most work organizations; and by self-selection amongst prospective recruits.

In the ideal-type bureaucratic system described by Weber (1948), forces for organizational change stemming from changes in values and abilities in grades as persons within them age and move on should also be minimal. The Weberian bureaucracy minimizes such forces, which would be disruptive to the working of the bureaucracy, in three ways. First, by insisting on an impersonal mode of operation, thus reducing or removing forces for change stemming from individual value-systems. Secondly, by rigorous selection based on ability, thus ensuring a high degree of uniformity in abilities. And thirdly, by promoting on the bases of seniority and ability, thus continuing to ensure uniformity in abilities in higher hierarchical levels, and also keeping the age in grade structure of the bureaucracy relatively constant.

From this it would tend to follow that the more bureaucratic is an organization, then the more immune it is from forces for change emanating from the personal development of its employees. Yet, as Argyris (1957) has suggested, these same conditions tend to obstruct the healthy personality development of the individual. This would suggest that the conflict inherent in the position of the individual in a work organization may be functional for the organization in that it will cause the system to change and develop as long as the organizational forces are not so strong as to swamp the effects of individual development. Even so, the conflict may put at risk the stability and long term survival of individual organizations.

I

REFERENCES

ARGYRIS, C. J. 1957. 'The individual and organization: some problems of mutual adjustment', *Administrative Science Quarterly*, 2, 1–24.

BECKER, H. S. 1952. 'The career of the Chicago public schoolteacher', *American Journal of Sociology*, 57, 470-7.

BECKER, H. S. and CARPER, J. 1956a. 'The development of identification with an occupation', *American Journal of Sociology*, 61, 289-298.

BECKER, H. S. and CARPER, J. 1956b. 'The elements of identification with an occupation', *American Sociological Review*, 21, 341–8.

BECKER, H. S. and STRAUSS, A. L. 1956. 'Careers, personality and adult socialization', *American Journal of Sociology*, 62, 253–63.

BECKER, H. S. 1960. 'Notes on the concept of commitment', *American Journal of Sociology*, 66, 32–40.

BERGER, P. L. 1964. 'Some general observations on the problem of work', in P. L. Berger (ed.), *The human shape of work*, New York: Macmillan.

BERLEW, D. E. and HALL, D. T. 1966. 'The socialization of managers'. *Administrative Science Quarterly*, 11, 207–23.

BIDWELL, C. E. 1961. 'The young professional in the army: a study of occupational identity', *American Sociological Review*, 26, 360–72.

BLAU, P. M., GUSTAD, J. W., JESSER, R., AMES, H. S. P. and WILCOCK, R. C. 1956. 'Occupational choice: a conceptual framework', *Industrial and Labor Relations Review*, 9, 531-43.

BLAU, P. M. and DUNCAN, O. D. 1967. *The American occupational structure*, New York: Wiley.

BRIM, O. G. 1966. 'Socialization through the life-cycle', in O. G. Brim and S. Wheeler (eds.), *Socialization after childhood*, New York: Wiley.

BUEHLER, C. 1935. 'The curve of life as studied in biographies', *Journal of Applied Psychology*, 19, 405–9.

BURNS, T. 1955. 'The reference of conduct in small groups', *Human Relations*, 8, 467–86.

CAPLOW, T. and MCGEE, R. 1958. *The academic marketplace*, New York: Basic Books.

CARPER, J. W. and BECKER, H. S. 1957. 'Adjustments to conflicting expectations in the development of identification with an occupation, *Social Forces*, 36, 51-6.

CHINOY, E. 1955. *Automobile workers and the American Dream*, New York. Random House.

CORWIN, R. G. 1961. 'The professional employee: a study of conflict in nursing roles', *American Journal of Sociology*, 66, 604–15.

DALTON, M. 1951. 'Informal factors in career achievement', *American Journal of Sociology*, 56, 407–15.

DALTON, M. 1959. *Men who manage*, New York: Wiley.

DAVIS, F. and OLESEN, V. L. 1963. 'Initiation into a women's profession', *Sociometry*, 26, 89–101.

DAVIS, J. A. 1961. *Undergraduate career decisions*, Chicago: Aldine.

DORNBUSCH, S. M. 1955. 'The military academy as an assimilating institution', *Social Forces*, 33, 316–21.

ENGLANDER, M. 1960. 'A psychological analysis of vocational choice: teaching', *Journal of Counseling Psychology*, 7, 257–64.

ERIKSON, E. H. 1968. *Identity: youth and crisis*, New York: Norton.

GEBHARD, M. E. 1948. 'Effects of success and failure upon the attractiveness of activities as a function of experience, expectation and need', *Journal of Experimental Psychology*, 38, 371–88.

GLASER, B. 1964. *Organizational scientists: their professional careers*, New York: Bobbs-Merrill.

GOLDTHORPE, J. H., LOCKWOOD, D., BECHHOFER, F., PLATT, J. 1968. *The affluent worker: industrial attitudes and behaviour*, London: Cambridge University Press.

HALL, D. T. and SCHNEIDER, B. 1969. 'Work assignment characteristics and career development in the priesthood', working paper, Yale University.

HALL, D. T., SCHNEIDER, B. and NYGREN, K. 1970. 'Personal factors in organizational identification', *Administrative Science Quarterly*, 15, 176–90.

HALL, D. T. 1971. 'A theoretical model of career subidentity development in organizational settings', *Organizational Behavior and Human Performance*, 6, 50–76.

HOLLAND, J. C. 1963. 'Explorations of a theory of vocational choice and achievement: II. A four-year prediction study', *Psychological Reports*, 12, 547–94.

HUGHES, E. C. 1937. 'Institutional office and the person', *American Journal of Sociology*, 43, 404-13.

HUNTINGDON, M. J. 1957. 'The development of a professional self-image', in R. K. Merton, G. G. Reader and P. L. Kendall (eds.), *The student physician*, Cambridge, Mass.: Harvard University Press.

JAQUES, E. 1965. 'Death and the mid-life crisis', *International Journal of Psychoanalysis*, 46, 502-14.

JENNINGS, E. E. 1967. *The mobile manager*, Ann Arbor: Michigan University Graduate School of Business Administration.

KAUFMAN, M. 1960. *The forest ranger*, Baltimore: John Hopkins Press.

KORMAN, A. K. 1967a. 'Self-esteem as a moderator of the relationship between self-perceived abilities and vocational choice', *Journal of Applied Psychology*, 51, 65-7.

KORMAN, A. K. 1967b. 'Ethical judgements, self-perceptions and vocational choice', *Proceedings, 75th Annual Convention, A.P.A.*

KOUFAX, S. with LINN, E. 1966. *Koufax*, New York: Viking.

MCCLELLAND, W. G. 1967. 'Career patterns and organizational needs', *Journal of Management Studies*, 4, 56–70.

MACMILLAN, B. 1971. 'Managerial mobility', paper given to the BSA Industrial Sociology Section.

MANSFIELD, R. 1971. 'Career development in the first year at work', *Occupational Psychology*, 45, 139–49.

MANSFIELD, R. 1972. 'Need satisfaction and need importance in and out of work', *Studies in Personnel Psychology*, in press.

MANSFIELD, R. and DAVIES, T. 1971. 'Occupational choice at Oxford', *Further Education*, 2, 60–3.

MASLOW, A. B. 1968. Personal communication to D. T. Hall reported in

131

D. T. Hall and K. E. Nougaim, 'An examination of Maslow's need hierarchy in an organizational setting', *Organizational Behaviour and Human Performance*, 3, 12–35.

MILLER, D. C. and FORM, W. 1951. *Industrial sociology: an introduction to the sociology of work relations*, New York: Harper.

MORSE, N. C. and WEISS, R. S. 1955. 'The function and meaning of work and the job', *American Sociological Review*, 20, 191-8.

MUSGRAVE, P. W. 1967. 'Towards a sociological theory of occupational choice', *Sociological Review*, 15, 33–46.

PAHL, J. M. and PAHL, R. E. 1971. *Managers and their wives*, Harmondsworth: Penguin Books.

PATERSON, D. G. 1962. 'Values and interests in vocational guidance', *Industrial and business psychology, Proceedings of the Fourteenth International Congress of Applied Psychology*, 118–25.

PELZ, D. C. and ANDREWS, F. M. 1966. *Scientists in organizations*, New York: Wiley.

PORTER, L. W. 1962. 'Job attitudes in management: I. Perceived deficiencies in need fulfilment as a function of job level', *Journal of Applied Psychology*, 46, 375–84.

PORTER, L. W. 1963. 'Job attitudes in management: II. Perceived importance of needs as a function of job level', *Journal of Applied Psychology*, 47, 141–8.

RAPOPORT, R. and RAPOPORT, R. 1971. *Dual-career families*, Harmondsworth: Penguin Books.

ROSENBERG, M. 1957. *Occupations and values*, Glencoe, Ill.: Free Press.

SEWELL, W. H., HALLER, H. A. and PORTES, A. 1969. 'The educational and early occupational attainment process', *American Sociological Review*, 34, 82–91.

SLOCUM, W. L. 1966. *Occupational careers*, Chicago: Aldine.

SOFER, C. 1970. *Men in mid-career*, London: Cambridge University Press.

SOFER, C. and TUCHMAN, M. 1970. 'Appraisal interviews and the structure of colleague relations', *Sociological Review*, 18, 365–92.

STRAUSS, A. L. 1959. *Mirrors and masks: the search for identity*, Glencoe, Ill.: Free Press.

SUPER, D. 1957. *The psychology of careers*, New York: Harper and Row.

UNDERHILL, R. 1966. 'Values and post-college career change', *American Journal of Sociology*, 72, 163–72.

WEBER, M. 1948. *From Max Weber*, tr. H. W. Gerth and C. Wright Mills, London: Routledge and Kegan Paul.

WILENSKY, H. L. 1960. 'Work, careers, and social integration', *International Social Science Journal*, 12, 543–60.

Social Relevance

5 The End of Management

COLIN FLETCHER

In the spring of 1969 I interviewed 75 managers to test the extent of stress in their jobs. That summer I fell silent. In alternating flashes anger and pity illuminated impotence and frustration. A cry caught in my throat.

I had begun work in the two factories with a measure of cunning. No one knew my purpose. I wanted to observe managers, but I didn't want them to see me. I stalked my respondents from a hide of hypocrisy. So we confided, laughed, and conspired, and I was drawn into their world. Soon I had lodged; my jollity left me too weak to resist.

Now trapped, I encountered the machine. Inside management was a gross inefficiency; corridors made a maze; all doors were to be avoided. My fuel about the place came from fear, suspicion, and servility. No one knew what was happening. We speculated about the months to come with patchwork clues and never using our hopes. We depended upon gossip but it rarely spoke of ourselves.

Few dared to think. We spoke of things and people as things. My slick, button-down, liberal image tore. I was catching managers' diseases and, in becoming as anxious as them, I lost nerve, grip, and purpose. I added hate to hypocrisy.

I had to get away. Nothing was going right for 'my managers'. Their jobs, careers and home life were absurd, precarious, and in conflict. I could find neither cause nor effect of this horror. I abandoned managers and thesis and fell to thinking. And when I had finished a long report on managers' stress at work I realized: 'it doesn't matter; management is about to end; the masters are making new hirelings'.

All that struggling with, and against, individual managers was in vain. I had assumed they were the enemy. I had cringed from anti-intellectual boors, I had chipped away beneath fascist clichés, I had tried to convince a few of their common cause with workers. But all on the assumption that they were part of the problem and that their personal problems proved this fact. No wonder the confused had remained confused. I had been busy scoring points and left the game intact. Meanwhile monopoly capitalism was becoming more international by the minute and these managers were being done out of a job. Yet I had sensed the drift of affairs; as a fledgling academic I was scared of managers; as a fledgling manager I was scared out of my wits. The latter fear was more important; for although I had not been trained to make sense of what I saw, I appreciated that if management is disappearing it makes a difference to what managers say. Their private fears cause some to buckle, some to bolt, and some to stand and fight.

I foresee the end of management and my reasoning makes the body of this essay. I hold that the current generation of managers cannot survive their employment conditions, that no future generations of managers are being trained, and that the alternatives exercised by managers indicate their knowledge of these facts.

The problem has been with managers all along. They have known the contradictions of their job. Now they are being exposed. Management is neither art nor science nor skill. At base there is nothing to do. A manager is hired for what he knows other firms do; what he can find to do, and what he can be told to do.

To begin:

Managers cannot survive their employment conditions

Although we know every occupation has its diseases we have yet to catch a headline reading 'Job Kills Man'. This omission depends on the staggering simplification that its a man's fault if he lets his job get him down. At informal postmortems one is likely to hear:

A: 'Of course he couldn't take it. He had his weak spots and they showed in the end.'

B: 'Yes, he was weak. If he didn't think he could do the job he shouldn't have taken it in the first place.'

A: 'He let it get him down. He let it play on his *nerves*.'

B: 'It was inevitable, he couldn't *manage* the job.'

136

All jobs seem to be so regarded: A man takes a job, makes a go of it, or lets it get him down. The man struggles with a monster within himself. A manager's job is especially so regarded. The man is bettering himself: in being a manager he is trying to get on. He must stand alone, initiated, individuated, and isolated.

Each manager is treated 'individually' in a structure which has very fine distinctions between every position. Management has the most intricate gradings of all the echelons in the firm's hierarchy. Yet there is no rational structure of reward: it depends on what the man has received before and how much he asks for. Newcomers get far more than long-standing employees.

But this does not mean that the long-standing manager is worse off; his 'survival factor' is higher. He keeps his job when others lose their heads. For although the manager is put alone and has to go it alone there are subtle groupings in the firm (and on the site) in which he has some part. The groupings are cliques and cabals (I take these terms from Melville Dalton's *Men who manage* and from Tom Burns).

A clique is a group of near equals whilst a cabal contains managers from dissimilar grades. Cliques lace across departments – they are mutual protection societies. Each department has its natural enemy:

> production *v.* inspection
> production control *v.* engineering
> purchasing *v.* production

with plant and personnel as everybody's targets.

The enmity is natural from the perspective of accountability. Departments expose each other's failures and examine each others' workings. The enmity can be turned to friendship if departments collude and corroborate each other's alibis. Cliques, therefore, stretch across departments that ostensibly police each other's actions and work by rigging meetings and decisions to support each others' accounts.

Cabals are more powerful than cliques. They include, at their head, a senior executive or even a Board member. The success of the most senior member brings a chain reaction for the rest in a short space of time. Cliques are defensive whilst cabals are on the offensive. For cabals are troubled by powerful isolates who can publicize their plans.

To survive, cabals have to work against the welfare of key isolates: bringing them in or pushing them right out. The directorate permit a cabal's vendetta and occasionally encourage it. A cabal can, however, be cast assunder by the 'fall from grace' of the man at the top. Consequently cabals make open oaths of loyalty to their leader and defuse the criticism of being a secret society.

Inside these groupings the manager is safe for the present, isolates are not. A manager may be a new boy, an ignoramus or an informer. These qualities isolate him from cliques and cabals. And isolation is an unsafe position. Already it has been said that cabals thrive on the warpath towards isolates. An isolate's empire can crumble *beneath* him. His access to information is chronically insufficient. His fortunes can be broken by his underlings – and they can be in a clique or cabal. A manager on his own is an unwanted guest rather than an honoured resident. He is unsafe.

Unsafe from what? Well, in addition to attrition by cabals there is the constant possibility of being planned out of the present job. The management hierarchy is regularly reorganized. A pendulum swings from central control to regional autonomy. New advisors; liaisons with accounts or finance; development teams; executive development programmes are all on the drawing board. Management is always susceptible to rationalization and middle management positions especially. A middle manager is a junior in a big department or the senior of a sprawling department. In either situation rationalization can make him technically redundant.

A new norm may be decided 'on consultants' advice . . . it involves a bit of a shake up, a complete face lift' or 'an organization set for the seventies'. Such plans seal an isolate's fate, his department is left as spoils and he is promoted beyond credibility.

Concurrent with planned change are surprise moves to subject the workforce to different pressures. A 'bull' can be put in a design department to shake them up. A 'maths man' can be put over production foremen to force them to account. A head can be removed while his staff guess about the reduction likely in their ranks.

The directorate relies largely on a clash between the manager and the managed to produce increases in results. The manager relies on the grapevine for tip-offs. Cliques and cabals can either nullify such changes or have them work in their favour. The isolate has the full brunt of the clash.

Meanwhile the manager is actually employed for his potential part in dreaming up rationalizations of management. This means that he must study other departments and screen his own from scrutiny. This part of his job is to simplify the paperwork by temporarily increasing it; to standardize control by temporarily suspending it; and to decrease costs by an increase in his own and ancillary labour. And yet this is not really what he is employed to do. The job is to control. The daily and hourly purpose is to control in order to be in control.

The manager's job is to get more from his workforce, to increase their use of machines and then the output from them. He is to contain this workforce whilst increasing its rate of production. He is to stall disputes to a stalemate or make the issue manageable for someone else. He is supposed to stand there and take it. He has nothing to give as he has no power over the number of people employed; the pay and conditions of work; or the machines at which his people work. To help him hold this situation he has immediate subordinates. They are to filter trouble, to enact changes in the size and use of the workforce, and to check the workers' production minutely. Some of the most convoluted relationships develop with these subordinates, the root problem being the impossibility of trust.

Managers dominate different subordinates in different ways. Some talk of being firm; of the need for control; of the inevitability of trouble below. Others talk of talk: of the value of decisions collectively taken and collectively binding. There is something of a choice open to managers – they can choose to be more or less boss over their subordinates. All the managers interviewed adovcated their own styles. In fact, two major styles became apparent. Two speeches have been made to illustrate them.

A speech for practical authority

There are few routines in our area. It's our job to work out routines that apply right across the place. I expect my men to organize their own departments. They are qualified professional men.

Delegation is an art: otherwise you are keeping a dog and barking yourself. I delegate my policy and they keep within it. They know my attitudes and take account of them. I'm only autocratic on policy and I set overall objectives. They can self-motivate but I have to motivate. I have to push them along that bit more.

We have planned action programmes and regular reviews. There is some popping into offices but I like them to get on with as little interference as possible. It builds up their personality and helps them develop.

I like to set an example, starting at 8.00 a.m., keeping the desk clear – that sort of thing. The object is that they produce results and work at a pace acceptable to me – within parameters to agreed objectives. You know, if I leave them alone they will fall asleep. Everybody wants to be monitored.

I regard myself as a parish priest. To avoid complacency I issue pats on the head and kicks in the backside.

I am the link-man in our operation.

In contrast, let us consider:

A speech for practical democracy

We work within the firm's policies and procedures as far as we can. I'm as democratic as possible. I ask a subordinate 'Have you tried?' If he hasn't I tell him to have a go.

Analysis of personality is the big management skill. You have to know your men, with their weaknesses and their strengths. Some are independent but others need a lot of attention. They are often coming for approval as much as decisions. You have to distinguish between their qualities and take an interest in anything they do. I'm constantly in touch – spot checks if you like.

I encourage consultation on all issues. They have unlimited access provided they've done their bit of thinking to start with. Some jobs are obviously politically important. Regular daily discussions iron them out before they get to be a problem. But I don't believe in frightening people. I like to point out the error of their ways. Overall they have established routines to go by. I don't discourage innovation but I like things done properly. On the whole, if they stick within the system, complaints won't stop at their door. They must follow a reasonable pattern.

I see myself as the captain of our team.

Both philosophies are meant to be 'practical'. They are of use to keep subordinates going. The crisis of trust is in the judgment that the manager can only trust his subordinates so far and that they must trust him fully. The hub of the problem being 'it's either me or them'. The philosophies, and the subordinates, are means to an end. And, in any case, the condition that the style be practical incorporates the manager's right to contradict himself. He can move towards the other style and try being 'one of the boys' or 'making sure they know who is the boss'.

The authoritarian might be addressed as John and the democrat make himself known as Jack. John looks upwards to his seniors, his loyalty being to their commands.

Jack averts his eyes from that which he cannot fathom: he looks downwards; his loyalty is to his department. They genuinely disagree over the ends to which their authority and democracy are put. To John the company's accounts are the clearest indication of purpose. To Jack an atmosphere of reason and absence of strife is the subtlest sign of his purposes achieved. John, of course, is not averse to the odd showdown with 'difficult customers'. Jack abhors this 'letting off steam' and does his best to prevent the contagion spreading to his department. In obvious ways they defend their work from the influence of each other. In hard times there can be endless, fruitless complaints over 'being out of touch' and 'spending too much time with his brood'. John is at best an elder brother and Jack a kindly uncle and this family metaphor is some indication of how long these philosophies take to develop,

A further philosophy practised by a few is that of Janus. This style professes neither authority nor democracy. Instead there are bitter words about subordinates, complaints of their complicity in undesirable practices with belief that they have defected to the side of the workforce. Janus pleads with and threatens his subordinates. He appeals for a new era, a new bright beginning in their relationship and he seeks the power to dismiss as many as possible. Janus is probably an 'authoritatively practical' out of his depth. He would like to be a leader and may well have been a successful leader in previous times. But his seeking of every conceivable weapon in the armoury of management signifies that he has lost control. So whilst appeal and abuse may figure somewhere in his style as a boss, his reliance is upon technical impersonality. The machine does his minding. He insists on machine perfection; of their keeping the closest watch on their workers' fiddles. Systematically he has withdrawn his personality from the relationship. He holds close and undisclosed his positional knowledge – his findings from committees and corridors. It is possible that his last vestige of control lies within the effect that this 'non-communication' has. Janus's ideal is martial law.

Two major philosophies have been outlined, those of practical authority and practical democracy. Both contain contradictions. They are undermined by their priority of practicality and unsettled by their implicit crisis of trust. Some managers have achieved working relationships in which case they come into conflict with each other. 'Newer' managers are achieving these styles. They uneasily oscillate between their purposes and practices.

Three more types are to be found. Janus has lost control and seeks orders rather than objectives, machines rather than the men. Janus is rare. Rare too are two types that have risen above the practicalities that make the problems. Young project managers and old department managers are literally on their own. They have distinctive work and, by inference, very supportive bosses. Both these rare types are regarded with pride by their superiors. Rarities that epitomize new style and old style management; wizzardry and reliability.

Meanwhile, each manager is being dominated as well as being dominant. He too is someone's subordinate. Each manager speculates as to what his boss *really* wants. Each manager at each level keeps a little of what is transmitted and a certain amount of his own translation. Each boss gives his subordinate some of his incomplete knowledge. Each boss has blind spots and makes indiscretions; his subordinate overlooks both. As a subordinate, the manager colludes with comparable subordinates to shield their boss and to appear as individuals before him. Weak cliques form and fragment according to the boss's style. But whatever the subordinate thinks, his first

instinct is that his boss is right. For the manager as a subordinate is clever to please, loyal to a name, and obedient to a
degree. Friendship is a problem. The boss can feel that friendship is a delightful compliment and that the subordinate is
trying to get round him. The subordinate can feel that he is
much safer as a friend than he is as an underling but that he
has put all his eggs in one basket.

Managers do not trust each other; a manager cannot fully
trust or disbelieve his own boss, his co-managers or his subordinates. The complex of these conflicts make him paranoid.
His paranoia is compounded by schizoid circumstances of work.

The manager is exhorted to *communicate*: the term 'communication' serving to confuse him further. He is encouraged
'to keep channels open', 'to have an open door'; to listen to
everything and talk with everybody.

The manager is exhorted to *co-ordinate*; to 'get things
moving' and 'achieve his objectives'. He is encouraged to
organize and re-organize, simplify, standardize, and rationalize
until he has 'tabs' on everything that happens.

The manager is exhorted to *control*; to keep a 'firm grip on
developments', to 'check every stage of the operation', to ensure
that he is the boss over everything that happens.

These terms are those of an *ideology*; they serve to direct
his attention, give his worries some objects and confuse him
as to the nature of his problems. For his problems are those
of the extrapolations of dominance. Communication is to
countervail secrecy, coordination is to exhaust sycophancy and
control is to extirpate sabotage. For it is the '3 S's' that are
happening and the '3 C's' that might be the managerial ideal.
Anyone, anywhere can stop telling the manager what he needs
to know, appease him with sweet talk, and plot his downfall.
Similarly lies can be told, false friendships can induce vital
confidences, and his ideas can be given the merets of trials.

The practical setting for confusion by ideology is that of the
committee. A manager is a negotiator, a dealer; a fixer of
contracts. He doesn't make decisions: he gets people to agree
to things with threats, praise, and promises and is treated the
same himself. He doesn't have power: he seizes and uses the
right to speak with some people and be a witness to the agreements engineered by others. The agreement-engineering
ceremonies are committees.

When the manager is in committee he is doing, and not doing, his job. He is doing his job because he needs to be there – just in case. For a fraction of the time he is on stage, his wits clenched, accounting for his failures and expressing his readiness to try again and to try even harder. For the rest he is bored: listening to snatches; thinking a little; letting nothing go and catching the odd good performance.

The meeting is a trial by attrition and has one of two forms: a departmental review or an interdepartmental discussion. The review is a postmortem and apportionment of blame. A light celebration is turning into an excruciating wake. The discussion is to wade through the porridge of procedures, incompetence, and vested interest to a new state of affairs. Everyone conceivably affected was called. Too many people; too long an agenda; their heads made vague by too much tobacco smoke. And the event lasts too long. The chairman has the power of judge and can force comparisons between the ambitious and the overstretched. The obvious parallel is the mother hen with her brood.

The manager churns on through this absurdity. And it pulls him out of shape. It makes him an expert in covering up, in being glib or aggressive. He feels he is not really doing his job. His job is in the office and around the department – finding out what they are doing and keeping them at it. But somehow it's more important to be in committee answering and observing for yourself than it is to do that which you are answerable for. This is absurd in itself and made more absurd by the pretence that those with whom one conflicts are one's colleagues.

Conflict and absurdity are the first two characteristics of the job of manager, stated in the preamble, that render the position untenable. The third characteristic is precariousness, and clearly its substantiation entails appreciating how managers recognize that it is *who they are* which makes them insecure. Their pasts are disinherited, they try to become their job. Managers conceal their backgrounds from other managers. But one aspect of past experience that is difficult to conceal is education because it shapes the managers' expressions. And management is anti-intellectual.

There is a general suspicion of the educated few. There is a prevalence of men 'who have worked their way up': who are unclear on how to take education and are resistant to it. There is antipathy towards 'la-di-da' accents and middle class effetism. For though there is respect for 'public speaking' the 'man with the mouth' and the 'genius with figures' is felt to be a 'con-man'. The few managers who are middle class by birth or who have a university degree square up to these disadvantages and apologize for them.

Pay and conditions are also considered unspeakable. For, like social class and education, their surfacing would produce conflicts over their discrepancies. There are differences of more than £2,000 per annum between comparable managers and on occasions a boss's salary is either barely above his subordinates or more than twice as much.

The higher paid managers have more of everything: office suites; expenses; cars and time to think. The resentment of middle managers is held at a grumble by the lack of firm evidence. Pay is a precarious asset for the manager because he doesn't know how well or how badly he is paid or for how long his pay will continue to arrive.

The manager is working hard to justify his job and thereby himself in it. The more the firm provides the more it demands. And all the while the manager says his wife and children come first, or that he works to get money to buy the things he wants. But the manager has very little time for these people and pastimes. He starts well before 9.00 a.m. and leaves well after 6.00 p.m. He takes work home most evenings. He stays exceptionally late at least once a week and works Saturdays or Sundays or both. The manager is working flat out keeping pace with his job as the Board incites other managers to make more work for him and encourages managers to standardize each others' work. Thus the manager is disabled from taking his holidays: if he really wants them they must be booked well in advance. Otherwise it's 'the works' fortnight' and a few odd days until yet again the manager is too late to seize the chance of rest.

Obviously the manager's family and social life are precarious by virtue of there being little time left to sustain them. The company comes first and must do.

In comparison the good old days of 'gaffers', 'gentlemen-farmers' and 'brilliant engineers' really do sound tolerable. In return for deference there was defence; managers felt permanent and the few of them seem to have been so. Now, I would

K

claim, 'it's wide open'. The ever-quickening pace is the dance before the death-throes. Managers feel trapped in the wild west: the fastest mouth wins only to be challenged by every newcomer and dirty fighter in the business. Managers' alienation, if this crisis of chronic conditions can be called such, is a burn-up affair with the firm. They are being worn out, literally, by work and worry – by trying to adjust to a disequilibrating momentum.

Thus the reasoning of this part of my argument shudders to its end. The current employment of managers is that of a man misshapen within the absurd, as man against man within the hierarchy and as man as manager against the competing, but vestigial, demands of his life. I reason that this situation cannot last indefinitely: either as a situation or as a man in such a situation.

No future generations of managers are being trained

In sketching the second arc of my argument I need to quibble with words. No more managers are being *trained*, I say. Clearly we now expect to be trained to be something: to be trained and certificated before taking responsibilities. We no longer expect to learn on the job. And so we are just beginning to accept the corollary: training shapes imagination and its horizons but does not teach responsibility.

I accept that the term 'manager' may be used for some time to come. But I argue that the youth being styled for management have a qualitatively different understanding of their work and are comparatively irresponsible. I suggest that this is the prevailing opinion of established managers.

New managers, tomorrow's managers, I shall term 'nouveau managers' to gain some connotations from the label 'nouveau riche'. The connotations I seek are those of striving, quasi-arrival, brashness, and gaucheness and yet, despite all, rejection by the riche propre. Nouveau managers are engaged as trainees. Young graduates are recruited by managers with particular responsibility for their selection, initial care, and training programme. The graduates come from the spectrum of availability: from the Oxbridge classics crust through to the wave of business studies from 'technological universities'. They are the children of the 'bulge' and grammar school education. They are a generation and have been treated as such all their lives. Consequently my elucidation begins with an account of the context of management in terms of its generations. Nouveau managers are ill fitted to what has gone before them.

The *old guard* are between 50 and 65 years old. They are middle managers and have held the same job whilst their departments have doubled, or even trebled, in size. They have kept up to date and installed cheaper, standardized methods as they were developed. They form a natural clique with memories of happier, less warlike days; they keep the myths alive. The myths are of a bygone age, of good, even-tempered experts as bosses, of workers giving their all for relatively low pay; of people in touch with each other and holidays as festivals.

The old guard keep their myths secretively, and do not make public declarations of their friendships. What is known about them is their membership of archaic local groups; churches; masonic temples; bowling clubs and leagues of hospital friends. The old guard have been lifelong members of the firm, and the local community. Often they made a journey of some distance to begin working for the firm. Having arrived, they worked their way up a ladder of which every rung was significant. They developed a style of practical democracy together.

Beneath the old guard are a few men of much greater rank. They are *ideas men*, brought into the company at considerable expense. They are 40–50 years old and have worked for at least three other firms. Their tasks are to stand outside the structure, pull together a future for the firm's products, and to engage in market research for new methods of production. They have no department and no immediate effect. For they counsel the Board. They are isolates and Apollos hired to carry out a mission.

Then comes *lumpen management*, those 35 to 50-year-old men on whom the day-to-day operations depend. They accept that, as the backbone of the hierarchy, they do the bulk of the 'real work'. They have worked for other firms, largely in the same locality. They have managed biscuits, pet foods, light and heavy engineering. Now they have the style of practical authority or that of Janus. If they are isolated, lumpen managers unite in cabals. They have gone as far as they can go, for strangely, their career prospects are those of the middle levels of middle management by the time they are middle-aged.

Finally there is a further interstitial grouping: the rare *hatchet men*. Their age is between 28 and 35. They joined the company as its earliest graduates and proved that they would do anything they were told. They are the 'highest flyers' of all being heads of departments, executives, and close confidantes of the Board. They enjoy being totally dependent on the firm and welcome any change they are told to make. Their security comes in this dependence and movement. They act as ideas men *within* their department; changing its structure; methods; personnel and title until it is dragged into the 1970s – less the greater proportion of its 'dead wood'. The hatchet men are held up as shining examples for the nouveau managers.

But there is no room immediately for the nouveau manager. He is given the task of being a personal assistant to another generational type with an understanding that though he will learn from his master he will not grow to be like him. For no one is quite sure what to do with these 'trainees'. They are attending to executives of high rank but obviously they are not understudies. They prepare letters, make calculations, and act as secretaries for discussion committees. They are intelligent and unaware and regarded with open contempt by lumpen management and pity by the old guard. The contempt is partly an extension of the dislike of education and partly disgust at how the nouveau managers shape up. For to lumpen managers trainees are spies and lap-dogs. They are circulating departments in the hope of an expression of slight preference and confidence; in the hope that they find something to do for long enough to be called a job. Naturally enough, the trainees band together whenever possible and make a clique in completing crosswords at dinner, and the occasional Saturday party. It is for them to prove themselves. This means they should compete with each other to make a few shine above the rest. The trainees are frankly unwilling to do so. To hardened managers trainees are cissies or even homosexual. Dull – deadly dull, no drive-guts or flair.

Lumpen managers demand to know what happened to the intelligent ones. They ask, 'Where did they go?' The trainees they have in no sense hurried to work. Few come to interviews at universities, many arrive after several months have elapsed, 'Where have they been?'

'Why do we get this lot? What is going on? The education

system keeps the bright ones until they are 21 and then they go elsewhere. We get trainees in the numbers we want – in the end! But look at them. They've no spirit. Of course, we know the university keeps the best ones but what about the second best? They've got no initiative. If they have got a spark they've gone within a couple of years. We spend a fortune finding them. They're not worth it but we've got to have them. And we pay them well until they find their feet. If they're any good they just walk off.'

This speech makes the phenomenon of *head starvation* manifestly clear. The firm is missing the cream and trying to sift the mediocre. Then the flock is resented for its sheepishness and the few leaders walk off alone.

The rather more sensitive souls of the trainees respond to these contradictions with an amalgam of passivity and cynicism. 'Why', they ask in their turn, 'should we worry? We get £1,500 to £1,900 per annum for what we do and a 40-year-old manager is probably only getting a few hundred more. And he's wearing himself out with work and worry. I'll stay here while the money's good and when it gets rough I'll go elsewhere.'

As a consequence of mutual misunderstanding, abuse, and exploitation passive cynicism develops and defends the nouveau manager. It also disqualifies him from replacing his mentors. His task is a miniature version of ideas men or hatchet men. In either case he is just brought along for the job and is moved on when, and if, it's done. For the nouveau manager jobs go on, and off, like switches. And to cope with being an employee who has but a hazy awareness of his employment, the trainee becomes heavily dependent on the firm. He is incorporated.

This process is akin to the suspension of disbelief necessary to the dramatic experience. In being absorbed into the firm the trainee substitutes the firm as employer for the firm as financier. The trainee becomes indebted to the firm.

The nouveau manager's adjustment to his situation is obviously appropriate: he takes the line of least resistance through to conformity. The directorate doesn't want more managers. They are cutting their losses in recruiting new managers together with those of the installation and maintenance of a computer. The Board wants fewer managers and more mobile, contract, technological operatives. The nouveau manager is to think like a director and act like a clerk. Rather than a management structure, fewer men are required to circulate in an amorphous quasi-management atmosphere. A few will be needed for the direct control of workers as foremen. A few will be needed as specialist combatants with workers over changing conditions. But for the rest what is required is clever, near-creative clerks to collect data and collate it for the Board.

The resentment from established managers comes because the nouveau managers have adjusted too readily. The trainees have not realized that managers work, in part, with each other, against the Board. And the changeover to the era of cartels, computers, and clerks has not been as easy as the firm wished. The Board expected managers to lay waste to their lifetime's work: to demolish the defences of the management structure itself. Calling nouveau managers 'managers', when in reality they control a secretary and share punch-card operators, is lip-service to lumpen management. And so far middle managers are just holding their own.

In part it is obvious that computers make levels of management redundant and in part it is clear that computers control administrative workers as production technology controls operatives. What is less satisfactory is arguing that computers have prevented new managers from developing. It is sufficient to say that nouveau managers are being cast in new moulds and their behaviour is indicative of more than 'a transitional phase in the evolution of management'.

Managers' plans belie their demise

Managers are not stupid. They can read the signs even when they appear to point in many directions. Managers think about their own future and in so doing calculate the life of their speciality, job, and employer. In this way managers make the future their own; they make a personal response to a social malaise. These responses are kept private. Yet as a confidante I was able to recognize consistencies in calculations. The consistencies do not emerge from managers *en bloc*. They are to be found as distinct for the three generations and the two rare groupings at their margins.

There are three generations of managers: those who remember the First World War, those who struggled to employment in the ensuing depression, and those who were educated out of the Second World War.

The 'elders' are at the point of psychological redundancy and retirement. They have held the same job and beliefs for a long time. They have become conspicuously old hat, for they talk of principles in a pragmatic age. A few of their number present some embarrassment to other managers. Their nostalgia is barbed. They say they don't know what it's coming to, that labour relations cannot worsen indefinitely, and that nobody takes any real responsibility. And those that are openly defiant are fully prepared to go. The elders are prepared to retire at 60 or even at 55. They have had enough and say so.

I do not mean that the elders are physically exhausted. Far from it. In comparison with lumpen managers they are in rude health. I mean that their words have a tone of powerless resentment. They do not see how the employment situation can last and therefore argue that it cannot really go on. This makes their powerlessness a burden. They have a 'camaraderie of the trenches' with old workers and yet they cannot oppose lumpen managers who exercise power over them. The elders are powerless to control mid-managers because they have not known them from their youth. The elders rely on informal control and lumpen managers will not be deterred from their ways by mild jokes.

Lumpen managers are most unwilling to go. There is nowhere for them to go to. They reached the middle levels of middle management by middle age. But they did not try to do so. Lumpen managers have been lifelong opportunists. Their careers only make sense with hindsight. They were brought on to their present positions by forces larger than ambition.

They began after the Second World War. Before this they held any number and type of job. Wartime service brought them on. If they were making weapons they rose to some sort of foreman by 1945. If they were in the army they rose up from the ranks and became NCOs or officers; if their path was the former, their promotion up the ladder has been steady since then. They have not sought status, their status has been increased to cope with increased production. They have been glad of the money and the change of bosses. And if their path was war service they express the onset of their career as: 'Then I came out into Civvy Street and this job came up.'

151

In taking their opportunities lumpen managers have learned to accept and work on most things that 'come up'. They have been prepared to move schools, homes, and regions at the instigation of their employers. They have been prepared to acquire most of the consumer desirables of the age. Their homes are mortgaged, their cars very nearly paid for, they have a telephone, television, 'fridge, washing machine, with perhaps a caravan or boat parked outside.

In consuming what was available, lumpen managers have used their local art gallery, swimming pool, library, and park on rare outings with their wives and children. Lumpen managers do not depend upon that which they consume. Their dependency is on the company.

Those that realize their dependency and have reached the ceiling of middle management have businesses elsewhere. Two production managers were respectively partner in a bookmaking chain, property developer and landlord, and partner in a sign-writing firm; whilst two inspection managers were respectively property developer and proprietor of a boutique with his wife, and director of a light engineering firm with his wife as a co-director and secretary. And, again, three other managers contributed to shops and businesses run by their wives.

All these after-hours entrepreneurs said their businesses provided interest, revenue, and independence. In this way they said some financial independence had helped in their job. They had got on because they were able to speak their mind. These men are now at the very top of middle management with an average of £5,000 per annum salary from two yearly contracts. There is nowhere for them to go. To go further up is wholly dependent upon the directorate recruiting into itself – and this would mean lumpen managers being able to get out of management.

In fact, though, 'getting out' may be the supreme act of opportunism in the lumpen manager's career. Four managers wanted to leave and become teachers. They were troubled in case nobody wanted them but they had already experimented with teaching on courses and in evening classes. They were ready to go – if there was anywhere to go to.

These entrepreneurs and educationalists were fully up the ladder and half out of the company. They had seen that there was 'no future in it for them'. Like other lumpen managers they did not see the company as their own. No one of this generation held shares in the company, nor would they unless the price were right. Lumpen managers seem just as privatized and instrumental as lumpen proletariat.

'Ideas men' are much more deeply committed. They love their work. In 1969 they had been with the company less than three years. They were pulled in from other, and bigger, companies and have accepted indeterminacy in return for big money. They are paid well over the odds in contrast to their previous jobs and comparable job holders. Despite being on short-term contracts they have home loans, money loans, and two litre cars from the company. Their staff is also specialist and well paid. They accept that a large proportion of their time is spent off the site, in their car and spending expenses. They have no illusions and anticipate that one day they will not return. Some other company will have made a much better offer and they had devoted their expertise but not themselves to their present employer. Ideas men read the *Daily Telegraph* on Fridays and the *Sunday Times* to observe trends in the employment of their expertise. Ideas men make themselves transient and say they are capitalizing on the transcience of their work. Ideas men make themselves able, scarce, and redundant.

'Hatchet men', on the other hand, are in league with the company. They cannot say no. They are ready to modify management and have it modified around them. They build up a personal history of successful executions and, they think, the gratitude of those on the Board whom they know personally. Their idea of career is a very highly paid series of jobs – pulled off in the company's firms at home and abroad. They run great risks being company faithfuls because they can be sacrificed in response to local pressure. Their sacrifice is subtle: they can be promoted to a non-existent position or their department can become the nucleus for all departments about to be rationalized by reduction. In the former case the ex-hatchet man is pushed out by promotion – to a cul-de-sac of fresh air with a grand title, no staff, and miles from production. In the latter the ex-hatchet man is brought down with an ever increasing load until it is impossible to administrate the sprawl for which he is responsible. Hatchet men respond to these risks lightly: 'If they come, they come. I'll go elsewhere. If they don't then I've done well and they'll look after me.'

Reviewing the plans of existing managers it appears clear that by and large each generation and grouping is ready to quit or to be sacked. Each type has its readiness and reasoning. And while the study was in progress the plans materialized as follows:

3 elders retired at the ages of 59, 61 and 63

1 lumpen manager left to teach in a primary school

6 lumpen managers had job changes which involved contractions of their departments, moves to smaller departments and demotions to satellite sites

1 ideas man had the sack with a week's notice

1 hatchet man was promoted to a non-job

2 hatchet men were moved to trouble spot sites and were rumoured to have failed.

It is not surprising, therefore, that two further plans were being discussed *by all types*. First, a return to paternalism was sought and thereby security for all employees. Thus managers sought staff status, sick pay, sports and social facilities, and guaranteed work in return for less pay for all employees. Many thought that this hope was unrealistic and that a better idea would be the unionization of managers. Consequently the revival of a defunct staff association was being canvassed. It presented some problems of realization as the company had formed it to give foremen a sense of status and now the managers were proposing to use it for security. Nevertheless, it was argued that it was worth accepting the implication of diminished status if it meant getting some bargaining power with the Board. To their suprise the managers found the Board amenable – only to realize that a staff association would forestall membership of the ASTMS which the Board had some reason to fear.

The nouveau managers knew nothing of existing managers' plans. They were consuming at the appropriate salary-credit-expenses level. They felt precarious and unwanted anyway.

Some were using the company for training and anticipating their first move. This proved difficult as very few jobs were advertised and they thought it necessary to appear competent and loyal rather than green and flighty. In fact, most trainees were without plans. They waited for 'the company' to decide what they should do next.

One nouveau manager, however, was a subversive. He had used the 'Weatherman' tactic of cutting his hair, wearing a suit, and listening. He was a confidante for those beneath him as well as those above. He was passing knowledge of intentions and personalities to key workforce personnel. He appreciated that he would have to leave if his actions were discovered. He had not told other nouveau managers in case they betrayed him. Nevertheless he thought one other trainee might be working similarly and was hoping to find out for sure.

To engage in a further prophecy, I do not think that the two action plans of managers and nouveau managers stand much chance of getting anywhere. That is, the unionization of lumpen managers and the politicization of nouveau managers are movements which can be accommodated by the company and have strong forces preventing them from sustaining momentum. Both generations recognize that their involvement in such activities involve exposure and the risk of expulsion. Moreover, there are conditions within the manager's present employment that make a collective action difficult to initiate.

For lumpen managers the problem is that their workload is already far too heavy. Unionization would be to engage in a struggle against the owners and is ultimately a counter-claim to this ownership. The lumpen manager is already supposed to be 'running the firm'. He does not want any more work than he's got – he wants less. It is difficult for him to dissociate himself from being a manager and to re-engage himself as a worker.

For nouveau managers politicization is difficult whilst practising the arts of concealment. Moreover, there is the practical problem that the dismantling of privilege and leadership of workers entails the development of mutual interests. Workers may be led from within; but leadership from above looks like a subtle revision of management. There is, then, the closedness of workers to such a development. Such closedness is amenable to change but this would depend upon fairly long-term familiarization. And here we confront the fact that nouveau managers are being groomed as mobile troubleshooters in an atmosphere, rather than a hierarchy, of control. They do not know anyone or live in a particular place or have much to do directly with the workers they rarely meet.

Thus both lumpen managers and nouveau managers are

dissuaded from purposive collective action, and thus, ineffectual in counteracting the curtailment of their employment. Lumpen managers have already had enough and nouveau managers have little in common with other groups in the company.

What, then, is the relevance of the argument advanced?

Facts in themselves have no authority (Hegel). It is argument that gives weight to facts and thereby draws strength to itself.

I have argued that 'manager' will cease to be a category of employee in the foreseeable future. I have not suggested that there will be no hirelings to subdue the slaves, but rather that within a company the intricate and delicate management structure will disappear and be replaced by a managerial atmosphere in which highly paid experts execute precise control, observation, and distraction tasks for their masters using machines which also control themselves. By attrition, redundancy, unionization, or revolution management will be finished, and managers themselves are facilitating their own end. This, then, is my prediction, made without qualification.

The argument may seem little more than a crude extrapolation. To be sure in the present – February 1972 – it is clear that scientific and managerial personnel are as readily redundant as shop floor workers. It is also becoming apparent that the proportion 'at risk' is probably higher in managerial workers. I accept that the argument is not my own. In fact I believe the argument to be a commonly held opinion. I have advanced my reasoning for two purposes and it is with the account of these purposes that I wish to close.

First, I wish to draw the attention of those who will hear to the continual crises of capitalism. I am ill equipped to provide a full analysis but I would suggest that the crisis condition in the labour of superintendence is indicative of a polarization of the capitalist block into masters and slaves whose management must then be military. It is not possible to say that something will happen or will not happen unless one is personally committed to seeing it through. I am opposed to the bolstering of capitalism.

Secondly, I feel that social scientists may tend to see managers as an enemy to them. As if managers embody capitalism and should therefore be ignored or contained. In advancing my argument I distinguished types of managers. I hope to have shown the contradictions in each social character and the way in which men become these types to the detriment of themselves. They are men trapped by self-seeking into socially useless pursuits and subject to a myriad of threats and privations. If social scientists were to relate to these men in terms of their demise, efforts could be made to draw them into their own struggle. As such, though management be validly 'finished', managers need not. They can be helped in their unionization and politicization. Once again, a prophecy may be purposely negated.

6 Industrial Conflict: Some Problems of Theory and Method

J. E. T. ELDRIDGE

INTRODUCTION

Clark Kerr, in his essay 'Industrial conflict and its mediation', provides us with one of the most succint statements that I have come across on the variety of forms which industrial conflict can take:

> 'Industrial conflict has more than one aspect; for the manifestation of hostility is confined to no single outlet. Its means of expression are as unlimited as the ingenuity of man. The strike is the most common and most visible expression. But conflict with the employer may also take the form of peaceful bargaining and grievance handling, of boycotts, of political action, of restriction of output, of sabotage, of absenteeism, or of personal turnover. Several of these forms, such as sabotage, restriction of output, absenteeism and turnover, may take place on an individual as well as on an organized basis and constitute alternatives to collective action. Even the strike itself is of many varieties. It may involve all the workers or only key men. It may take the form of refusal to work overtime or to perform a certain process. It may even involve such rigid adherence to rules that output is stifled.' (Kerr 1964: pp. 170–1)

In this paper I want to explore a number of paradigms which have been constructed by sociologists and within which attempts have been made to explain the patterns, rate, and intensity of industrial conflict in one or more of its manifestations. This will be done in the hope that at least we will know what we are taking on board when we are asked to accept an explanation. At best there may be grounds for suggesting that certain kinds of explanation are to be preferred.

THE PLURALIST PERSPECTIVE

A great deal of contemporary discussion and analysis of industrial conflict takes place within what has come to be termed a pluralist framework. I want to indicate some of the conceptual ambiguities which can arise, the prescriptive elements which can be encountered, and the images of society which serve as a backcloth for sociologists operating within this perspective.

Written into the notion of pluralism in the most formal sense is an idea of competing social forces which constrain and check absolutism. We may recall that in Schumpeter's *Capitalism, socialism and democracy*, the theory of competition for political leadership is likened to the economic concept of competition. But the application of 'perfect competition' to social life is judged an unrealistic ideal. However: 'Between this ideal case which does not exist and the cases in which all competition with the established leader is prevented by force, there is a continuous range of varieties within which the democratic method of government shades off into the autocratic one by imperceptible steps' (Schumpeter 1943: p. 271).

This in any given case would lead to the empirical question of where within the range of variation a particular society was located – what kinds of imperfections and inequalities in the competitive struggle existed – and the interpretive question of whether particular expressions of conflict were reflections of the existing balance of power or were attempts to change that balance. Theoretically we may note that in so far as we identify the social forces model with perfect competition we are imparting notions of diffusion of power and of segmented antagonism, that is conflict between relative equals. As we move away from that, questions of inequality between competitors enter in. Conflict in terms of domination, based on varying degrees of power concentration, has to be accounted for.

At the level of the total society, pluralism finds impressive advocacy in Durkheim with the thesis that the development of intermediate groupings between the state and the individual is

159

desirable if one is to avoid the opposing evils of state domination or anomie (with its connotations of normlessness or unregulated competition). Since competition was of the essence of social life for Durkheim, the key problem for him was how to regulate it effectively and thus enhance human freedom. Much later we find Kornhauser arguing in similar terms that the presence of such intermediate groupings promotes stability and defends liberal democracy against mass society on the one hand (broadly equivalent to Durkheim's anomic state) and totalitarianism on the other. Kornhauser stresses both the importance of a range of secondary associations existing and of individuals having multiple affiliations on the grounds that extensive cross-cutting solidarities promote a high level of freedom and consensus and prevents one line of social cleavage from becoming dominant (Kornhauser 1960: p. 80). Although hierarchical elements within social organizations are not eliminated from his model, it is clear that Kornhauser's portrayal of his idea of liberal democracy implies more or less perfect competition between interest groups: 'A plurality of independent and limited function groups supports liberal democracy by providing social bases of free and open competition for leadership, widespread participation in the selection of leaders, restraint in the application of pressures on leaders, and self government in wide areas of social life. Therefore, where social pluralism is strong, liberty and democracy tend to be strong' (Kornhauser 1960: pp. 230–1).

What happens when pluralist analyses of industrial conflict are pursued? Clark Kerr's liberal pluralism is of seminal significance here (Kerr 1964). For him the relation between managers and managed in a complex industrial society is an acute problem. Since he stands for a position which opposes centralized power in society (and this especially means state power) he wants industrial relations to proceed autonomously. This entails managers and managed coming together to construct and maintain rules and institutions for conflict regulations. Thus he advocates collective bargaining, the setting up of appropriate forms of mediation and arbitration procedures, and the use of the strike as a weapon of last resort. The rationale for this position is clearly spelled out: such conflicts are more limited than industrial conflicts which spill over into the political arena. This is reflected in his attitude to the Taft-

Hartley Act: 'It is questionable whether there should be any general labour law on labour legislation, since a general law particularly invites an attempt to cover all possible abuses by the antagonists and encourages a large scale political battle' (Kerr 1964: p. 18). Further, within an autonomous industrial relations framework Kerr evidently prefers overtly organized and voluntarily accepted forms of conflict regulation as against individualistic or group conflict of a covert nature such as sabotage, restriction of output, or absenteeism, which are less manageable. Hence essentially conflict which is open and institutionalized is seen as a safety valve which serves to maintain a free society. It is for him the golden mean between anarchy on the one hand and total domination by one party on the other. The prescription therefore is to search for 'practical' adjustments around the golden mean in order to maintain the pluralist system in a dynamic-equilibrium. The forms and expressions of industrial conflict are consequently evaluated within that paradigm. It is accordingly, in effect, treated as functional or dysfunctional for society as a whole. One of the problems here is of confusing the model with reality – of assuming what one should in fact be demonstrating, namely that there is a good fit between the two – and then evaluating patterns of industrial conflict in functionalist terms. In this way a radical critique of society which might involve a re-interpretation of industrial conflict is defined away. If, for example, there is empirical evidence available which reveals wide disparities in the distribution of wealth and property in capitalist industrial societies, then it at least becomes arguable that the real function of the routinization of industrial conflict is to institutionalize inequalities between manager and managed. Miliband's observation here is pertinent:

'What is wrong with pluralist-democratic theory is not its insistence on the factor of competition but its claim (very often its implicit assumption) that the major organized "interests" in these societies, and notably capital and labour, compete on more or less equal terms, and that none of them is there-fore able to achieve a decisive and permanent advantage in the process of competition. This is where ideology enters and turns observation into myth.' (Miliband 1969: p. 146)

The significance of this is, at least in part, that instead of analysing industrial conflict in terms of three possibilities – does it promote authoritarianism, does it lead to anarchy, or does it contribute to the maintenance of the pluralist system, one should allow for the possibility of different kinds of pluralism with different degrees and kinds of inequalities present. To admit the possibility of this is to recognize that what might be regarded as disorderly and undesirable industrial conflict from one pluralist perspective might from another pluralist perspective be regarded as promoting a new and more desirable form of integration. But it is precisely this which is ignored in the way the problem of industrial conflict is typically formulated and which makes for conceptual and methodological weaknesses in analysis.

In the context of industrial relations in Britain the industrial sociologist Alan Fox has raised the question why is there a problem of keeping industrial conflict within socially tolerable bounds and how may it be solved. His perspective is similar to and in part explicitly derived from Clark Kerr. In his widely read paper 'Industrial sociology and industrial relations' (Fox 1966), the main answer would appear to be that management have a faulty ideology: a unitary rather than a pluralist view of the nature of authority in the enterprise which leads to a failure to appreciate the realities of industrial relations. The failure to recognize that there are divergent interest groups with particular loyalties, all with competing claims, is to be empirically at fault. The team view of the industrial enterprise – a common purpose and a single source of authority – means not only that the real nature of industrial conflict is misunderstood but also that it gets in the way of the orderly conduct of industrial relations. Hence:

'Like conflict, restrictive practices and resistance to change have to be interpreted by the unitary frame of reference as being due to stupidity, wrong-headedness or out of date class rancour. Only a pluralistic view can see them for what they are: rational responses by sectional interests to protect employment, stabilize earnings, maintain job status, defend group bargaining power or preserve craft boundaries. The unitary view must condemn them as morally indefensible: the pluralistic view can understand them and by understanding is in a position to change them'. (Fox 1966: p. 12)

But in a later paper written jointly with A. Flanders, 'The reform of collective bargaining: from Donovan to Durkheim' (Fox and Flanders 1969), a more detailed answer is offered. The points that I want here to highlight are these:

(1) The whole analysis of industrial conflict is couched in a general orientation addressed to the problem: how can integrative conflict in a pluralist society be maintained and enhanced? The problem is set against two other major alternatives: repressive measures to suppress conflict in an authoritarian society or unregulated conflict in which the mechanisms of social control are generally weakened, described as anarchic. This general orientation is very similar to Kerr's. The move to anarchy is seen as a threat to pluralism in its own right and also as encouraging a political solution of an authoritarian kind rather than simply trying to reconstruct a more effective pluralist order.

(2) In a pluralist society it is recognized that some measure of disorder is a built-in risk (Durkheim's mild anomie). The main thesis appears to be that cumulative disorder in which the normative order is fragmented derives from power disparities which are themselves a product of the general level of employment.

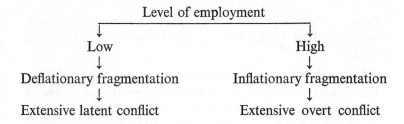

Deflationary fragmentation exemplified in the inter-war years is primarily described in terms of employers setting the system of normative regulation on one side and imposing inferior conditions on their employees, who while deeply resentful were unable to mobilize power to resist.

Inflationary fragmentation is related by Fox and Flanders to the post-war British scene. The basic idea is of inflation promoting and in turn being exacerbated by unrestrained competition. Such competition is portrayed as having several

163

dimensions – employers bidding up the price of labour in local labour markets over the agreed rates, unions in leap-frogging competition over wages and working conditions for their members, and particular groups of workers changing their views upwards concerning their relative worth vis-a-vis other groups, that is their sense of a 'fair' return for their labour. Given a diagnosis of acute anomie in the economic sphere, Fox concludes that 'what is at stake is whether the whole normative framework governing the production and distribution of wealth becomes further fragmented and splintered in a manner which threatens cumulative disorder, or whether we are still capable of reconstructing larger areas of agreement upon which larger units of regulation can rest' (Fox and Flanders 1969: p. 174). In order to achieve this, faith is placed in a multi-pronged policy of reform of bargaining structures at plant and industry level together with indicative planning and monitoring devices at industry and national level. As in the case of Kerr scepticism is expressed about the efficacy of legal sanctions in regulating conflict. The solution offered is essentially one of reconstructing the system of industrial relations to make possible orderly conflict. The paradigm in and through which industrial conflict is analysed is a functionalist treatment of the industrial relations system as a plurality of groups in dynamic equilibrium. A departure from this desirable integration is viewed as unstable giving rise to 'profound and serious consequences'. This is instructively illustrated in the following passage:

> 'The proliferation of norm-creating groups – the resulting multiplicity of normative systems may produce a degree of disorder which is felt to impede and imperil vital functions of social life and government. In industrial relations the economic consequences are not confined to strikes and other distractions of the productive process. The loss of integration and predictability is also expressed in such things as chaotic pay differentials and uncontrolled movements of earnings and labour costs.' (Fox and Flanders 1969: p. 162)

What this approach does is insulate a pluralist model of industrial relations from the wider social structure, thus leaving untouched any analysis of structured inequalities in the total society. Yet one may postulate that the way such inequalities are perceived and experienced may well contribute to an understanding of industrial conflict. Thus what is described in the above quotation as a loss of integration could from another perspective be analysed in terms of encroaching control – a response to inequalities no longer regarded and accepted as legitimate or inevitable.

INTERACTIONIST PERSPECTIVES

Herbert Blumer has argued:

'The study of interaction would have to be made from the position of the actor. Since action is forged by the actor out of what he perceives, interprets and judges, one would have to see the operating situation as the actor sees it, perceive objects as the actor perceives them, ascertain their meanings in terms of the meaning they have for the actor, and follow the actor's line of conduct as the actor organizes it – in short, one would have to take the role of the actor and see the world from his standpoint.' (Blumer 1966: p. 542)

This is the basic position of what non-pejoratively one might term a subjectivist sociology, which it is claimed can promote a realistic analysis of social processes and by the same token avoid the dangers of reification of those whose point of departure is the social system or social structure. It brings the issue of consciousness into social explanation in a very central way. I want to offer qualified support for this perspective: support because it faces the question of the meaning to be given to social action, qualified because in Blumer's formulation at least it leaves certain questions unanswered.

First, it can be observed that while the emphasis on studying social processes springs from an impulse to 'tell it how it is', in fact metaphors and analogies are not necessarily eschewed as an aid to understanding. Let us take the game analogy applied to industrial conflict as an example. In so far as bargaining between parties is a major element of conflict regulation in industrial relations the game analogy employing concept of players, spectators, rules, moves, tactics, strategies, termination, and outcomes has obvious attractions. We may indeed take this as a filling out of Simmel's approach to sociology as a study of social interactions. On what basis does interaction take place and how does it proceed?

If one treats industrial relations with reference to the game analogy one might inquire: (1) What are the ground rules which define the game and make is possible? The fact that the game is played at all implies a notion of reciprocity between the players and from this moves, tactics, and strategies follow.

(2) Can any 'rules of preferred play' (Garfinkel's term) be discerned? In a chess game, for example, the Sicilian Defence might supersede the Caro-Kann defence as a generally preferred mode of play amongst chess players. Both are consistent with the ground rules and therefore in that sense legitimate, but one comes to be preferred to another for various reasons. But the implications of following one defence rather than another can be far-reaching in terms of tactics and strategies. As the interaction proceeds certain possibilities and certain constraints exist within the rules for both parties while certain others are removed. So in an industrial conflict the parties may play to settle the matter within the plant; on other occasions they may prefer to widen the dispute by bringing in outside union officials and employers' associations; sometimes a union will strike when procedures are exhausted, sometimes it will agree to arbitration.

Ethnomethodologists such as Garfinkel and Cicourel have argued the usefulness of the games analogy because the notion of rules of the game conveys a sense of what once learnt is taken for granted, and of the meaning which may be attached to certain events – what is permissible, what is permissible but surprising, what is illegitimate, and so on. We may pause to emphasize that there is a learning process – so that there are players who may have to play games with which they are not familiar, or players with differing degrees of skill and ability.

The learning problem is instructively illustrated in an account of the Rabaul, New Guinea strike of native indentured labour in 1929 by Margaret Mead. When the Europeans called for their tea and shaving water one morning, they were surprised and annoyed to find no servants ready to answer the call. They were surprised that given different tribal loyalties among the labourers, it was even possible to organize a strike. The idea had been imparted to them from visiting American Negro seamen: 'A "strike" as the natives understood it after listening to the tales of the visiting seamen, meant that you, all together, planned secretly, absented yourself from work, and refused to come back until higher wages were promised' (Mead 1956: p. 79). But what does one do when the claim is rejected? This they had not learnt or worked out.

> 'When they were told to come back to work, they replied they wanted an increase in wages. They were told they wouldn't get it and to come back to work at once: and they did. No one had told them what strikers did when those against whom they struck didn't accede to their demands.' (Mead 1956: p. 80)

The development of rules of the game in industrial relations can be applied, as Clark Kerr has done, to indicate that the opposing parties recognize implicitly or explicitly that it is in their mutual interests to routinize conflict and contain it in normative bounds. He states:

> 'Rules which guarantee the independent sovereignity of each party, which raises the cost of fighting . . . which set some fairly precise norms for settlement . . . which prohibit use of certain provocative means of contest, which limit conflict to intermittent periods, which confine the subjects for disagreement to some reasonable area at any one time – all aid the non-violent settlement of industrial disputes. The rules of the game aid rationality – knowledge of costs and consequences – and thus diplomatic resolution of controversies.' (Kerr 1964: p. 199)

From this writers in the Kerr school tend to treat industrial relations in evolutionary terms, towards a movement of growing rationality and peaceful regulation of industrial conflict – as such conflict is routinized and ritualized. Sometimes this is linked with a view that industrial relations are becoming more game like, not only in a developed sense of procedures and what is appropriate, but also in the bounded character of the game. It is set off against other games – segregated for example from the political game. On this certain observations may be offered:

(1) Obviously the growth of procedures can be described in many industrial societies – from early patterns of repression

167

and collective bargaining by riot, through to the struggle for union recognition, towards a position of institutionalized collective bargaining and equality before the law. Studies by Knowles and Phelps-Brown, for example, discuss this in the British context (Knowles 1952, Phelps-Brown 1959).

The United States, Taft and Ross point out, has had the bloodiest and most violent labour history of any industrial nation in the world, which tended to appear in its most violent form when employers attempted to crush a union or to deny union recognition (Taft and Ross 1969). In their survey they note that on at least 160 occasions state and federal troops have intervened. Violence has not disappeared. In the 1960s important examples could be found of sabotage. The Alabama Power Company was on the receiving end of fifty acts of sabotage in 1966 including the draining of oil from transformers, placing of chains across powerlines, severing of guy wires on transmission line poles, and the destruction of power equipment by gunfire. But Taft and Ross argue that the overall evidence is of a decline of violence since the second world war:

'This diminution of labour violence was not a temporary phenomenon but endured the strains of major and minor wars, a number of business cycles, and substantial changes in national and local political administrations . . . The reconversion of American industry after World War II brought on the greatest strike ever in our history. Yet these mammoth strikes were accompanied by virtually no violence, completely at variance with the experience after 1918.'(Taft and Ross 1969: pp. 379–80)

(2) One should be aware of the pitfalls of the rationality concept in this context. It is important to recognize that games theorists themselves treat the concept of rational behaviour as a limiting case. Having made a basic distinction between zero-sum and non-zero-sum games the rational gamester makes his play for a best course of action. This has to take account of what he expects his opponent to do and how he expects his opponent to respond to what he does. In real life situations many imperfections can creep in related to the skills of the players, the ways in which collective decisions are made by the various parties (which one could see as a series of sub-games), the nature of the communications and informations systems of

an inter-party and intra-party character. The ramifications here are enormous as recently demonstrated in fine fashion by Goffman in his discussion of expression games and strategic interaction (Goffman 1970). Indeed, given these imperfections when it comes to bargaining situations between management and unions it may not always be clear or agreed within or between the parties whether the bargain involves a mutually advantageous adjustment or a distributive bargain in which one gains at the expense of the other. A productivity bargain, for example, may be portrayed as the former by management seeking a bargaining initiative, but whether it is integrative or experienced as that by the union is quite another matter. Or a bargain may be labelled a productivity bargain and presented to a government department set up to monitor agreements, even when the bargaining parties know that it was a distributive bargain. If that is the way to get the agreement through then one dresses it up with fashionable though meaningless accoutrements.

Further, rationality need not imply that both sides have available identical moves or the same range of moves. This is the important refinement made formally by Schelling in which he rejects the definition of rational play with symmetrical moves (Schelling 1963). By 'moving' here he has in mind possibilities such as threats, promises, operating sanctions, and interfering with the communications system. One does the best with what one has. However we make the point that the outcome does not depend on skill differences in bargaining though one need not doubt the importance of this, but also in part of the resources one has to mobilize. In some bargaining situations it is as though, to return to our chess illustration, one side did not have a bishop or a knight while the other side was fully manned. Or again thinking of the succession problem, one takes over a game from someone else in which a number of constraints are already operating and a number of options closed.

In other words, it would not be correct to derive from Kerr's comments on 'rules of the game' either a view of bargaining parity between the antagonists or of rough equality of skills. These are essentially matters for empirical investigation although the difficulties of such investigations are very great, if only because some of the moves are concealed deliberately by the participants. But what we can say is that while it is important to understand the normative constraints which bind the parties in industrial relations and to recognize that these are in part reinforced and in part modified by actually playing the game, the question remains what are the social givens from which these norms which constitute the rules of the game are derived? This points to the sociological question of the sources of legitimacy in a particular social order: a question from which we should not be distracted by fascination with the minutiae of the game, but about which the game might tell us something as we see what the participants take for granted. So certain kinds of conflict may be taken for granted within the game, but other conflict generating moves may be seen as dubious within the rules or even of such a character as to transform the nature of the game. How, for example, does one interpret the work-in of the Clydeside shipyard workers, or the workers occupation of the Plessey engineering factory in Scotland within the British context? Again in the case of the miners' strike in Britain in the opening months of 1972, the refusal of miners in many areas to attend to safety precautions were justified on the grounds that one shoulp exercise maximum pressure on the NCB in the dispute. NCB officials frequently presented the view that not only was this self-destructive because potentially it destroyed jobs as well as machinery, but that it was not fair. An NCB official in Kent surveying the situation reflected the ambiguity when he commented: 'We are very lucky in Kent. The union members are playing the game – whatever the game is' (*Sunday Times* Business News, 30 January 1972).

(3) The game analogy can of course be overdone. The institutionalization and isolation of industrial conflict postulated by Kerr and Dahrendorf for advanced industrial societies is in a sense encouraged by a bounded conception of rules of the game. But the reality may not be so tidy. Long has given a sense of this in his paper 'The local community as an ecology of games'. In it he argues for a conception of a territorial system in which can be observed a political game, a banking game, an ecclesiastical game, and so on. But he points out that an individual may play a part in more than one game and that separate games may become connected. The game image is maintained by Long but an Alice in Wonderland element is introduced:

'Sharing a common territorial field and collaborating for different and particular ends in the achievement of overall social functions, the players in one game make use of the players in another and are, in turn, made use of by them. Thus the banker makes use of the newspaperman, the politician, the contractor, the ecclesiastic, the labour leader, the civic leader and all to further his success in the banking game – but reciprocally, he is made to further the others' success in the newspaper, political, contracting, ecclesiastical, labour and civic games. Each is a piece in the chess game of the other, sometimes a willing piece, but to the extent that the games are different with a different end in view.' (Long 1966: pp. 150–1)

So then the participants in industrial conflict may form part of the political game and the industrial game. The players may not always be sure or aware what game they are playing in. Was the 1971 Post Office strike in Britain only an industrial game? Was the government's political game involving prices and wages policy a separate matter? If not, how were the games connected? Again we may recognize that different parties may label a strike as political and economic: indicating disagreement as to what game is actually being played. Such disagreements have relevance when it comes to checking the score. So the Department of Employment in the U.K. is instructed not to count political strikes in the statistics on industrial disputes. In 1971, for example, strikes against the Industrial Relations Bill involving many thousands of workers were defined as political and accordingly were not counted.

But suppose we try and follow Blumer more literally and do not permit metaphors to intervene in the analysis of industrial conflict? Industrial conflict in common with other social processes presents the sociologist with the problem of interpreting data. There are initial difficulties of deciding what counts as data, of how much data that one judges to be relevant is available, and of how consistently records from which data are extracted have been kept. I have discussed a number of these matters elsewhere particularly in relation to strike data (Eldridge 1968). But the problem goes deeper because the same outward act, say a strike, may mean different things to the participants in different times and places *and* different outward

171

acts, say output restriction and absenteeism, may sometimes have roughly equivalent meanings attached to them.

The term vocabularies of motive is explicitly used in Wright Mills (Mills 1963) although the sense of it is clearly conveyed in a number of key sociological figures including Weber, Simmel, Mead, and Mannheim. It refers to the justifications which are given past, present, or future forms of conduct. But the concern is not with idiosyncratic statements but with social motivation, that is with the motivation of groups of people in particular social contexts. These motivations may be articulated from time to time but quite often they are taken for granted. The 'reason' for this action is 'obvious', at least to the participants. The motives are standardized and serve as a sanction for some acts, while discouraging others.

One recent stimulating reference to vocabularies of motive relating to industrial conflict is located in Taylor and Walton's discussion of sabotage (Taylor and Walton 1971). From a wealth of examples the writers suggest three somewhat different forms of motivation may be discerned in acts which are all labelled 'sabotage'. They may be intended to reduce tension and frustration, to facilitate the work processes, or to assert some form of direct control. It is suggested that the prevalence of one or other of these three types may serve as an indicator of the nature of the conflict situation.

> 'Unplanned smashing and spontaneous destruction are the signs of a powerless individual or group . . . where there is a lack of any general shared consciousness amongst the workers . . . Utilitarian sabotage . . . is to be expected principally in industries where the worker has to "take on the machine" in order to push up his earnings – his working against the clock encourages such secondary adjustments . . . Where sabotage of Type 3 is encountered, we expect to find a history of militant activity and generalized recognition of the target for attack and a readiness to sacrifice short-term gains for long-term objectives in a situation in which the opportunities for official protest are circumscribed.' (Taylor and Walton 1971: p. 242)

It was not possible for the authors to link the typology in any statistical sense to the situations outlined, partly no doubt because of the obvious problem of data collection. One study

172

which does attempt to do something of this kind with strike data is Turner, Clack, and Roberts' study *Labour relations in the motor industry*. There it is suggested that

'. . . car firm strikes . . . have had their roots in a pattern or complex of conscious grievances which are "real" in the sense that one can see that they might very well – applied to oneself for instance – be an adequate motive for action and that this pattern of grievance is reflected with a high degree of correspondence in the pattern of state strike-causes.' (Turner *et al.* 1967: p. 333)

These were seen as a response to perceived inequities of wage structure and workloads and to insecurity of employment. And adequate motivation is seen as varying with the employment cycle with wage disputes increasing in boom periods and (more obviously) redundancy strikes in recessive periods. In the study of industrial conflict this is one of the most interesting attempts made to link causal adequacy with adequacy at the level of meaning.

We may take one final example – this time one in which different actions are accorded rough equivalence in terms of social motivation. Handy has argued that absenteeism, strikes, labour wastage, and accidents can and have been utilized as alternative expressions of discontent in the British coal-mining industry in the post-war period (Handy 1968). In particular it is observed that there has been a drastic decline in strike activity since 1957 in proportion to the employed mining population, but an increase in absenteeism, voluntary leaving, and accidents per 100,000 manshifts. It is pointed out that between 1957 and 1960 the NCB pursued a stock-piling policy and there were many reported expressions of the miners' view that by not turning up for work they were doing the Coal Board a favour by reducing the stock a little. Absenteeism in this context serves as a form of output restriction and this was pursued in relation to observable economic conditions. 'That coal miners should reflect their discontent in this form rather than in strike action since 1957 would seem quite rational when one considers the short-run financial disadvantages to them of strikes as compared with absenteeism' (Handy 1968: p. 50).

A concern then with vocabularies of motive does raise ancient but still critical questions concerning the relationship

en motives and action. Further, it encourages us to
line the structure in which particular social motivations
expressed. The only cautionary note which may be sounded
is that there is a tendency to equate the establishment of
adequate motivation with rational behaviour. What had
formerly been regarded as 'irrational' by the uninitiated is
depicted as rational because meaning can be attached to the
act. The connection does not always hold if rationality is to
cover both the meaning of the act and its anticipated consequences. For example, one could in principle explain in terms
of adequate motivation the British Post Office workers' strike
of 1971. But in terms of consequences a series of planned
guerilla strikes might well have proved less costly to the union
and more damaging to the Post Office and in that sense more
rational given the end in view of the employees.

Part of one's reservation about Blumer's position is that it
can lead to a concept of definition of the situation of a somewhat free-floating sort so that consciousness is treated in
idealist terms. An alternative view is that

'the construction of realities may be more influenced by
power relations, socialisation processes and class structures
than by the creative interpretation of the actors engaged in
interaction . . . the social world is not only structured by
language but also by the modes and forces of material
production and by the systems of domination . . . the basic
rules of everyday life . . . are not necessarily a free product
of the subjectivity of members in search for meaning. These
rules can also be a result of factors outside the intention of
the members' activities and interpretations.' (Dreitzel 1970:
pp. xvi–xvii)

An illustration of what is implied in such a statement is to be
found in Baldamus's discussion of industrial conflict which
hinges around the phenomenon of wage disparity (Baldamus
1967). Given that wages are a cost to the enterprise and that
work effort involves certain kinds of deprivation which may be
treated as a cost to the employees, there is an inherent conflict
of interest in the wage bargain. The price paid for labour is the
value placed on effort. Industrial conflict is thereby seen as the
struggle which goes on to change effort values in favour of
employer or employee. Conflict may be expressed in the form

of official and unofficial strikes, labour turnover, absenteeism, quota-restriction, gold-bricking, and slow-downs.

In certain circumstances the bargain can operate in favour of the employee (positive wage disparity). One example is when there is a growth in capital investment per unit of labour. There is also the familiar situation of inflation and full employment: 'The most obvious effect is an overall improvement in the wage earner's bargaining position, with the familiar results of absenteeism, declining factory discipline, increased wage demands and so on' (Baldamus 1967: p. 120). But Baldamus takes the view that these are short-run gains and that in the long run some measure of negative wage disparity appears as a permanent institutional condition of industrial enterprise. Why is this? Partly because work obligations are institutionalized as part of the socialization process, '. . . to accept work deprivations as a duty can only mean in terms of the distributive process that *to some extent* effort is surrendered to the employer free of compensation . . . the more powerful the employee's sense of obligation, the greater is the scope for increasing wage disparity in a given situation' (Baldamus 1967: p. 111). The other reason is that positive wage disparity is only possible for short periods because it eats up a firm's capital reserves and reduces profit margins. In a capitalist economy, therefore, industrial conflict has to be understood in relation to a concept of exploitation. Baldamus comes close to elaborating a thesis of internal contradictions when he argues as follows:

'. . . the very methods that are the main administrative instrument of effort intensification, such as payment by results, make the process of effort compensation and particularly the relation of effort to earnings, more and more transparent. The growing pre-occupation with the administration of effort values may thus possibly reach a point where the normative aspects of industrial work are less concealed or less taken for granted than at present . . . Unless a new pattern of social support emerges the disruptive effect of industrial conflict can then no longer be absorbed, as they have been hitherto, by the employee's tacit acceptance of moral obligations.' (Baldamus 1967: p. 112)

We see from this that the analysis, while referring to the same kind of empirical phenomena as writers such as Fox and

175

anders, operates from different assumptions concerning the mployment contract. The question for him becomes how is exploitation institutionalized and what factors lead to the unmasking of particular forms of exploitation.

THE DIALECTICS OF STRUCTURE AND PROCESS

What is implied in the preceding sections is that at some point a term denoting social structure has to be introduced. Of course it is a conceptual abstraction, but then one does not literally describe reality when labelling social processes, no matter how 'naturalistic' or close to everyday life one tries to be. Here one may recall that the point at issue was well appreciated by Simmel in his influential essay on conflict (Simmel 1955). There he develops a dialectical treatment of structure and process, the usefulness of which he seeks to establish by illustration. A relevant and important example is his discussion of the growth of employers and workers' organizations in Germany and England in the late nineteenth century. He observes that as a trade union grows in size it may centralize its administration. Its officers may then prefer to meet a united employers' organization to avoid duplicating negotiations and coping with a range of employer positions. The employers for their part have grounds for reciprocating. A form of antagonistic cooperation develops with both sides operating on the principle that the benefits of the arrangements outweigh the costs:

> 'For although the result of such organisation was that an incipient strike could rapidly spread and last a long time, this was still more advantageous and economical for both parties than were the many local quarrels, work stoppages and petty conflicts which could not be arrested in the absence of strict organisation of the employers and workers.' (Simmel 1955: p. 90)

What is emphasized here is the idea that the mode in which conflict is expressed is in principle related to a notion of structure (petty conflicts with small groups, institutionalized bargaining, and sometimes long strikes with centralized, relatively co-ordinated groups) and that the participants in a given situation can interact in a way which modifies the given structure and hence affects potentially the mode and intensity of conflict

176

expression and the manner of its regulation. The participants are, in a word, determined and determining. Elsewhere Simmel argues that Marx was right when he maintained that the condition of labour was conditioned by the objective conditions and forms of production. As a proposition this does not depend for its truth on man's acknowledgment, but once acknowledged the nature of the conflict relation alters. From personal battles, the issues are 'objectified'.

'In Germany, this objectification was started more recently by means of a theory, in as much as the personal and individualistic nature of antagonism was overcome by the more abstract and general character of the historical and class movement. In England, it was launched by the trade unions and was furthered by the rigorously supra-individual unity of their actions and those of the corresponding federations of entrepreneurs. The violence of the fight, however, has not decreased for that. On the contrary, it has become more pointed, concentrated and at the same time more comprehensive, owing to the consciousness of the individual involved that fights not only for himself, and often not for himself at all, but for a great super-personal aim.' (Simmel 1955: p. 40)

Hence the actor's consciousness is of great importance in Simmel's treatment of conflict. It may be recalled that when Simmel writes of the parties engaged in antagonistic cooperation he comments that 'they are surrounded in their whole enterprise by a social power which alone gives meaning and certainty to their undertaking' (Simmel 1955: p. 37). This really prompts the question: if they are aware of social power, how do they define and experience it and how do they respond to it? How are they determined and determining? The work of Reinhard Bendix offers, I think, an instructive approach to such an answer (Bendix 1962, 1963, 1965). He begins with the suggestion that we do better to conceptualize social structure, not as a natural system with defined limits and invariant laws governing an equilibrating process, but as a system of historical discussions which we can examine in terms of piecemeal solutions which men have found for the characteristic problems of that system. He is critical of the natural systems formulation because it tends to a view of social structure as an interrelated

M

functioning whole with systematic prerequisites, properties, and consequences. Fundamentally he thinks this approach leads to a reification of the social structure concept. In arguing for a historically informed sociology he suggests that social structures be defined in terms of the characteristic areas of contention among the constituent groups of society. 'If we say then that one social structure has ceased to exist and another taken its place, we mean that the terms of reference have changed by which issues are defined, relationships are maintained, or contentions resolved' (Bendix 1965: p. 174). Bendix suggests that this approach enables one to take into account the terms in which the participants define issues but that 'it is also necessary to go beyond that [subjective] dimension and define the social structure which eventually results from all these contentions, and that cannot be done in subjective terms alone' (Bendix 1965: p. 76).

The sociological possibilities of this approach to social structure are in my opinion exemplified in Bendix's own study *Work and authority in industry* (Bendix 1963). The strategy of that book was to look at how comparable groups in different societies confronted a common problem and how they resolved it. And the problem was how could discipline and subordination be maintained in economic enterprises. The problem is analysed with reference to totalitarian and non totalitarian regimes and with reference to early and later periods of industrialization. Bendix looks at ideologies used to justify and attempt to legitimize managerial control. Such ideologies – for example the human relations ideology in America or the ruling party ideology in Russia and East Germany – are seen as 'formulated through the constant interplay between current contingencies and historical legacies' (Bendix 1963: p. 443). So, to take the Russian example, Bendix argues that when Lenin urged the need for iron discipline of the worker to the Soviet leader, this reflected not only a response to revolutionary emergencies but the legacies of Tsarist rule in which employers and workers had been subject to authoritative control.

However, notwithstanding ideologies which appeal to 'co-operative team work', 'national interest', or a 'classless society' as a source of managerial legitimation, Bendix also notes the widespread character of strategies of independence on the part of subordinate work groups, that is activities which express attempts to gain independence from managerial control. He has in mind group activities such as output restriction, working to rule, and concealment of information. While there is a common problem arising from the superordination/subordination dichotomy, the structure of controls and sanctions employed can of course be considerably different as between different societies, hence both in the imposition and response to them a different vocabulary of motives justifying the exercise and resistance to managerial power may be discerned. Not only this, but where sanctions can be effectively deployed against overt subordinate resistance, industrial conflict may be evident in more covert forms. Bendix makes the point, for example, in the case of East Germany that worker opposition

> 'takes the form of production slow-downs, momentary but demonstrative work stoppages, rejection of "voluntary obligations" or of proposed speed-ups and many others. All these methods have in common that they afford the individual worker a high degree of anonymity, and thereby minimise the danger of detection by the Secret Police.' (Bendix 1963: p. 410)

Similarly Neumann argued that in Nazi Germany the workers responded to the Fascist party's attempts to raise labour productivity by various forms of passive resistance:

> 'The slow-down staged by the German workers is certainly not an open or very marked policy, which would spell death for the leaders and concentration camps for the followers. It consists in the refusal to devote all energy to work, and sometimes in the determination to give much less than the normal.' (Neumann 1966: p. 344)

What needs to be remembered is that interest in the vocabulary of motives of participants does not lead to undisciplined subjectivism and it is related to a concern with structure. Mills makes clear that this is his own view. But he properly observes that in complex urban societies 'varying and competing vocabularies of motive operate co-terminally and the situations to which they are appropriate are not clearly demarcated' (Mills 1963: p. 449). This makes life difficult for the sociologist – but it should put him on his guard, not only because the actor may be the possessor of a sophisticated vocabulary of motives – so

179

the sociologist's model cannot afford to be too crude – but also because an actor may switch vocabularies and hence the sociologist needs to be sufficiently flexible to allow for this.

If, for example, one wished to explore the possibility that a worker's 'image of society' affected his attitude towards industrial conflict one would have to discover with great skill what these images were. Willener and Lockwood among others have attempted to do so (Willener 1957, Lockwood 1966). So with Lockwood suggestions are made that workers may have a 'power', a 'prestige', or a 'pecuniary' model and these are tentatively linked to work and community situations, with the implication that these images of society might well condition the willingness of individuals to participate in group terms in overt industrial conflict such as striking. More recently Brown and Brannen have suggested from their study of shipbuilding workers that individuals may not always be clearly located in one or other of the three categories (Brown and Brannen 1970). Consequently empirical work leads to a construction of models which can allow for overlapping. Something of a pay-off for this is perhaps evident in Cousins's recent article 'The non-militant shop steward' (*New Society*, 3 February 1972), which was also concerned with shipbuilding workers. Survey data from the shipyard studied revealed that shop stewards were more likely to vote Conservative than the men they represented and that they were more concerned to follow procedures before striking and support productivity bargaining than their men. At the same time the researchers observed in the yard overtime bans, go-slows, token strikes, unofficial strikes, and an official strike lasting five weeks. How does the conservative and the militant behaviour co-exist?

'It is as if workers had two separate systems of understanding: one reflected in general attitudes and responses to the industrial and normative systems of order and drawn from public attitudes; the other with potentially more radical implications, reserved for concrete, interpersonal inter-pretations, and drawn from specific experience of injustice and conflicting life styles . . . Amongst the men, a potentially militant sense of unjust and inferior treatment can *co-exist* with conservative attitudes towards procedure based partly on deference, partly on a desire to be accepted and partly on a desire to build up regularities of behaviour that could ensure respect.' (Cousins 1972: pp. 227–8)

In other words more than one vocabulary of motives could be utilized in defining the situation – and flipping to militancy would have to be understood through a precise appreciation by the sociologist of the context. It may well be that this kind of sensitivity (which still does not abandon the concept of structure for a free-floating 'consciousness') could be extended to other contexts, as for example when white collar workers in response to what they perceive as managerial injustice, say a specific case of victimization, decide to join a union with all the implications for the patterning of industrial conflict which that decision will entail.

Another instructive example of an attempt to link structure and process in analysing industrial conflict is that of Ralph Dahrendorf (Dahrendorf 1959). In his account of industrial relations in 'post-capitalist' societies he explicitly derives from Kerr the thesis that the violence and intensity of industrial conflict has diminished as compared to capitalist societies as a result of the development of collective bargaining and procedures of mediation, conciliation, and arbitration. Further, he does not only advocate like Kerr that political and industrial conflict should be isolated to prevent social division on a large scale, but argues that this situation is mirrored in post-capitalist societies:

'We assert that in post-capitalist society the rulers and the ruled of industry and society are tendentially discrete groups. This means that membership in an industrial class leaves open to which political class an individual belongs, since independent determinants and mechanisms of allocation are effective in the associations of industry and political society.' (Dahrendorf 1959: p. 271)

This he depicts as a situation of social pluralism. It is explicitly set against a ruling class thesis of post-capitalist society. But, at the same time, he has a strong sense of the significance of hierarchy in social organization as productive of conflict. Indeed one of his major contentions is that 'the fundamental inequality of social structure, and the lasting determinant of social conflict is the inequality of power and authority which

181

inevitably accompanies social organization' (Dahrendorf 1959: p. 84). Thus asymmetry in terms of power relations is built into his model even in a situation defined as social pluralism. Even if one allows parity between the bargaining parties to exist, workers' organizations as they become bureaucratized become yet another imperatively coordinated association: 'This again, promotes a new type of conflict, intra-union conflict, and one for which wild-cat strikes provide some evidence. It is hard to see how trade unions propose to check this development' (Dahrendorf 1959: p. 279). It is this sense of the on-going significance of the struggle for power (which at least in part always has to be seen as a zero-sum game) that prevents him from offering or advocating a simplistic integrationalist view of industrial conflict:

'. . . our analysis is not intended to suggest that all trouble in industry is past. For one thing it is never possible simply to extrapolate historical developments. The fact that industrial conflict has become less violent and intense in the last century does not justify the inference that it will continue to do so. On the contrary experience shows that in the history of specific conflicts more and less violent, more and less intense periods follow each other in unpredictable rythms. It is certainly conceivable that the future has more intense and violent conflicts in store.' (Dahrendorf 1959: pp. 278–9)

The sociological problem then becomes to identify particular forms and expressions of industrial conflict and to tease out their significance for the social order in which they take place. To pursue this goal can be something other than an ideological rationalization. For although necessarily judgmental and inter-pretative qualities on the part of the sociologist are demanded, a willingness to sift through the evidence (whether one thinks of particular industrial disputes or indices of industrial conflict) may lead to conclusions that he would prefer not to reach. When one contemplates the relevance of sociology to the affairs of men, that may be a slender gain, but, one may suppose, not to be discounted in the quest for knowledge about the social world. The general issue underlying this point was well put by Mannheim:

'. . . let it be said that there exists a fundamental difference between, on the one hand, a blind partisanship and irrationalism which arises out of mental indolence, which sees in intellectual activity no more than arbitrary personal judgments and propaganda, and on the other a type of inquiry which is seriously concerned with an objective analysis and which, after eliminating all conscious evaluation, becomes aware of an irreducible residue of evaluation inherent in the structure of thought.' (Mannheim 1960: p. 89)

REFERENCES

BALDAMUS, W. 1967. *Efficiency and effort*, London: Tavistock.

BENDIX, R. 1962. 'Comparative sociological studies', in *Transactions of the Vth World Congress of Sociology*, vol. 4.

BENDIX, R. 1962. *Work and authority in industry*, New York: Harper.

BENDIX, R. 1965. 'The comparative analysis of historical change', in T. Burns and S. B. Saul (eds.), *Social theory and economic change*, London: Tavistock.

BLUMER, H. 1966. 'Sociological implications of the thought of George Herbert Mead,' *American Journal of Sociology*, 71, 535–44.

BROWN, R. and BRANNEN, P. 1970. 'Social relations and social perspectives among shipbuilding workers', *Sociology*, 4, 71–84, 197-211.

COUSINS, J. 1972. 'The non-militant shop steward', *New Society*, February 3rd.

DAHRENDORF, R. 1959. *Class and class conflict in industrial society*, London: Routledge and Kegan Paul.

DREITZEL, H. P. (ed.). 1970. *Recent sociology, no. 2*, London: Macmillan.

ELDRIDGE, J. E. T. 1968. *Industrial disputes*, London: Routledge and Kegan Paul.

FOX, A. 1966. *Industrial sociology and industrial relations*, London: HMSO.

FOX, A. and FLANDERS, A. 1969. 'The reform of collective bargaining: from Donovan to Durkheim', *British Journal of Industrial Relations*, 7, 151-80.

GOFFMAN, E. 1970. *Strategic interaction*, London: Blackwell.

HANDY, L. J. 1968. 'Absenteeism in the British coal-mining industry: an examination of post-war trends', *British Journal of Industrial Relations*, 6, 27–50.

KERR, C. 1964. *Labour and management in industrial society*, New York: Doubleday.

KNOWLES, K. G. J. C. 1952. *Strikes*, London: Blackwell.

KORNHAUSER, A. W. 1960. *The politics of mass society*, London: Routledge and Kegan Paul.

183

LOCKWOOD, D. 1966. 'Sources of variation in working class images of society', *Sociological Review*, 14, 249–67.

LONG, N. E. 1966. 'The local community as an ecology of games', in L. Coser (ed.), *Political sociology*, New York: Harper.

MANNHEIM, K. 1960. *Ideology and Utopia*, London: Routledge and Kegan Paul.

MEAD, M. 1956. *New lives for old*, New York: Mentor.

MILIBAND, R. 1969. *The state in capitalist society*, London: Weidenfeld and Nicolson.

MILLS, C. W. 1963. *Power, politics and people*, London: Oxford University Press.

NEUMANN, F. 1966. *Behemoth. The structure and practice of national socialism 1933–44*, New York: Harper.

PHELPS-BROWN, E. H. 1959. *The growth of British industrial relations*, London: Macmillan.

SCHELLING, T. 1963. *The strategy of conflict*, London: Oxford University Press.

SCHUMPETER, J. 1943. *Capitalism, socialism and democracy*, London: Allen and Unwin.

SIMMEL, G. 1955. *Conflict*, New York: Free Press.

TAFT, P. and ROSS, P. 1969. 'American labour violence: its causes, character and outcome', in H. D. Graham and T. R. Gurr (eds.), *Violence in America*, New York: Bantam.

TAYLOR, L. and WALTON, P. 1971. 'Industrial sabotage: motives and meanings', in S. Cohen (ed.), *Images of deviance*, Harmondsworth: Pelican Books.

TURNER, H. A., CLACK, G., ROBERTS, G. 1967. *Labour relations in the motor industry*, London: Allen and Unwin.

WILLENER, A. 1957. *Images de la société et classes sociale*, Berne.

7 Industrial Relations: A Social Critique of Pluralist Ideology

ALAN FOX

The principal purpose of this essay is to offer an examination and critical appraisal of the pluralist ideology in its application to the study of industrial relations.

The starting point will be the distinction, outlined by the author elsewhere (Fox 1966), between the pluralistic and the unitary frames of reference. Apologies are offered to those already familiar with it, though even for them a brief re-capitulation may be useful in recalling the terms of the argument. After suggesting possible pluralist criticisms of the unitary approach, some practical consequences of the two perspectives will then be exemplified in a comparison of the (Donovan) Report of the Royal Commission on Trade Unions and Employers' Associations with the Industrial Relations Act of 1971. This will be followed by a critique of the pluralist position itself and an attempt to evaluate its uses.

Since pluralists are doubtless of many varieties and emphases, even in the field of industrial studies, the concern will be with the brand of pluralism which has been widespread (though certainly not universal) among those academics, both in Britain and the United States, who have been termed 'institutionalists', who have taken an active role in the realm of public policy (and sometimes private consultancy), and who have been foremost in shaping the teaching, research, and literature of the subject.

The essay expresses, as much as anything, the author's consciousness of his own need to clarify and, above all, make explicit the strengths, weaknesses, and underlying ideological assumptions of the pluralist position. In that sense it is tentative, exploratory, and very much open to counter-argument. It is intended as a contribution to a debate in which the crucial assumptions and broader standpoints of the contestants (if we must use the language of the arena) have not always, to put it mildly, been clearly and explicitly stated: a situation bad for the debate and for students whom we rightly encourage to take part in it.

THE UNITARY IDEOLOGY

We begin, therefore, by recapitulating briefly the main features of the unitary perspective. Perceived through this frame of reference, the 'organizational logic' of the enterprise is seen as pointing towards a unified authority and loyalty structure, with managerial prerogative being legitimized by all members of the organization. This accords with the emphasis that is placed on asserting the common objectives and the common values which unite and bind together all participants.

The assumption of fully shared interests shapes the unitary attitude towards all work group 'custom and practice' or union rules which management experience as seriously irksome. Given that management goals and policies are seen as 'rational', it follows that only in so far as employee behaviour is congruent with those goals and policies is it likewise rational. This view was characteristic of many popularizers and camp-followers of the early Human Relations school, which worked with an ideology strongly unitary in nature.

> 'In the attempt to account for "resistance" to orders, "restriction" of production, absenteeism, and other problems, management-oriented students discovered that an informal organization exists among workers that sometimes runs contrary to management's plans. They imputed the rise of informal organization to the non-logical, emotional, and sentimental nature of the workers. On the other hand, they conceived management's behavior to be guided by the logic of cost and efficiency.' (Miller and Form 1964: p. 245)

It is only a short step to the triumphant conclusion that the workers' irrational behaviour is contrary to their own interests.

It is not difficult to see how, on this view, the failure of some groups of lower, and sometimes even of middle, rank participants fully to acknowledge management's prerogative and its demand for obedience and loyalty comes to be seen as springing from responses of doubtful validity and legitimacy. It follows that conflict which is generated by organized – or even unorganized – oppositional behaviour on the part of employees tends likewise to be seen as lacking full legitimacy.

Along with a liberal use of 'team' or 'family' metaphors inspired by this presumed unity is apt to go a strong belief that in a properly ordered world managerial prerogative could always be enforced against the few malcontents by means of coercive power if necessary.[1] The greater the tendency to see the 'true' nature of industrial enterprise as unitary, and to see any challenge to managerial rule as of doubtful legitimacy, the greater the disposition to view the enforcement of prerogative by coercive power as desirable and justified. The time-consuming and patience-straining process of 'winning consent' through consultation and negotiation may appear not only burdensome in practice but even pusillanimous in principle. Observation suggests that this stance is apt to predispose its holders to beliefs which may in some circumstances prove to be wishful thinking – that power does in fact lie to hand in sufficient measure not only to make immediate coercion possible, but also to suppress, control, or eliminate any possible adverse long-run consequences which might otherwise outweigh the benefits of applying it. In other words, the notion of the unitary perspective includes the hypothesis that managers holding it are disposed, at times of special stress, crisis, or emergency, to attempt to fall back on coercive means of enforcing their will if challenged.

Given the unitary assumptions, such behaviour may not be difficult to justify. If it is believed that, whatever appearances exist to the contrary, or despite the diversionary temptations and distractions to which all organizational members are prone, the really fundamental interests are shared by management and managed alike, then management may have to be cruel to be kind by overriding what it asserts to be 'irrational' beliefs,

---

[1] Experience has taught the author that the term 'coercive power' is sometimes interpreted simply to mean that of the police and armed forces. In fact, of course, any kind of sanction whether physical, economic, religious, moral, or whatever, can be used in sufficient strength to be experienced as coercive.

purely short-term preoccupations, and limited perspectives produced by ignorance. Still more is it disposed to feel justified in coercing subversives who would otherwise destroy the system.

Similar behaviour is observable in other social structures which are seen as unitary in nature. Father may try to impose his will on the children, regarding himself as trustee of their 'true' interests. The team manager feels justified in imposing rigorous training and disciplinary schedules upon his players, convinced that despite protesting muscles and a puritanical regime they share his will to win. A military unit offers the most obvious example, however, of a leadership which combines the team ideology with total enforcement of prerogative and elimination of subversives.

Holders of the unitary perspective may extend these attitudes and beliefs to the use of coercive power by the law. The conviction is not simply that the law can usefully play a greater part in industrial relations (a proposition which would be supported by many who do not embrace the unitary view) but that increased legal intervention can and should take the form of regulating men's behaviour directly and enforcing this regulation by direct punitive legal sanctions. This stance extends to the role of law the same assumptions about the practicability and net usefulness of using coercive power that were noted in connection with beliefs about the assertion of managerial prerogative. One would expect, then, those who continue to assert the viability of the concept of prerogative also to be found asserting the value of direct legal regulation backed by coercive sanctions.

These implications of the unitary perspective for the issue of compliance can be brought out in yet another way. We invoke here the distinction (drawn by, among others, Merton 1966) between two contrasted types of transgressor: the 'aberrant' and the 'nonconformer'. The aberrant acknowledges the legitimacy of the norms he violates, while the nonconformer does not – indeed he repudiates them. Among the important consequences of this distinction may well be a sharp difference in the responses to punishment. On condition that the aberrant perceives his punishment as fitting the crime, he may be able to accept that he is only being required to do what at a considered level he knows to be right. By contrast, the nonconformer's rejection of the norms in question will of course be heightened still further in terms of moral outrage when he is punished for non-compliance. Thus punitive action which may succeed in regulating the behaviour of aberrants without any offsetting disadvantages may only arouse nonconformers into open rebellion, or at the very least a total withdrawal of good will and positive commitment (Fox 1971: Chapter 2 for a development of this argument).

We may hypothesize that the subscriber to the unitary ideology will tend to define transgressors as aberrants. His own conviction of the rightness of management rule and the norms issuing from it may create difficulty for him, not simply in acknowledging the legitimacy of challenges to it, but even in fully grasping that such challenges may at least be grounded in legitimacy for those who mount them. Surely the transgressors must know in their hearts that they are doing wrong, behaving foolishly, defying proper authority, hurting others needlessly, acting perversely or maliciously? Such is the will to believe this (and thereby validate their own authority to themselves as a justification for imposing punishment), that subscribers to the unitary view look round for any argument which enables them to assert that the transgressors must be considered as acknowledging the legitimacy of the norms they are defying. It will be urged that simply by accepting the employment contract, or by signing for a copy of company rules, or by being covered by a collective agreement concluded with a trade union, or even, perhaps, by being subjects of a political regime that has enacted certain legislation by 'democratic' processes, they must be said to be legitimizing the norms that govern them, thereby laying themselves open to justified punishment whenever they need recalling to the paths of righteousness. As we have noted, the unitary frame of reference tends not to promote recognition of the problematical nature of these dynamics of compliance and legitimacy. Fully to accept that the recalcitrants may be nonconformers who totally repudiate the norms in question and see their own repudiation as fully legitimate would be to take the first step away from the unitary pole of the continuum towards the pluralistic pole.

Reference to trade unions reminds us that holders of the unitary perspective live, work, and possibly manage in a society where trade unions and collective bargaining, with their encroachments on managerial prerogative and their rejection of the unitary conception, are deeply rooted and recognized facts. How do subscribers to the unitary view assimilate these facts into their ideology? There are three points to be made here. (1) Unions may be seen as an historical carry-over, brought into existence originally by unenlightened and shortsighted policies on the part of too many employers in the past who foolishly failed to see that 'sensibly' humane treatment of their employees was good business. They have to be tolerated, but have no real rationale in enlightened modern business except possibly, in certain situations, as a bureaucratic mechanism serving the requirements of effective communications, regulation, and compliance – though even here a dependent 'company union' or staff association would fulfil the same function less threateningly. (2) Unions may be seen as an outcome of sectional greed, or of an imperfect understanding of elementary economics or the 'national interest' or even where their own best interests lie. Again, they have to be endured but, as before, their rationale is shaky and their legitimacy dubious. (3) Unions may be regarded, whatever their manifest purposes, as also having the latent function (or rather dysfunction) of serving as power vehicles for those who seek to subvert the existing social order. Suppression is impracticable, but they remain suspect and must be controlled.

Thus a widespread sufferance of trade unions and collective bargaining can coexist with a conviction that at best they are unfortunate necessities of doubtful legitimacy which violate the organizational logic of business enterprise, and at worst a threat to the established order. Managers whose mental and emotional responses are shaped by the unitary ideology (whether or not they pay lip-service elsewhere), may find difficulty in escaping an uneasy feeling that the presence of trade unions in their organization indicates an unhealthy situation. Something has gone wrong: things should not be like this. Perhaps, given a superhuman effort in searching for the 'right' policies and the 'right' managerial style, the proper unity could be restored. They see trade unions as Thomas Hobbes saw autonomous associations within the body politic: as 'lesser Common-wealths in the bowels of a greater, like wormes in the entrayles of a naturall man'.

Finally, this brief summary of the unitary view might usefully note that it tends to be associated with a conservative social and political philosophy: a fact suggesting that it is part of a class ideology which comes readily to those who rule. This ideology has its origins, needless to say, far back in history; in the constantly asserted and enforced 'right' of the master to demand unquestioning obedience from his servants. With the common law development of contract this ideology passed into the assumptions of the employment contract.

> 'In this important respect the modern law of employment drew heavily on the old law of master and servant. The main contribution of the old to the new was the traditional authority of the master to control the workman . . . The main outcome was to continue, in the heyday of contract, the traditional law of subordination.' (Selznick 1969: p. 132)

The employment contract became 'a very special sort of contract – in large part a legal device for guaranteeing to management the unilateral power to make rules and exercise discretion. For this reason we call it the *prerogative contract*' (*ibid.* p. 135). The unitary perspective thus has deep roots in the historical texture of class, status, and power. Even the traditional terminology long persisted. Not until 1875 did master and servant legislation become the Employers and Workmen Act. Change of terminology could not, however, easily change centuries-old assumptions and expectations deeply ingrained in social attitudes, institutions, and culture, and despite such lip-service as is given to 'democracy' in this field there is still evident in *behaviour* a surviving attachment to master-servant relations.

Such, then, are some of the suggested characteristics of the unitary perspective. It would be difficult to substantiate any assertion that, as a set of working beliefs and assumptions, it is necessarily and invariably, from the managerial point of view, an inadequate tool. The usefulness of any tool depends on one's purposes and the nature of the situation within which one seeks to realize them. There are, in all industrial societies, enterprises whose history, organization, and culture are such that the unitary perspective can still serve managerial purposes. Small establishments; old family firms; paternalist concerns with many long-service employees and a charismatic figure at the top; firms in relatively isolated areas where alternative jobs are few and the writ of traditional authority still runs; cultures or sub-cultures which still fully legitimize the rule of the boss: these are among the situations where a unitary frame of reference may still appear to be 'functional' for managerial purposes.

One alternative perspective which has developed, however, asserts the unitary view to be diminishingly useful. The increasing size and social complexity of work organizations; shifts in power relations within politics and industry; changes in social values; rising aspirations; the weakening of traditional attitudes towards officially constituted governance: these are among the factors which are sometimes said to require managers to develop a new ideology and new sources of legitimation if they are to maintain effective control. This alternative perspective has, in fact, long been evolving, rarely stated explicitly but often implicit in the industrial policies of some western governments and of the more sophisticated companies. It has long been embodied also in the teaching, writing, and public policy activities of industrial relations academics both in Britain and the United States.

THE PLURALIST IDEOLOGY

In describing an ideology there is always the difficulty presented by the existence of many individual variants. Some adherents accept while others may reject each given item of the syndrome. Only a generalized picture can therefore be offered. This means that a person subscribing to any one particular pluralist belief presented here cannot be regarded as necessarily identifying with, or even being aware of, the others.

Seen from this generalized perspective the enterprise is not a unitary structure but a coalition of individuals and groups with their own aspirations and their own perceptions of the structure which they naturally see as valid and which they will seek to express in action if such is required. The term 'coalition' is used, for example, by Cyert and March (1959). It includes the notion that individuals and groups with widely varying priorities agree to collaborate in social structures which enable all participants to get something of what they want. The terms of collaboration are settled by bargaining. Management is seen as making its decisions within a complex set of constraints which include employees, consumers, suppliers, government, the law, the local community, and sources of finance. It is in response to the pressures of these organized constraint mechanisms that management forges its compromises or rises above them with some new synthesis, and in their absence pluralists would be profoundly doubtful if even the roughest of distributive justice would be likely to emerge.

Thus the enterprise is seen as a complex of tensions and competing claims which have to be 'managed' in the interests of maintaining a viable collaborative structure within which all the stakeholders can, with varying degrees of success, pursue their aspirations. There are felt to be no clearcut criteria which can measure how well this aspect of the management task is being performed. A certain amount of overt conflict and disputation is welcomed as evidence that not all aspirations are being either sapped by hopelessness or suppressed by power. On the other hand, conflict above a certain level is felt to be evidence that the ground rules need changing; that marginal adjustments in rewards or work rules are required; that management is failing in some way to find the appropriate compromises or syntheses.

To be sure, perceptions by the participants of conflicting interests need not be seen by pluralists as a *logical necessity* of the industrial enterprise. However, even if we consider only the various groups of employees we can see an empirical probability that in a competitive society where, for example, money is universally desired but limited in supply, employee groups will periodically disagree among themselves and with management about what constitutes fair shares. The pluralistic view assumes, therefore, that given the divergent pressures and claims to which managers are subject they may on this and on many other issues be tempted to govern their 'human resources' in ways which one or more subordinate groups experience as arbitrary, summary, or contrary to their own interests, and which they are likely to seek to challenge through independent collective organizations. It therefore sees trade unionism not as a regrettable historical carry-over, but as just another manifestation of one of the basic values of competitive, pressure group, 'democratic' societies of the western model – that 'interests' have rights of free association and, within legal limits, of asserting their claims and aspirations. It also sees trade unions or organized work groups as being able in some situations to readjust the power balance within the enterprise to such effect as to enable subordinates to impose *their* preferences in ways which *management* finds arbitrary and summary. Trade unions are nevertheless accepted by pluralists as legitimate expressions of legitimate challenges to managerial rule. Indeed they are positively welcomed as giving expression to a mode of joint rule-making by managers and managed which is valued in its own right, simply 'as a method of regulating relationships between people in industry', whether or not it succeeds in 'pushing wages as high as possible' (Clegg, n.d.).

The pluralist seeks to persuade the manager, too, to accept this perspective in fully legitimizing the role and functions of trade unions and organized work groups.

'To the champion of pluralism as an instrument of democracy, tolerance is the live-and-let-live moderation of the marketplace. Economic competition is a form of human struggle . . . in which each combatant simultaneously acknowledges the legitimacy of his opponent's demands and yet gives no quarter in the battle . . . Tolerance in a society of competing interest groups is precisely the ungrudging acknowledgment of the right of opposed interests to exist and be pursued.' (Wolff 1965: p. 29)

Where such a perspective is combined with an awareness that combination allows subordinates to assert their claims and grievances with some vigour, it suggests the conclusion that the whole question of managerial governance must be regarded as problematical, and that management may not be able to enforce without serious loss to itself a total assertion of prerogative in areas of policy where it is challenged by a determined union or work group. The pluralist urges upon managers the full acceptance of what he sees as the implications of this frame of reference – that the legitimacy of their rule in the eyes of subordinates is not automatic but must be actively pursued and maintained; that the 'interest group' structure of the enterprise calls for coalition-type bargaining based on frank recognition of divergent group perceptions; that management's power superiority is no longer sufficient to permit the luxury of imposed solutions; that 'leadership' in a coalition structure has to be defined quite differently from that in a unitary structure; that ideologies and rallying cries based on unitary assumptions may prove counter-productive in a pluralistic situation and, finally, that in current circumstances their best chance of being able to control events lies in their being ready to share that control with the groups they are seeking to govern.

It is characteristic, therefore, of pluralists to criticize the unitary perspective for failing to analyse carefully enough the distribution of power; for assuming that management or the state has more than may in fact prove to be the case; and for giving too little consideration to the long-term disadvantages of relying on coercion. One would also expect a tendency for those of this persuasion to be doubtful about the efficacy of attempts to apply the law directly to enforce certain patterns of behaviour, on the grounds that if enough people are determined enough to refuse to submit, the law is impotent. They accordingly rest more hope on winning consent to those desired patterns.

It would be regarded as a weakness of the unitary view that, by underestimating the problematical nature of management rule, and overestimating the long-term practicability and net usefulness of prerogative and coercive power as a basis for industrial order in our kind of society, it undervalues the significance of negotiated, agreed, normative codes for coalition-type collaboration, and of the need to explore the dynamics of legitimacy and consent as the stable bases of such codes. Pluralists would see part of the difficulty as lying in the fact that subscribers to the unitary view are reluctant to define the enterprise in coalition terms.

It would also seem plausible to suggest that whereas subscribers to the unitary view may prefer to define transgressors as aberrants who legitimize the relevant norms and can therefore properly (and without adverse consequences) be punished, pluralists are likely to see most transgressors as nonconformers for whom punishment would be futile and indeed counter-productive, and whose repudiation of the relevant norms must be met by a negotiated reconstruction of those norms to the point where they meet at least the minimal needs of all the parties.

Such an approach would hardly make sense without an accompanying assumption that the normative divergencies between the parties are not so fundamental or so wide as to be

195

unbridgeable by compromises or new syntheses which enable collaboration to continue. Clark Kerr has observed that 'a pluralistic industrial system . . . can only operate well if the ideology impelling its important groups is consistent with pluralism, i.e. a philosophy of mutual survival' (1954: p. 12). Bakke had earlier defined the desirable situation as one in which, 'although pursuing each his own interest, the parties recognize their mutual dependence upon each other, agree to respect the survival needs of the other, and to adjust their differences by methods which will not destroy but rather improve the opportunities of the other' (1946: p. 81).

Pluralists would argue that the situation in most advanced western industrial societies does in fact bear a rough approximation to this picture of a basic procedural consensus. They make, therefore, the working assumption that, given 'good will' and such external stimulus, help, and structural support as may prove necessary, managements and unions will always and everywhere be able ultimately to negotiate comprehensive, codified systems of regulation which provide a fully adequate and orderly context making for the promotion and maintenance of orderly behaviour. The Donovan Report, 'seeking to identify the underlying causes of unofficial strikes', considered 'the root of the evil' to be the 'present methods of collective bargaining and especially our methods of workshop bargaining', and 'the absence of speedy, clear and effective disputes procedures' (1968: para. 475). Reform of these methods and procedures was expected to reduce very considerably the problem of 'disorder'. Clearly the assumption was being made of a widespread basic consensus which needed only the 'right' institutional forms in which to emerge.

What are the fuller implications of these attitudes? The first is that every industrial conflict situation can, in sufficiently skilled and patient hands, be made to yield some compromise or synthetic solution which all the interests involved will find acceptable and workable – that no group, for example, retains a continuing concern with maintaining what other groups define as 'disorder'. This in turn requires that each party limits its claims and aspirations to a level which the other party finds sufficiently tolerable to enable collaboration to continue. On the basis of a shared confidence that they both subscribe to this philosophy of 'mutual survival', the parties are able to operate procedures of negotiation and dispute settlement characterized by a consensual code of ethics and conduct which includes, for example, the principle that, provided certain jointly agreed processes of consultation and participation in decision making are followed, culminating in freely, equitably, and honourably negotiated agreements, the participant groups will regard themselves as morally committed to observing the terms of the resulting decisions.

The concept of honour is important in bringing out the pluralistic assumption of a rough balance of power. Pluralists would acknowledge that, more commonly in the past than the present, 'agreements' might be concluded that are so manifestly and blatantly imposed coercively by greatly superior power that they must be seen as accepted only 'under duress' and therefore not morally binding. Half-starved workers of the past who were admitted back to work after an employers' lockout on condition that they renounced union membership for ever have not been seen as behaving dishonourably when they resumed union activities. The normal pluralist stress on the moral obligation to observe agreements therefore implies a belief that power is not so unevenly matched as to introduce the extenuating concept of duress.

'Good will' therefore turns out to mean a readiness to accept the basic consensus. It would obviously be possible for one party to make claims which the other found totally unacceptable and on which compromise or synthesis proved impossible. The pluralist presumption would be that in such a case the consensual ethic governing joint regulation would be ruptured, and collaboration would be resumed only when one party succeeded in coercing the other. The operation of a pluralistic system requires that such situations be the exception rather than the rule, and that in the main the claims of each party fall within the range found bearable by the other.

Such a situation bears a clear resemblance to a Parsonian consensus. The assumption is being made that while, to be sure, conflicts arise over the terms of economic collaboration, values and norms are not so divergent that workable compromises cannot be achieved. Underlying the cut and thrust of market-place and organizational encounters, in other words, lies the rock-firm foundation of a stable and agreed social system. Men may disagree about the distribution of the social product and other terms of their collaboration – and it is healthy and desirable that they should – but their disagreements are not so great and so lasting that they seek to destroy the system or even put it under serious hazard. In order to maintain that system they submit to compromise and find themselves able, for this purpose, to share moral beliefs which teach the importance of observing agreements freely and honourably undertaken.

It is clear that the beliefs and assumptions of pluralism as applied to industrial relations are broadening out, in terms of our argument, to beliefs and assumptions about society as a whole. Here we move beyond the perspective that might reasonably be seen as implicit in a certain view of industrial relations. In this wider sense, pluralism is a philosophy which rejects both the classical liberal tradition, in which the legalisms of 'free and equal contract' between atomistic individuals facilitated exploitation by masking gross disparities of power, and the 'social integration' of totalitarian (unitary) societies, in which an imposed 'common' ideology and set of values are used to mask manipulation and coercion by a dominant ruling group. Free and independent combination among the weak which enables them to enhance their strength, and a judicious curbing of the power of the strong, together with the mechanisms of party political democracy and a free market in ideas, are seen as the best ways of avoiding these two rejected images of society. '. . . pluralism's goal is a rough parity among competing groups . . . (Wolff 1965: p. 58). In the words of another American theorist, pluralists 'see society as fractured into a congeries of hundreds of small special interest groups, with incompletely overlapping memberships, widely differing power bases, and a multitude of techniques for exercising influence on decisions salient to them . . .' (Polsby 1963: p. 118). 'Freedom' plays an important part in the argument. 'As a theory of the social foundations of freedom, pluralism rests its hopes on civil antagonism. It sees in group conflict a benign disorder . . .' (Selznick 1969: p. 41). This approach sometimes leads to what Pen describes as 'an extremely innocent view of society'. The 'criss-crossing of small conflicts has stabilizing functions; this fits into the picture of a pluralistic society. One step further and we arrive at a balance of forces . . .' (Pen 1966: pp. 278-9).

Thus pluralism is often associated with a belief that there

can and should be, or indeed even is, a balance of power as between the principal interest groups of society. 'The various conceptions of "pluralism" in contemporary sociology and political science are models of systems of intercursive power relations' (Wrong 1968: p. 47). *Intercursive* refers to 'relations characterized by a balance of power . . . where the power of each party . . . is countervailed by that of the other, with procedures for bargaining or joint decision making governing their relations when matters affecting the goals and interests of both are involved' (*ibid.* See also Miliband 1969).

Industrial relations pluralists have articulated such views with respect to their own special interest. Clark Kerr echoes Galbraith's principle of 'countervailing power' (1952) in arguing that 'The state at least should seek to effect a balance of power among the private groups . . .' (1954: p. 10), while Selekman has asserted that shifting alliances and coalitions, temporary or long-term, already operate to effect balances of power – 'The equality of strength brought about by these alliances prevents the establishment of any single dominant overriding power for any length of time' (Selekman and Selekman 1956: p. 162). 'We end up with a pluralistic system of power, the parts checking and counter-checking each other . . .' (*ibid.* p. 181).

Besides using its weight 'to make sure that no major interest in the nation abuses its influence or gains an unchecked mastery over some sector of social life' (Wolff 1965: p. 19 – he is expounding the view, not identifying with it), central government must 'set the rules of the game' within which 'the conflict among the several power elements in a pluralistic society' takes place (Kerr *et al.* 1962: pp. 290–1).

UNITARY IDEOLOGY AND THE INDUSTRIAL RELATIONS ACT 1971

Two recent major events in the field of public policy on industrial relations will now be examined in terms of the foregoing analysis in the belief that they offer examples of the practical manifestation of the unitary and pluralistic ideologies. These events are the (Donovan) Report of the Royal Commission on Trade Unions and Employers' Associations (1968), and the Industrial Relations Act (1971), which will be examined first.

The values underlying the Industrial Relations Act reveal a variety of influences (including the pluralistic), but those of the unitary approach play a part in some of its most important provisions. This is revealed at the outset by its attitude towards trade unions.

The fact that the legal right to be a union member is 'balanced' by the legal right not to be a member[1] – with the individual permitted to opt out 'on grounds of conscience'[2] – suggests the view that trade unions remain somewhat suspect organizations which still bear traces of their historical taint of doubtful legitimacy simply on account of their tendency to challenge the authority rights of their masters. Whatever was in the minds of the drafters, the language of the Act appears to keep alive and extend social approval to a certain attitude towards managerial rule. It perpetuates the situation in which trade unionism is still not totally assimilated to the expectations of the industrial citizen.

Even more significant is the unitary approach which the Act brings to bear upon so-called 'disruptive' and 'disorderly' behaviour. Many of its major provisions have as their underlying emphasis the aim of reducing such behaviour of work groups by strengthening the direct external legal controls that can be brought to bear on them. This is pursued through attempts to reverse the tendencies frequently portrayed as characteristic of the post-war period – the partial shift of power from management to shop floor, and from union hierarchy to rank and file. Restoring power to management is sought through making all written collective agreements, awards, and

---

[1] In fact, of course, this lawyer's equation is not a 'balance' at all. The more people exercise their legal 'right' not to be a union member, thereby reducing collective strength, the less those who choose differently can effectively pursue the pressure group activities which are the major purposes of unions, the purposes for which they need their right to join. The non-member's enjoyment of his right *not* to join is not prejudiced, however, by the different choices of his fellows.

[2] It remains to be seen how the phrase 'grounds of conscience' is interpreted by local industrial tribunals, i.e. whether it will be strictly limited, say, to members of certain small religious sects or come under pressure for extension to cover 'social' grounds on which individuals may consider it 'wrong' to join a union for the purpose of challenging management authority. Now that the principle has been enshrined in legislation, there may be attempts to have social as well as religious conscience admitted as a justification for non-unionism. It will be remembered that trade unionists, out of general hostility to the Act, may refuse to serve on these tribunals, possibly leaving an opening for certain types of argument to get a more serious reception than they would otherwise enjoy.

decisions legally enforceable contracts unless an express disclaimer is included. This is felt to be specially significant in relation to procedure agreements (regulating the forms and procedures for handling conflict), where the hope is that work groups which now make free with disruptive action will be forced to observe peaceful constitutional forms, at least until the agreed procedure is exhausted. Since the unions which are parties to these agreements will be held responsible, under threat of penalty, for seeing that they are observed, the unions will, it is assumed, be placed under powerful incentives to reassert control over their agents and members at the workplace. There are many other patterns of behaviour defined as 'unfair industrial practices' which come under the same kind of direct penalty imposed by an external agency.

It could also be thought characteristic of the unitary aspects of this legislation that, along with the emphasis on the need and the viability of direct legal control and punitive sanctions, goes a total lack of interest in the practical mechanics of winning consent from the governed. Despite its major preoccupation with securing desired patterns of behaviour, the Act expresses no concern with the specific practical means by which those in official positions (the state, managers, and trade union officers alike) might hope to secure the commitment of the governed to the rules which govern them.[1] Control is seen in excessively simple terms. On those aspects of decision making where a challenge is presented by union or work group, management is presumed to conclude collective agreements which the union is then expected to enforce upon its members. On the question of the forms, modes, practices, and institutions by which union officers inform, consult, and win the consent of their members the Act reveals no awareness of there being a problem. The union simply exercises its authority. If some members or groups of members demur, it must enforce its rule decisively. There is

[1] Neither does the *Code of Industrial Relations Practice* (Department of Employment, June 1971), the professed 'purpose of which is to set standards and give practical guidance on the conduct of industrial relations'. If the argument is that the Act could not be expected to concern itself with such matters, the counter-argument would be that in laying down, in clause 45, the conditions under which a union, or joint negotiating panel of unions, can apply for protected status as 'sole bargaining agent', the Act recommends the Commission on Industrial Relations to take into account whether the unions have 'sufficient trained officials available for purposes of collective bargaining'—a very direct concern with the practical mechanics of regulation.

no recognition of, or interest in, the fact that these questions of compliance and enforcement may present practical difficulties. This stance emerges in its extreme form in clauses 35 to 39, providing for the possibility of a procedure agreement being imposed on the parties which the relevant union then becomes legally responsible for imposing on its members 'as if a contract consisting of those provisions had been made between the parties'. Again, simple assumptions are made that the law can effectively coerce the union, and that the union can effectively coerce its members. There is also the implicit assumption that any ill-consequences for industrial relations of this neglect of consent will not outweigh the benefits.

In sum: a pluralist might argue that while there are important respects in which the Act succeeds in coming to terms with the emergent pattern of employment relations, there are clear signs of a failure to rise above perspectives which have their roots in an historical pattern of class, status, and power. The emergent approach which some pluralists see evolving views the enterprise as an association of 'interests' which fully and exhaustively negotiate the terms of their continuing collaboration; an association in which traditional class and status assumptions of command and subordination give place to organizationally protected participation and 'due process' in respect of all the issues with which the 'interests' are conscious of a concern; an association within which the search for order takes the form not of the integrative strategies prompted by the unitary perspective but of the accommodative strategies logically implied by the pluralist conception. '. . . accommodation – the mutual adjustment of groups that preserve their distinctive identities and interests – is the only road to harmony consistent with the political model of industrial organization' (Selznick 1969: p. 119). From this view, the Industrial Relations Act, while taking a guarded step towards this conception, nevertheless retains one foot in that world where master-servant nostalgia prevails and where trade unions are still seen as somewhat raffish organizations appealing to the less attractive traits of the (otherwise splendid) British working man. The 'law of governance' necessary to crystallize, codify, regulate, and encourage these emergent trends has yet, pluralists might argue, to find its way to the statute book. The desirable approach can be found, instead, adumbrated in the Donovan Report where, though in need perhaps of elaboration, the essential ideas can be found.

PLURALISM AND THE DONOVAN REPORT

The Donovan Report reveals implicitly if not explicitly many of the characteristic features of the pluralist perspective. Space limitations preclude an exhaustive analysis and some awareness of the Report's general texture and argument will be assumed.

The pluralist frame of reference emerges early in its pages with a statement about the nature of the business enterprise.

'The running of large businesses is in the hands of professional managers . . . While in the long term shareholders, employees and customers all stand to benefit if a concern flourishes, the immediate interests of these groups often conflict. Directors and managers have to balance these conflicting interests, and in practice they generally seek to strike whatever balance will best promote the welfare of the enterprise as such.' (Donovan 1968: para. 18)

A selection of specific issues enables us to point the contrast with the unitary aspects of the Industrial Relations Act. First, and of basic significance, is the very status and social justification of trade unions. It is possible for pluralists to conceive, and approve of, an industrial society in which it is assumed that wage-earning and salary-earning groups *should* generate their own claims and aspirations; that they *should* challenge managerial authority in the pursuit of them; that the complexities of large-scale organization make it inevitable that the regulation of industrial relations *should* be handled jointly through independent representative associations, and that any plea by particular individual employees to be allowed to contract out of these institutional arrangements is as irrelevant as a plea to be allowed to contract out of income tax. These attitudes are implicit in much of the Donovan Report, and come very close to the surface in its arguments for rejecting any prohibition of the closed shop. 'As part of the argument for prohibition it might be said that since we suggest elsewhere that any condition in a contract of employment that the employee shall not join a union is to be void in law, it would be right to treat in the same way a condition that the worker *shall* join a union. However, the two are not truly comparable. The former condition is designed to frustrate the development of collective bargaining, which it is public policy to promote, whereas no such objection applies to the latter' (para. 599).

Secondly, a pluralistic bias, with its insistence on seeking always to understand group behaviour in the light of the group's own social location and goals, can lead towards a more searching examination of the concepts of so-called 'disorderly' and 'restrictive' behaviour by work groups. As against a tendency for those holding the unitary view to regard 'restrictive practices' as irrational, the pluralist perspective of the Donovan Report sees overmanning, for example, as being 'used in the rational pursuit of the interests of workers, narrow and shortsighted though these interests may sometimes be' (para. 310).

Thirdly, a view of the enterprise as a pluralistic rather than a unitary structure disposes its holders to respond to disruptive behaviour not by attempting direct suppression but by pursuing a patient unravelling of causes. Reform of wage systems and pay structures, of disputes procedures, of the content and institutions of company and plant regulations generally: reforms stimulated and guided by public agencies equipped to offer help – such is the Donovan emphasis. 'By far the most important part in remedying the problem of unofficial strikes and other forms of unofficial action will however be played by reforming the institutions of whose defects they are a sympton.' Disruptive behaviour would continue 'until the confusion which so often surrounds the exercise by management of its "rights" has been resolved by the settlement of clear rules and procedures which are accepted as fair and reasonable by all concerned' (para. 454). The pluralistic assumptions described earlier are here plain to see.

Finally, and most fundamentally, the pluralistic perspective leads towards the proposition that in western societies legitimacy is less problematical when regulation on contentious issues is conducted jointly by the parties directly involved than when it is imposed by either party on the other or by some external agency upon both. In the words of the Donovan Report: 'In industrial relations, "law and order" can be created only by adequate collective bargaining arrangements' (para. 505). The Report was far from ruling out legal intervention *in toto*, but a major emphasis in this respect was to regard as futile and self-defeating any attempt through direct legal sanctions to control industrial relations behaviour. 'As long as no effective method for the settlement of grievances exists no one can expect a threat of legal sanctions to restrain men from using the advantage they feel able to derive from sudden action in order to obtain a remedy for grievances which cannot be dealt with in an orderly fashion' (para. 505).

CRITICISMS OF PLURALIST IDEOLOGY

Pluralism thus presents itself as an altogether more 'realistic' and sophisticated frame of reference than the unitary. This does not save it, however, from the continued resistance of those still wedded to unitary beliefs, values, and assumptions, nor from criticism from a very different direction which entertains serious doubts, in its turn, about the realism and sophistication of the pluralist analysis.

Criticisms from those occupying a traditional stance on manager-worker relations are not difficult to predict. There are many features of the pluralistic perspective which the early industrial entrepreneur would have seen as profoundly destructive of initiative and control, and it is still seen by some managers today as a disturbing and pessimistic doctrine which threatens their confidence, authority, and leadership in a manner suggesting little hope for really effective management in the future. They may take exception to any encouragement of employee groups to mobilize power and use it against management; may distrust the threat to hierarchical rule and authority that is represented by the whole pluralist notion of divided power, checks, and balances. There are few reasoned arguments for the unitary view, however, which attempt to meet pluralism on its own ground, and the more common course is either to practise 'double-speak', i.e. to make an initial verbal genuflection to the pluralist idea and follow this with unabashedly unitary sentiments, or to pay lip-service to pluralism while behaving in ways clearly motivated by unitary attitudes and principles. In the absence of a coherent argument from the unitary direction, therefore, the emphasis here will be on criticisms from the other source.[1]

[1] Criticisms of pluralist ideology in the political context are, of course, numerous. One useful way into the debate is via Mills 1959, Wolff 1965, Gitlin 1965, and Castles *et al.* 1971.

Perhaps the most fundamental reason for rejecting the pluralist position would be a belief that industrial society, while manifestly to some extent a congeries of small special interest groups vying for scarce goods, status, or influence, is more convincingly characterized in terms of the over-arching exploitation of one class by another, of the propertyless by the propertied, of the less by the more powerful. By this view, any talk of 'checks and balances', however apt for describing certain subsidiary phenomena,[1] simply confuses our understanding of the primary dynamics which shape and move society – a useful confusion indeed for the major power holders since it obscures the domination of society by its ruling strata through institutions and assumptions which operate to exclude anything approaching a genuine power balance.

Again, by this view it would follow that any strategy by a class-conscious 'proletariat' to take up the class war against the 'bourgeoisie' could hardly be reconciled with the pluralist notion of mutual survival. The drive behind such a strategy would not be to 'live and let live', but to test class relations to destruction. From this perspective the interests of the bourgeoisie could not be seen as legitimate, and an ideology which formally recognized them as such would be strengthening the exploiters against the exploited, whether it was aware of doing so or not. It would be said that instead of drawing the attention of the propertyless to the facts of their subjection, pluralist ideology presents the owners and controllers of property as simply one group of claimants among many. It thereby becomes another of the conditioning influences which indoctrinate the victims of an exploitive set of economic and social relations into accepting the system.

The force of this mode of analyses does not depend on accepting the oversimplified terms in which it is sometimes presented or the political prescriptions which sometimes accompany it. There is only space here to note the obvious point that private ownership is not the only source of control over economic resources and therefore not the only source of economic power over people. Nevertheless it is from a perspective

---

[1] '... there is some reality in ... romantic pluralism ... : it is a recognizable, although a confused, statement of the middle levels of power ... But it confuses, indeed it does not even distinguish between the top, the middle, and the bottom levels of power' (Mills 1959: p. 244).

similar to this that a radical analysis can be offered which is highly damaging to the generalized pluralist view presented here. It asserts as its starting point a great disparity of power as between, on the one hand, the owners and controllers of economic resources and, on the other, those dependent upon them for access to those resources as a means of livelihood.[1] This power is exercised not only directly in industry, business, commerce, and financial institutions, but also indirectly in a multitude of ways. Gouldner enumerates some of them.

'The rich exercise power, including political power . . . through their control of great foundations, with their policy-shaping studies and conferences and their support for universities; through a variety of interlocking national associations, councils and committees that act as legislative lobbies and as influences upon public opinion; through their membership among the trustees of great universities; through their influence on important newspapers, magazines, and television networks, by virtue of their advertising in them or their outright ownership of them, which, as Morris Janowitz once observed, sets "the limits within which public debate on controversial issues takes place"; through their extensive disproportionate membership in the executive branch of the government, their financial contributions to political parties . . . and through their control of the most important legal, public relations, and advertising firms.' (Gouldner 1971: p. 300)

This view of the American scene differs only in detail from that in other western societies. An exhaustive account would have to include many other ways in which the influence of the rich and powerful pervades and permeates the texture of our every-day life, usually so impalpably that, like the air we breathe, we do not register them.

Such an account contrasts sharply with the one which figures, explicitly or implicitly, in so many pluralist statements, of a rough balance of power among 'the congeries of hundreds of small specialist groups' in society. There is, of course, no

[1] Perhaps it is hardly necessary to emphasise that the debate about the nature of the power structure in western industrial society is highly controversial and revolves around not only what are believed to be 'facts' but also interpretations of those facts and, most fundamentally of all, the selection of some facts as more significant than others.

question but that, in respect of capital–labour relations, the disparity of power can be, and has been, mitigated. The propertyless are indeed dependent upon the propertied for access to resources, but the latter are also dependent upon the former for getting work done, and combination enables employees to offset somewhat the power of their masters. Yet to enjoy control of resources – a control upheld by the law and in the last resort by the armed forces of the state – seems such a decisive advantage that the fact of many people believing in the existence of a power balance presents us with a puzzle. In Gouldner's words: 'anyone with an ounce of empirical curiosity could not help but wonder how it could be possible for the man with a million dollars to be content to have no more of a vote than the man living on public welfare, particularly since the latter could vote to tax his fortune' (1971: p. 299). By no means all of those who believe in a power balance are property owners whose selective perceptions can easily be understood – there are many even in the wage-earning class who now consider organized labour to have a power superiority, which incidentally is misused.

How is this puzzle to be explained? If property owners and controllers do enjoy great superiority of power, how are we to account for this impression that organized labour, far from suffering a great power disadvantage, has gone far towards levelling up the score and has even, in many instances, overshot the mark?

One important fact which enables such a view to prevail is that the owners and controllers of resources very rarely need to exert publicly and visibly in open conflict more than a small part of the power that lies at their disposal. This is important because unless power is being actively and visibly exercised in terms of sanctions its effect on behaviour often passes unnoticed. In fact, of course, it is in precisely those power relationships where the power disparity is greatest that its active exercise is least necessary. Consciousness even of the implicit threat that remains unspoken bends our minds towards whatever pattern of behaviour is required to prevent the threat being made manifest. The behaviour of those dependent in any way on the powerful is 'continually influenced by the *awareness* . . . that superiors can give or withhold at will things that men greatly want . . .' (Gouldner 1971: p. 294). The impact of power on behaviour is therefore all-pervasive despite the absence of obvious evidence. It is the absence of obvious evidence, however, which is likely to influence popular assumptions on the subject.

A further reason why the powerful rarely need to make their power visible and obvious is that all the social institutions, mechanisms, and principles which it is crucially important for them to have accepted and legitimized are accepted and legitimized already and come under no serious threat. These range far beyond such basics as the institutions of private enterprise and profit making. They cover such matters as the influence of wealth and resource control over economic, social, and political decision making; over the content of the mass media and communications generally and thereby, for example, over the major objectives of the economic system. Crucial for them, too, is the virtually universal acceptance of class and status stratification, and of the hierarchical organization of work, with its massive inequalities of authority, reward, status, and job autonomy. Essential, in turn, for the acceptance of these inequalities are such cultural beliefs as, for example, that those in authority 'ought' to enjoy higher rewards than those they command, and that the alleged (and probably engineered) scarcity of a particular skill, talent, or ability justifies its holder in demanding a larger share than those of more common or modest attainments.

If we ask how it comes about that this widespread legitimation and acceptance exists of institutions, mechanisms, principles, and beliefs so necessary and convenient for the owners and controllers of resources the answer is, of course, that, as was noted earlier, their very power affords them the facilities for creating and maintaining social attitudes and values favourable to that acceptance. The greater the extent to which power can be used indirectly to shape perceptions and preferences, the less the need for it to be used directly in ways which make it visible. We also need to note that power often creates its own legitimation in a sense described by Gouldner. 'Those who obey because they are afraid do not like to think themselves unmanly or cowardly; in an effort to maintain a decent regard for themselves, the fearful frequently find ingenious ways in which they can define almost any demand made upon them as legitimate' (Gouldner 1971: p. 293).

o   209

Provided these essential strategic institutions, principles, and beliefs remain major built-in features of the social structure, the owners and controllers of resources can be said, to use an exceptionally appropriate colloquialism, to have it made. Society is already in the shape which serves their essential interests and purposes, thanks to the power and influence exerted to this end by past as well as present generations of property owners and their many agents and sympathizers.

Perhaps it is hardly necessary to point out that this analysis requires no assumption of malign conspiratorial intent on the part of power holders. The ideology (and its practical embodiments) which they urge upon the majority would soon start to fail in its effects if they were not themselves sincerely convinced of its validity. Exactly how this conviction expresses itself through a multitude of subtle and not-so-subtle social mechanisms and interactions it is the task of sociology – and social psychology – to explore.

But however widespread the acceptance of the 'master' institutions of society, there remains an ever-present need for what might be called 'fine tuning'. Flanks have to be protected, fences mended, new doors to power opened as old ones close, new and subtler techniques developed of exercising it. In the field of work, as elsewhere, many marginal issues have to be resolved – exactly how much authority for a given level of management; exactly how much more financial reward for this work group as against that; exactly what pattern of work organization in this particular factory. Meanwhile, however, pressures develop from below for some voice in these decisions. But the essential protections for wealth, privilege, and power are still largely accepted by those mounting these pressures. Their aspirations are for marginal improvements in their lot, not for eliminating private property, destroying hierarchy, repudiating the principles which support great inequalities of wealth, income, and opportunities for personal fulfilment. They can therefore safely be allowed a foothold in the making of certain types of decision bearing on their terms and conditions of employment. Indeed, such a concession is only judicious in that, by meeting modest and marginal aspirations, it avoids the risk of their being inflamed by frustration into more fundamental and dangerous demands. More positively, the satisfaction of these marginal aspirations strengthens the legitimacy of the system in the eyes of those subordinated to it, thereby not only enhancing rather than weakening managerial effectiveness but also stabilizing the wider economic, social, and political systems. 'Collective bargaining', wrote Harbison in a sustained panegyric, 'provides one of the more important bulwarks for the preservation of the private-enterprise system' (1954: p. 274), a view supported in essence by Dubin, who refers to 'its stabilizing influence upon the whole society' (see under Harbison 1954).

These arguments suggest that the sufferance which owners and controllers of resources extend to organized interest groups among the propertyless, and which some theorists elevate into 'ungrudging acknowledgement of the right of opposed interests to exist and be pursued' (Wolff 1965: p. 29), is far removed from any balanced reciprocation of mutual rights as between groups of equal power, status, and respect. It is heavily conditional upon the interest groups concerned being prepared to accept as given those major structural features which are crucial for the power, status, and rewards of the owners and controllers.

It is because this condition is usually fulfilled that owners and controllers are rarely driven to call upon their reserves of power in any overt and public exercise. Only the margins of power are needed to cope with marginal adjustments. This, then, is what accounts for the illusion of a power balance. Labour often has to marshal all its resources to fight on these marginal adjustments; capital can, as it were, fight with one hand behind its back and still achieve in most situations a verdict that it finds tolerable. Only if labour were to challenge an essential prop of the structure would capital need to bring into play anything approaching its full strength, thus destroying at once the illusion of a power balance. For example, a demand backed by strike action that wage earners receive equal rewards with management would soon demonstrate which side could, and would feel impelled to, last out longer.

The power balance illusion thus rests on the continuing acceptance by the less favoured of social institutions and principles which support wealth and privilege, and which the wealthy and privileged would exert their great power to defend if that acceptance were to pass into attempts at repudiation. But conversely, the illusion contributes towards acceptance, for by veiling gross disparities of power it fosters the belief that all the principal interests, at least, of society complete 'fairly' for its rewards, thereby helping to legitimize the system. Thus does pluralism make its small contribution towards keeping society safe for wealth and privilege.

The critique of pluralist ideology cannot, however, end there. The point was made earlier that for management to concede collective bargaining and other means by which employees or their representatives can participate in the making of some kinds of decision may well strengthen rather than weaken their control. This argument now needs elaboration.

Despite the rejection by some employers and managers of pluralist notions and values, it is not difficult to argue that such an ideology represents, in the context of modern business, a high point in enlightened 'managerialism', in the sense that it serves managerial interests and goals whether pluralists themselves identify with those interests and goals or not. Admittedly it urges the full acceptance by managers of rival focuses of authority, leadership, and claims to subordinate loyalty. It recommends the limited sharing of some rule making and decision taking. It deprives managers of all theoretical justification for asserting or claiming prerogative. Yet the outcome of these concessions is visualized, not as the weakening of managerial rule as we now understand it, but as its strengthening and consolidation. Pluralism would certainly be defended by at least some of its exponents partly on the grounds that it is more likely than the unitary view to promote rational, efficient, and effective management.

The author of this essay has made this point himself in the past. 'The pluralistic frame of reference, which openly concedes the severe limitations on management power, constitutes thereby a source of potential strength rather than weakness' (Fox 1966: p. 14). Similarly Flanders: 'The paradox, whose truth managements have found it so difficult to accept, is that they can only regain control by sharing it' (1970: p. 172), and Chamberlain: 'Thus it is only good management to seek to secure consent of the governed who could otherwise make it impossible for management to achieve the very objective which it has set for itself' (1963: p. 190). Finally, the Donovan Report itself argued that a whole-hearted acceptance by management of comprehensive, speedy and equitable negotiation and grievance procedures would promote pay structures which were, *inter alia*, 'conducive to efficiency' (para. 183).

Certainly support for pluralism can spring from other values as well, such as those underlying the notion of self-determination by self-defining 'interest' or 'opinion' groups. Nevertheless the pluralist position remains open to the interpretation of being no more, or no less, than enlightened managerialism, for there are signs that where the objectives of efficient and effective management conflict with the objectives of would-be self-determining work groups, pluralist concern tends to be directed towards finding ways by which the latter can be contained within a regulative framework that promotes and maintains the former. The post-war trend in Britain towards workplace bargaining characterized as 'largely informal, largely fragmented and largely autonomous' (Flanders 1967: p. 28) was described by the Donovan Report as conferring the 'important benefits' of 'a very high degree of self-government in industry' (paras. 129–30). The Report condemned it, nevertheless, and proposed reversing the trend by means of comprehensive, systematic company and factory agreements, on the ground that

'the benefits are outweighed by the shortcomings: the tendency of extreme decentralization and self-government to degenerate into indecision and anarchy; the propensity to breed inefficiency; and the reluctance to change – all of them characteristics which become more damaging as they develop, as the rate of technical progress increases, and as the need for economic growth becomes more urgent' (para. 130).

Such propositions as these suggest that pluralists do not envisage as the outcome of joint regulation by management and labour any major change in the organization of industry, in the fundamental distribution of power and control, or in the broad objectives towards which the industrial effort is directed. Rather is it assumed that there is broad basic agreement on these issues and that pluralistic mechanisms must be valued, not only as ends in themselves, but also as means for articulating, institutionalizing, and resolving marginal discontents and disagreements which, though of considerable significance for the immediate parties, leave the essential structure of control basically intact.

Pluralism could be presented, in fact, as the far-seeing manager's ideology for a future in which those in positions of rule come increasingly under challenge, have to seek new legitimations, and must turn intelligence and patience towards the growing and never-ending task of winning consent. It becomes the recommended frame of reference most likely to enable present and future managers to pursue their purposes successfully amid the multiple values, the diverse and rising group aspirations, and the shifting power relations of a complex society undergoing an accelerating rate of economic and social change. From this view, either management learns these new modes of governance or it will suffer, at worst, the destruction of its present form or, at best, obstruction so severe as to render it incapable of pursuing adaptation and growth.

Seen in this light, the pluralist ideology would be the choice of a structural-functionalist seeking to identify the appropriate integrative mechanisms for industrial relations systems in western industrial societies – appropriate, that is, whatever its professed intentions, in maintaining the *status quo* of highly unequal power, wealth, and privilege. The very concept of the industrial relations *system* would then take on a theoretical significance familiar in the United States but going well beyond what has usually been given it by most academic industrial relations specialists in Britain. For the latter, 'system' has borne only its weak sense of a set of related behaviours, norms, and values which can usefully be studied together for their significance and meaning with respect to a selected field of interest. Located, however, within a body of assumptions about basic consensus, the concept might appear to bear a much stronger sense. The behavioural norms, procedures, and values of joint regulation would be viewed by some theorists as an integrative sub-system which acts as one of the self-equilibrating mechanisms ensuring the survival and adaptation of the total system. These notions that an institutionalizing of conflict and an open coming-to-terms with dissident groups under one's command may be positively beneficial for the manager are, of course, familiar in sociological theory. The idea that the functionalist approach could not deal with conflict had to be laid to rest as it became increasingly clear that institutionalized mechanisms for identifying and regulating conflict could, given certain conditions, be defined not as a threat to, but as a prerequisite of, social stability and integration in its deepest sense (Silverman 1970: p. 47). American exponents of pluralism have, as we have noted, been insistent on the value of such mechanisms in providing 'very substantial support for our system of democratic capitalism' (Harbison 1954: p. 276).

Such notions appear to have achieved their apotheosis of practical application in being given the accolade by that ever alert bulletin of trendy management, the *Harvard Business Review*. In an article entitled 'Make conflict work for you', Mr J. Kelly argues that

'old concepts of human relations, including the notion that conflict *per se* is harmful and should be avoided at all cost, do not square with the facts any longer. Indeed, the new approach is that conflict, if properly handled, can lead to more effective and appropriate arrangements . . . The way conflict is managed – rather than suppressed, ignored, or avoided – contributes significantly to a company's effectiveness.' (July-August 1970: p. 103)

However, let us imagine a pluralist interjecting at this stage to defend his position. 'What', he might ask, 'is wrong with the situation being described? Management is shown as becoming more effective in handling and coordinating the human beings under its governance. How is this greater effectiveness shown as being achieved? By coercion, underhand manipulation, trickery, "human-relations" gimmickry? Not at all. It is shown as being achieved, first, by frank and open recognition of divergent group interests and values, and secondly, by a patient and honest working through of these differences towards a compromise or synthesis which is freely accepted by all parties as being fair. If this more effective management can be achieved *through* greater self-determination and self-respect on the part of the labour force, within a regulative framework that contains the more powerful groups from exploiting their strength at the expense of the others, are we not achieving a happy combination of good things? Effective management based on pluralistic attitudes and methods is not only an end in itself, as a civilized way of conducting the unavoidable hierarchies of modern business, but also a necessary means to other ends such as an all-round rise in living standards and a bigger margin for social services.'

Given certain preconditions this case could probably be made unanswerable. To illustrate these preconditions a highly fanciful

215

hypothetical situation must be invoked. Let us suppose a work organization being set up by a group of people who come together freely and spontaneously for the purpose. They are all independent and autonomous persons; none having power over another either to control his behaviour directly or to control it indirectly by arranging for him to be indoctrinated with beliefs and values convenient for the power holder. They are equal also in their sense of their own worth.

After free and equal discussion they reach a consensus. They agree on the primary goal of efficiency and agree, too, that this will be best served by setting up a hierarchy marked by differential roles, rewards, degrees of autonomy, and status. After some dickering and higgling, they agree on what these roles and rewards are to be. Since technological and market changes will require marginal adjustments in them from time to time, they regard it as self-evident that the decision-making structure must include representation of those affected.

In this fantasy world,[1] a pluralist ideology could certainly be claimed as offering social arrangements of a very superior order which serve both economic and human values. Comparison with the world of reality, however, at once reveals the claim to stand in need of severe qualification. People do not come together freely and spontaneously to set up work organizations; the propertyless many are forced by their need for a livelihood to seek access to resources owned or controlled by the few, who derive therefrom very great power. The few can use this power, as we have seen, not only directly in determining the behaviour of the many, but also indirectly through their effect on the many agencies of socialization, communication, and attitude forming, in inculcating beliefs, values, and assumptions which render the many amenable and submissive to the social structures which the power holders wish to maintain. Thus is promoted the high degree of acceptance of the *status quo* which is such a marked feature of our society. Thus is promoted the acceptance of the social institutions, principles, and assumptions which embody and generate inequality of rewards, privileges, and other life chances.

[1] Fantasy though it be, some structural-functionalist writings give the impression of being haunted, consciously or unconsciously, by some such vision as this version of the social contract; of free and equal citizens meeting under the village oak tree to arrange their mutual relations.

It is a tendency of socialization and social conditioning, moreover, for the conditioned to be unaware that the beliefs, assumptions, and institutions which they accept are conventional and artificial in the sense of being open to conscious, collective choice and change, and are in no way inevitable or the consequence of natural laws inherent in the cosmos. It is probable that for much of the time most men do not perceive the conventional and arbitrary nature of many of the social arrangements under which they live, and suppose them to be the only possible ones given 'the nature of things' – a notion which usually includes a belief in an unchangeable 'human nature'. This unawareness itself helps to make possible the continuance of the existing order. And in this context it must always be borne in mind that the conditioners are themselves conditioned.

What all this means is that when union or work group representatives take their place with managers at the negotiating table, they do so not as free and equal citizens in the sense described in our fantasy world, but as men who have already been socialized, indoctrinated, and trained by a multiplicity of influences to accept and legitimize most aspects of their work situation; a situation designed in the light of the values and purposes of the major power holders.

'. . . The goals for which interests struggle are not merely given: they reflect the current state of expectation and acceptance. Accordingly, to say that various interests are "balanced" is generally to evaluate the *status quo* as satisfactory or even good; the hopeful ideal of balance often masquerades as a description of fact.' (Mills 1959: p. 246)

Those aspects of their situation and of the economic and social order which the bargainers do not legitimize they may nevertheless acquiesce in because to challenge such fundamentals seems futile. Perhaps in any case they appear inevitable. Thus the 'harmony' that is engineered by the pluralist's 'accommodation – the mutual adjustment of groups that preserve their distinctive identities and interests' (Selznick 1969: p. 119), is only possible because the representatives of labour leave unchallenged those institutions, principles, and assumptions which ensure to the owners and controllers by far the greater part of their privileges and power. The two sides cannot be seen, then, as moving off from the same start line to settle jointly the nature and terms of their collaboration. Overwhelmingly the greater part of the collaborative structure and its mode of operation is settled already; settled on terms and principles which discriminate in every important respect in favour of its owners and controllers, and which the rank and file do not contest. If we ask the reason why they do not, we note, of course, their consciousness of the power confronting them, but we are noting also their social conditioning which tells them that to challenge the basic structure which relegates them to inferior status, rewards, and life chances generally would be to challenge the unchangeable; to challenge what is inevitable; to challenge the unavoidable dichotomy of 'them' and 'us' and the certainty that 'they' must, and perhaps even should, enjoy superior status, rewards, and rights of command. The conditioning which promotes legitimacy is important, for what determines men's behaviour in the face of greatly superior odds is not some 'objective' fact about the odds themselves but the interaction between the odds and the nature and strength of their motivations and aspirations. Men passionately convinced of the legitimacy of their cause can defeat a superior force; men doubtful of it can be checked by a weaker one. The second half of this proposition underlines the significance of the point made earlier that the rich and powerful are themselves socialized and conditioned. If they are taught to see their superior rewards and privileges as matters of unquestioned right they will assert them all the more confidently; conversely if that confidence is undermined by a very different ideology their exercise of power may come to lack conviction, to become uncertain, and to be more easily discouraged by determined and resourceful opposition.

Conditioning and power combine, then, to produce acceptance and submission. If inequalities are being imposed upon people by forces which they shrink from challenging, one way by which they can avoid psychological discomfort is to be receptive to all those influences, direct and indirect, explicit and implicit, crude and subtle, which assure them that the inequalities are necessary and legitimate, are accepted as natural by the other groups in society, and are inevitable in some form or another the world over.

It is in this context that the activities, writings, and utterances of industrial relations pluralists cannot help but take on an ideological significance, however unintended. They focus their interest on the substance and methods of rule making and conflict regulation within the existing and given institutions and objectives of work. Their 'problem areas' they tend to share with individuals, groups, and agencies who are concerned with the practical application of those forms of economically rational, efficient, and humane management which, directed though they may be to profit making, are seen as producing such incidental benefits as lower cost operations, better terms and conditions of employment, and 'mutually satisfactory' procedures of joint regulation and conflict resolution. These individuals, groups, and agencies include 'progressive' managers, some employers' associations, certain voluntary organizations concerned with managerial problems and techniques, government departments, and public agencies with the relevant terms of reference. The interest is in 'order' – not an imposed order but an order negotiated with representatives of participant interests.

It is being argued here, however, that this negotiation of order within the enterprise takes place only at the margins. Management and the interests do not jointly build their collaborative structure from the ground floor up. Power and social conditioning cause the employee interests to accept management's shaping of the main structure long before they reach the negotiating table. Thus the discussion may be about marginal adjustments in hierarchical rewards, but not the principle of hierarchical rewards; about certain practical issues connected with the prevailing extreme sub-division of labour, but not the principle of extreme sub-division of labour; about financial (extrinsic) rewards for greater efficiency, but not about the possibility of other types of (intrinsic) reward with some sacrifice of efficiency; about measures which may achieve company expansion and growth, but not about the benefits and costs of company expansion and growth; about how the participant interests can protect and advance themselves within the structure operated by management to pursue its basic objectives, but not about the nature of those basic objectives.

By accepting this definition of 'problems', those working with a pluralist framework implicitly accept the master institutions, principles, and assumptions of the *status quo* as nonproblematical. In doing so they add their professional status,

219

personal prestige, and influential involvement in public policy making to the forces and influences which lead subordinate groups to continue seeing the *status quo* as legitimate, inevitable, unchangeable, 'only to be expected', subject only to changes at the margin. Compared with these forces and influences, those which point out that the institutions, principles, and assumptions determining the context and experience of work are 'open' and changeable in the sense of being subject to men's collective choices are insignificant to the point of being negligible.

The ideological commitment implied by the pluralist position is further revealed in the response to situations where the basic consensus, which it is assumed will normally provide the foundation for compromise given the necessary marginal adjustments, is ruptured. These are situations in which events and ideologies have driven the parties so far apart as to rule out, for all practical purposes, the likelihood of a negotiated settlement being forthcoming.

Pluralism here brings into play its assumptions (*a*) that given skill and patience, agreed and fully legitimized procedure agreements can be reached which offer every group a speedy remedy for grievances, and (*b*) that the small number of situations in which work groups break their moral obligation to observe these procedures by resorting to unconstitutional, disruptive methods are due to ill will. The categories offered by the Donovan Report to describe these situations are those 'in which strike-proneness is due to irresponsibility or to agitation by eccentrics or by subversives' (para. 508). Against activities of these kinds 'it would be neither unjust nor futile to apply legal sanctions' (para. 509). The same view prevails in the United States. Clark Kerr, after stressing the importance of the pluralistic consensus in the stability and effectiveness of the industrial relations system, declares that 'No significant group can be allowed to sabotage it because of a conflicting exclusive ideological orientation' (such as a philosophy of class war). 'The effective response to such tactics does raise real questions about the role of compulsion in a democracy in the handling of such groups and individuals' (Kerr 1954: p. 12). And indeed, what reasonable person is likely to question the use of sanctions where sabotage, 'irresponsibility or ill-will is the root cause of the evil' (Donovan 1968: para. 509)?

The implications are plain. This is the language in which one describes political enemies and 'social undesirables'. Any frame of reference which automatically relegates nonconformers who do not share the basic consensus to categories like these is performing the function of supporting and justifying the existing order. This point is being made not in the interests of decrying such treatment of nonconformers, which is a subject in itself. This essay is about analysis, not prescriptions. The point is made in the interests of being quite clear about what we are doing.

Given the pluralistic assumptions this kind of response to the 'odd men out' is not unreasonable. If the belief is, first, that economic and political groups compete on not too grossly unequal terms for political power (through which is decided the basic structure and institutions of society), and secondly, that within the work organization management and labour, again on roughly equal terms, negotiate their particular sector of order, there is likely to be little patience with the few who refuse to be reconciled to this apparently admirable system. It will seem that they wilfully reject the principle of majority decisions; prefer anarchy and disorder; are maliciously disposed against their society on personal grounds. And indeed it may well be true that they include some whose behaviour owes more to their own psychological quirks than to any considered preferences of social and economic organization. But it is a further demonstration of the ideological content of pluralism that it leads logically towards categorizing *all* nonconformers in these terms.

For those who find the preceding critique persuasive, however, there is an alternative possibility – needing always an empirical check but at least offering a more comprehensive framework of analysis. Individual or groups of employees (or individuals leading groups) who perceive their situation in terms of the critique may see what pluralists define as 'free and equal joint regulation' as no more than 'bargaining under duress'. If they aspire towards demands which would represent a repudiation of all or some of the conventionally-received notions which are the condition of their negotiating activities being tolerated by the major power holders, and they are conscious of being contained within the conventional bargaining limits by those power holders, they are likely to see such negotiating as they are permitted as being under duress.

Despite frequent management complaints of being helpless

before union or work group demands, employees who have broken away from conventional beliefs and assumptions about their due rewards and the the general conduct of industry may be well aware that the widespread acceptance of these conventions is due, in part to a sense of overwhelming odds which it would be futile to challenge, in part to deep doubts about the legitimacy of such a challenge. Seeing both these responses as the outcome of greatly unequal power, the nonconformers might view the whole apparatus of joint regulation as just another mystification which confuses industry's rank and file about the nature of the system (Cliff 1970).

Given a consciousness of bargaining under duress, what happens to the moral obligation to observe agreements 'freely and honourably negotiated'? Those who feel coerced feel no obligation. Appeals from persons of high status and power to behave 'responsibly' by keeping agreements may be regarded by nonconformers as the culminating frustration, especially when accompanied by threats of legal coercion. The whole structure may appear as no more than a confidence trick; the praise bestowed on 'responsible' behaviour as no more than a variant on the technique of 'cooling the mark out';[1] and the 'dignity' and 'self-respect' displayed by employees and their leaders within this pattern of joint regulation as no more than the much praised behaviour of Uncle Tom, dignified and uncomplaining under exploitation.

Pluralism has, then, as strong an ideological content as any other viewpoint examined in this essay, despite a tendency of some to write as if pluralism were above the battle. In past strictures upon the unitary standpoint the author has himself expressed propositions which carried this flavour – for example in Research Paper 3 for the Donovan Commission. But vastly more significant is the fact that in the wider field of political theorizing and discourse, pluralism has been closely associated with the so-called 'end of ideology' widely touted in the 1950s.[2]

[1] A process examined by Goffman (1952: pp. 482–505). The 'mark' is the con-man's victim; cooling the mark out is an exercise in the prudent art of consolation—'An attempt is made to define the situation for the mark in a way that makes it easy for him to accept the inevitable and quietly go home'.

[2] For a statement of pluralistic end-of-ideology in industry viewed against the wider background of political pluralism, see Kerr et al. 1962, Chapter 10. Rousseas and Farganis (1965) offer a critique of the 'end of ideology' standpoint in American politics.

Pluralism is apt, indeed, to convey this impression to many. While being 'realistic' about 'conflict', it does not question the major assumptions and principles upon which work and industry are based and which the vast majority of people have been trained to accept. Thus it appears to combine realism with neutrality. 'Does it not', writes Wolff, 'accord a legitimate place to all groups in society? How then can it be used to justify or preserve the dominance of one group over another?' Given these characteristics, 'One might think that whatever faults the theory of pluralism possessed, at least it would be free of the dangers of ideological distortion' (Wolff 1965: p. 48).

When the pluralist offers his practical help and advice in the field of public policy there may be no great problem for the analytically sophisticated bystander in gauging the ideological implications. But those unversed in such skills may suppose the pluralist to be speaking with the authority of objective science when in fact his method of analysis, his recommendations, and indeed his very selection of 'problems' deemed worthy of attention, spring from a body of values, assumptions, beliefs, and preferences which are apt to remain unspoken. He may, for example, approve the existing power structure of society, its values, and its distribution of life chances. Or he may strongly disapprove yet believe that fundamental change, violent or otherwise, might finish by leaving most people in a worse state, that many good things would be lost in the process, and that the fortunes of even the humblest strata are likely to be at least as well served by maintaining the existing type of social order while trying to strengthen the power of weaker groups to assert their claims. Even so it can fairly be argued to be incumbent upon the pluralist to draw attention to those elements of the existing order which he is prepared to accept as given. For while *he* may be prepared to accept those elements as given, there is no call upon others to do so. But can they not make their own assessments, it might be asked, without his needing to have any part in that process? The answer must be that, as we have noted already, for much of the time most men do not perceive the conventional and arbitrary nature of many of the social arrangements under which they live and suppose them to be part of an inevitable and unchangeable order (Goldthorpe 1969). It is one important aspect of the social scientist's professional obligation, therefore, to make himself and others

223

aware that this is not so. It is part of his responsibility to make clear that the existing order is in no way determined by laws inherent in the universal nature of things; that its most hallowed features are conventional in the strictest sense and thus subject to change originating from men's deliberate choice; and that the selection of some features of the current scene as 'problems' and the denial of the same status to others is determined, not by objective and 'neutral' considerations, but by decisions (which may well be implicitly rather than explicitly formulated) as to what is to be accepted as fixed and unchanging. The pluralist may consider he has the best of considered reasons for accepting many conventionally received notions as given, and changing them, if at all, only at the margin. He may, indeed, be convinced that this acceptance is a necessary price to pay if he is to have any influence in the field of public policy for improving society's economic performance – a prerequisite, perhaps, in his view for bettering the lot of its humbler members. These are perfectly valid, legitimate, and socially responsible positions. Yet, considered within the whole dialogue concerning desirable social change and reform, are they not weakened by appearing to be open to the charge that in failing to be explicit about power relations and the conventional nature of work organization they help to sustain a social order marked by great inequalities and privilege? Conversely, would they not be strengthened by such explicitness accompanied by a reasoned argument which supports the acceptance of certain 'givens' of our social and economic structure?

Be that as it may, the whole of the preceding argument can, from one point of view, be seen as leading up to an ethical issue which can be artificially sharpened for discussion by invoking, first, an imaginary situation and, secondly, an imaginary argument.

For the first, let us suppose that all members of society, contrary to what has been suggested here, are in fact fully cognisant of all the facts as they have been argued in the preceding pages not only about the great disparity of power in society but more especially about the conventional assumptions relating to authority, hierarchy, privileges, and rewards. Let us suppose that they weigh the probable costs and benefits of campaigning and bargaining at the margins of the existing order, as against those of campaigning and bargaining for more radical change, and that they decide in favour of the former – for reasons which may include their own appraisal of the likelihood of success, the desire for a quiet life, and any other consideration they see as relevant. In such a case their situation might begin to approximate to that of 'free and equal' citizens, with full knowledge, making a considered choice as autonomous moral agents. From that point of view, then, this essay would be no more than a statement of 'what everyone knows'. We would all, managers, employees, and academics alike, be proceeding with knowledge of the facts and nobody would be leaving himself open to any charge of deceiving himself or anyone else, wittingly or otherwise.

If, however, there is any reason to believe that the participants are not cognisant of the facts, and that their aspirations and claims, and their responses to the aspirations and claims of others, are affected by this ignorance, then are there any legitimate grounds on which social scientists could consider it 'socially responsible' not to labour at emphasizing these facts? At this point we conjure up an imaginary argument. Let us suppose someone to assert that if all men were to become fully aware of the conventional nature of the social order which regulates their aspirations and behaviour, the stability not only of that particular order but of any kind of order – certainly any kind of 'democratic order' – would be seriously threatened. This argument is termed 'imaginary' only in the sense that, to the author's knowledge, it forms no part of industrial relations pluralism. In the wider field of politics it has of course figured in many conservative arguments dating from Edmund Burke's reply to Tom Paine and the Natural Rights movement.

It can take many forms, including that which urges us all, unexceptionably, to think and act responsibly in the light of the probable consequences. But is it possible to resist the conclusion that they can all be reduced, in the last analysis, to an argument that, for the sake of stability and order, certain facts believed to be true must not be encouraged for popular consumption; that other men cannot be trusted with the full knowledge of their condition? Are there any conditions under which this is valid? In particular, has it any validity for modern industrial societies which claim to be mature, 'politically educated' democracies? If it has, is there not something to be said for being more modest about that claim?

P

One thing seems certain. Anyone who considers, as does the author, that the 'full knowledge' of which we are speaking is not widespread must certainly accept that if it becomes so the search for stability and order will become far more difficult. Although there is not the slightest vestige of an historical reason to suppose that in advanced countries trade unionists conscious of having much to lose would put it all at serious risk by socially destructive behaviour, we could well expect them to formulate their claims within the bargaining framework on different lines and according to different aspirations from those we are accustomed to. We would expect, too, the wider political democratic process to be put under strain, and we would soon find fishing in those troubled waters many whose values we might or might not respect. What responsible person, indeed, can fail to take all these consequences into account?

But men thinking hard and honestly about the same arguments can reach different conclusions. For the author of this essay, at least, the idea of a society prepared to face the profoundly disturbing consequences of 'full knowledge' as defined here, while also remaining determined to retain what is good in the present order, represents an attempt to grapple with the full implications of increasing literacy, growing insistence on the citizen's right to formulate his own beliefs and aspirations in the light of the facts available, and a diminishing disposition to define conventions as unchangeable laws.

Meanwhile, however, we have the widespread conviction that there are many reforms worth pursuing within the existing set of power relations, beliefs, assumptions, and conventions. 'Reform' is a term of many ambiguities – it is used here to mean marginal improvements which leave the master institutions and assumptions of society still in clearly recognizable shape, as against change of a more fundamental kind. Although the former shade into the latter there is a difference which most of us are prepared to recognize as meaningful and worth making. The concluding section of this essay will suggest that those applying themselves to this field of public policy involvement in reform will tend, whatever their personal beliefs, to be obliged to behave 'as if' they subscribed to the pluralist ideology.

THE APPEAL OF PLURALISM

There is no space here to explore the reasons why in the political field a pluralistic orientation to society appears to carry both plausibility and attractiveness. One might hazard that among them is a sheer will-to-believe in an interpretation which salves consciences and legitimizes existing social arrangements. In Mills's view

> 'The greatest appeal of romantic pluralism to those of conservative yearning is that it makes unnecessary any explicit justification of the men who are ostensibly in charge of public affairs. For if they are all in balance, each of them really quite impotent, then no one set of higher circles and no manageable set of institutional arrangements can be held accountable for the events and decisions of our time.' (Mills 1959: pp. 336–7)

Pluralism has many other kinds of appeal, but the one that has made itself most apparent in this essay with respect to industrial relations would seem to be its appropriateness as a set of 'working assumptions' for those interested in the formulation and application of public policy. Irrespective of personal philosophy, a working acceptance of the basic structure, objectives, and principles which characterize industry is usually a condition of being able to exert influence towards reform. Government ministers, higher civil servants, staffs of public agencies, trade union officers, employers, and managers alike, work within constraints of power and expectations which severely limit their choices, and unless would-be advisers also take these constraints into account their advice and help is likely to be useless for practical purposes.

To make the point concrete we might imagine a pluralist academic advising a government department on incomes policy. Were he to start by urging a completely open-ended and free-ranging discussion of the basic principles by which managerial and non-managerial work should be rewarded his listeners would no doubt indicate politely but firmly that they only had one lifetime and were rather hoping to get something done. They would feel, perhaps, like the lost motorist who asks the way to Birmingham and is told: 'If I were you I wouldn't start from here.' Reform, as the term is being used in this essay, is a matter of changes at the margins of established institutions and assumptions, and the reformer is like to be found, implicitly if not explicitly, and whether he is aware of it or not, using for working purposes a set of assumptions which can be seen as pluralist in nature.

But what has 'reform' meant for industrial relations academics? Only one reform tradition will be touched on here, but one sufficiently important to be seen, perhaps, as the main stream. Within the industrial relations scene in Britain, and to a significant extent also in the United States, the early interest and involvement of some of the most prominent academics was marked by special sympathies not with the managerial role but with the trade union and labour role. In America, the liberals of the thirties and forties identified with the unions in their challenge to, and distrust of, big business and its creed of profit and prerogative; and support for trade unionism and collective bargaining became an automatic item in voting the straight progressive ticket, though this is far from true today. Similarly, in Britain, the early post-war development of academic interest stemmed most importantly from those with labour sympathies who considered that practical reforms worth having could and needed to be pursued in the short and medium run, and that effectiveness in this endeavour meant taking many other things for granted. Whether they articulated their working assumptions or not, these tended to take a form approximating to that described here as pluralism. At that time their recommendations for 'progressive reform' were predominantly addressed to the unions. If later they came to believe that they should increasingly address the managers this indicates no change of colours on their part, but rather a conviction that the pursuit of 'progressive' social ends which they valued lay indirectly through enlightened initiatives by management to which unions could – indeed would have to – respond.

If, therefore, pluralists are to be charged with managerialism, on the grounds that their perspective helps managers to be more effective in handling the complex human problems of modern industry, it must be on the understanding that such an approach can stem not necessarily from personal identification with the values and private goals of managers as such, but from a belief that management based on pluralist attitudes and methods is not only an end in itself, as a more civilized way of conducting the hierarchies of modern business, but also a necessary means to other ends such as, for example, a rise in living standards for the less favoured and a bigger margin for social services. This approach expresses a belief that there are reforms and objectives worth pursuing within the *status quo*, but it may also be accompanied by a conviction that a radical analysis going beyond pluralism is not only of greater intellectual validity but is also a necessary stimulus and guide to the pursuit of more fundamental change. Such, at any rate, is the approach of the author of this essay.

It does not follow, of course, that an acceptance of the radical critique of pluralism presented here necessarily shapes, still less determines, political attitudes and policy prescriptions along any particular lines. It would be possible, for example, for a member of a power-holding group to accept such an analysis and regard the situation as perfectly satisfactory provided he remained on top. Machiavelli's Prince would probably have no difficulty. Most power holders prefer, however, to veil the stark realities for themselves as well as for others, and a radical analysis of society will appeal most to those who wish to change it.

While that analysis is the starting point, the consequential need for evaluation of, and response to, the social situation once analysed takes us into a wider universe of values, conceivable alternatives, probable consequences, and choices. A valid analysis is indispensable: by providing us with a convincing picture of what is, it enables us the more clearly to think about what might be, and moreover helps each of us to judge for himself the value of any proposed change or reform. But it does not of itself throw up unique prescriptions as to how we should respond to the situation it reveals.

Meanwhile, those who accept it as a stimulus and guide to social change while also accepting the need for immediate reform face the problem posed in this essay. In so far as we use a pluralist framework as a set of working assumptions in pursuing reform within the *status quo* we shall seem to give credence to a view of society which seriously misleads its less favoured members. This is the sort of dilemma that is no doubt responsible for the charge sometimes directed at reformers that 'reform is the enemy of revolution', where revolution is defined as radical social change. It is of course true by definition that all behaviour which is not directed towards making the present system unworkable contributes to its survival, and reform is thought to delay the millennium still further by blunting the edges of discontent and muffling the dialectical clash of the system's internal contradictions. It follows, however, that the casualties, victims, and underdogs of our society can expect no help from the sources of such arguments as these. Indeed, more misery must be created in the hope of hastening revolt.

In all reform-seeking behaviour there is some degree of acceptance of the *status quo*. Every reformer is answerable to himself on the question of how much. But each of us may be helped in formulating the answer if there proceeds, concurrently with reform of the social order within the assumptions of its master institutions, the pursuit of a deeply searching analysis which questions and goes beyond those assumptions to illuminate what is possible as well as what is not.

What seems to emerge from these arguments, therefore, is that one may use, or work to the assumptions of, either the pluralistic model or the critique of it presented here, according to one's current purposes – which may indeed alternate between involvement in, and detachment from, the 'applied' field of public policy. In the practical field there have been Communist trade union leaders who, while active in party counsels and policy, have played a role in industrial relations which was 'as if' they accepted pluralist assumptions and values. In the academic field it is possible to reject pluralism as an analytical framework in favour of the more critical perspective presented here, while still believing that existing society is, for all its many morally disgusting features, an advance in important respects on most societies of the past, and that its master institutions should not be put at serious hazard until there is a high probability of something better replacing them. Such a stance would rest on the belief, emphasized earlier, that our response to what we perceive as social evils has to be mediated by cost-benefit considerations bearing upon the alternatives, and would put high priority on efforts to reform existing institutions.

If we take men to be of equal worth, however, each must weigh these considerations and probabilities for himself. The raw materials for this assessment must include insight into the nature of past and present as well as estimates of the shape of possible futures. The task is taxing and we need help from many quarters, not least from sociology. Sociology as a discipline confers its greatest strength when it helps us at least to some limited degree to reduce our dependence on the blinkers of our own social conditioning and thereby to escape from the self-fulfilling prophecies of 'what is must be'.[1]

The critique of pluralism advanced in this essay, then, seeks to encourage the use of a particular kind of appraisal of past and present in the belief that it reveals, whereas pluralism obscures, certain social mechanisms of great significance for the debate. Unquestionably the pluralistic perspective has vital uses as a working instrument when we involve ourselves in public policy. In such contexts pluralism might be said to serve as something in the nature of a Platonic 'noble myth'. But it is a further implication of the reasoning of this essay that pluralism may also operate as an ignoble myth by offering a misleading picture of the realities of social power, thereby serving those who, by the test of 'cui bono', have an interest in the propagation of a comforting and reassuring message.

[1] This is, of course, a highly ideological statement. Those who inherit the tradition of Burke and other conservatives down the ages would argue that it is precisely the danger of sociology that by encouraging this detached perspective on social institutions it threatens what is at best a precarious order. However, there is hardly need to stress here that sociology, too, has its conservative tradition, manifested currently in structural-functionalism.

REFERENCES

BAKKE, E. W. 1946. *Mutual survival: the goal of unions and management*, New York: Harper and Row.

CASTLES, F. G., MURRAY, D. J., POTTER, D. C. (eds.). 1971. *Decisions, organizations and society*, Harmondsworth: Penguin Books in association with the Open University Press.

CHAMBERLAIN, N. 1963. 'The union challenge to management control', *Industrial and Labour Relations Review*, 16, 184–92.

CLEGG, H. n.d. *Purpose of the unions*, London: National and Local Government Officers' Association.

CLIFF, T. 1970. *The employers' offensive: productivity deals and how to fight them*, London: Pluto Press.

CYERT, R. M. and MARCH, J. G. 1959. 'A behavioral theory of organizational objectives', in M. Haire (ed.), *Modern organization theory*, New York: Wiley.

DONOVAN, LORD. 1969. *Report of the Royal Commission on Trade Unions and Employers' Associations*, 1965–1968, London: HMSO, Cmd 3623.

FLANDERS, A. 1967. *Collective bargaining: prescription for change*, London: Faber and Faber.

FLANDERS, A. 1970. *Management and unions*, London: Faber and Faber.

FOX, A. 1966. *Industrial sociology and industrial relations*, Research Paper 3, Royal Commission on Trade Unions and Employers' Associations, London: HMSO.

FOX, A. 1971. *A sociology of work in industry*, London: Collier-Mac millan.

GALBRAITH, J. K. 1952. *American capitalism: the concept of countervailing power*, New York and London: Hamilton.

GITLIN, T. 1965. 'Local pluralism as theory and ideology', in H. P. Dreitzel (ed.), *Recent sociology no. 1*, London: Collier-Macmillan, 1969.

GOFFMAN, E. 1952. 'On cooling the mark out: some aspects of adaptation to failure', in A. M. ROSE (ed.), *Human behaviour and social processes*, London: Routledge and Kegan Paul, 1962.

GOLDTHORPE, J. H. 1969. 'Social inequality and social integration in modern Britain', *Advancement of Science*, December 1969, 190–202.

GOULDNER, A. W. 1971. *The coming crisis of western sociology*, London: Heinemann.

HARBISON, F. 1954. 'Collective bargaining and American capitalism', in A. Kornhauser, R. Dubin, A. M. Ross (eds.), *Industrial conflict*, New York: McGraw-Hill. For other essays in the same volume which stress the 'stabilizing' effects of 'institutionalized conflict', see Chapter 1, 'Problems and viewpoints', by the editors, and Chapter 3, 'Constructive aspects of industrial conflict', by Robert Dubin.

KERR, C. 1954. 'Industrial relations and the liberal pluralist', *Proceedings of the Seventh Annual Meeting of the Industrial Relations Research Association*, 28–30 December 1954.

KERR, C., DUNLOP, J. T., HARBISON, F. H., and MYERS, C. A. 1962. *Industrialism and industrial man*, London: Heinemann.

MERTON, R. K. 1966. 'Social problems and sociological theory', in R. K. Merton and R. A. Nisbet (eds.), *Contemporary social problems*, 2nd ed., New York: Harcourt Brace.

MILIBAND, R. 1969 *The state in a capitalist society*, London; Weidenfeld and Nicolson.

MILLER, D. C. and FORM, W. H. 1964. *Industrial sociology: the sociology of work organizations*, 2nd ed., New York: Harper and Row.

MILLS, C. WRIGHT. 1959. *The power elite*, New York: Oxford University Press.

PEN, J. 1966. *Harmony and conflict in modern society*, London and New York: McGraw-Hill.

POLSBY, N. W. 1963. *Community power and political theory*, New Haven: Yale University Press.

ROUSSEAS, S. W. and FARGANIS, J. 1965. 'American politics and the end of ideology', in Horowitz, I. L. (ed.), *The new sociology*, New York: Oxford University Press.

SELEKMAN, S. K. and SELEKMAN, B. M. 1956. *Power and morality in a business society*, New York: McGraw-Hill.

SELZNICK, P. 1969. *Law, society, and industrial justice*, New York: Russell Sage Foundation.

SILVERMAN, D. 1970. *The theory of organizations*, London: Heinemann.

WOLFF, R. P. 1965. 'Beyond tolerance', in R. P. Wolff, B. Moore Jr., H. Marcuse, *A critique of pure tolerance*, London: Jonathan Cape, 1969.

WRONG, D. 1968. 'Some problems in defining social power', in H. P. Dreitzel (ed.), *Recent sociology no. 1*, London: Collier-Macmillan, 1969.

8 Organization: a Choice for Man

JOHN CHILD

'For much of the time most men do not perceive the conventional and arbitrary nature of many of the social arrangements under which they live and suppose them to be part of an inevitable and unchangeable order. It is one important aspect of the social scientist's professional obligation, therefore, to make himself and others aware that this is not so. It is part of his responsibility to make clear that the existing order is in no way determined by laws inherent in the universal nature of things; that its most hallowed features are conventional in the strictest sense and thus subject to change originating from men's deliberate choice.' (Alan Fox, Chapter 7 above, pp. 222–4)

Social science can assist the process of change through its scrutiny of the conventional wisdom, ideology, and prejudice which still pervade many aspects of our social life. By identifying social conventions for what they are, the social scientist helps to create an awareness of the possibilities for alternative modes of action and organization which may provide benefits not previously achieved. He can stimulate this awareness through clarifying the assumptions contained in influential theories and beliefs and then critically examining these against relevant empirical evidence. The social scientist may also through his work be able to expose hitherto unappreciated consequences which the characteristics of one institutional area in society have for those in another area. This may point to the existence of conflict between accepted criteria of performance applied to different facets of social activity, and in this way make us more aware of the social policy choices with which we are confronted.

In regard to industry, the social scientist's role in creating an awareness of available choices therefore requires him to examine the empirical foundation for existing theories, especially those which can be used to justify prevailing modes of work organization. Many writings on organization refer to a rationale of administrative effectiveness. This rationale is often taken to imply that only a certain form of organizational structure will in given circumstances be conducive to a high level of organizational performance, and little prospect is held out for substantial changes in industrial organization without incurring serious economic penalties. But how adequate is such a theme when set against empirical evidence? The social scientist can, in addition, consider whether the forms of work organization which do characterize industry today have any serious consequences for the achievement of desirable ends in other areas of social life. In particular, is there any conflict between managerially defined criteria of effective organizational performance and 'social' criteria which are established by reference to the quality of men's lives both inside and outside the workplace?

These questions provide the framework of the present chapter. This expresses the view that many (though certainly not all) writers on organization have worked with a perspective on organizational design which is open to qualification both on empirical and normative grounds. The approach adopted in this chapter has been influenced by earlier critiques of conventional organization theory such as Argyris (1964) and Silverman (1970). It seeks to draw attention to the likely availability of choice in organizational design and to the wider social importance of recognizing, investigating, and acting upon that availability. Indeed, it concludes that any approach to organization which ignores its social relevance will become untenable as a guide to acceptable practical action in the developing climate of advanced societies.

CONVENTIONAL WISDOM ON ORGANIZATION

An important theme in writing emanating from managerial sources was, for a long time, the claim that the design of organization should be treated as a purely technical matter. This was clearly stated in a seminal paper which Urwick wrote in 1933:

235

'It is the general thesis of this paper that there are principles which can be arrived at inductively from the study of human experience of organization, which should govern arrangements for human association of any kind. These principles can be studied as a technical question, irrespective of the purpose of the enterprise, the personnel composing it, or any constitutional, political or social theory underlying its creation. They are concerned with the method of subdividing and allocating to individuals all the various activities, duties and responsibilities essential to the purpose contemplated, the correlation of these activities and the continuous control of the work of individuals so as to secure the most economical and the most effective realization of the purpose.' (1933: p. 49)

This approach to organization as a technical question implies that considerations of economic administration are of overriding significance regardless of the values which may underlie the creation or maintenance of an 'enterprise'. In so far as only a particular form of organization would best satisfy these considerations, it was concluded that there is little room for choice in organizational design. This is what Lupton has called the 'universalistic' approach to organization (1971).

In early writings on organization, this approach was expressed by the search for generally applicable principles and techniques for allocating tasks, controlling the work done, motivating those doing it, and rewarding their accomplishment. Both the so-called 'classical' theorists and members of the early human relations school accepted that there was a 'logic of efficiency'. This logic was generally interpreted to mean the establishment of bureaucratic modes of control, with narrow supervisory spans, closely prescribed duties, and a clear and formal definition of procedures, areas of specialization, and hierarchical relationships. It was believed that the technically efficient organization was one in which unity of effort was achieved through the limitation of individual discretion and the elimination of ambiguity, both achieved through the use of routine procedures and systems. The earlier human relations writers did not so much suggest that this rationale be rejected as that some bridge had to be built between it and the needs of employees for socially satisfying relationships in the workplace.

236

The gap could be bridged, they thought, through the medium of an appropriate supervisory style and workgroup structure. Again, universal prescriptions were laid down for this style of leadership and for the design of work groups.

The universalistic approach to organizational design has today been widely rejected in favour of a 'particularistic' perspective. This regards the design of an effective organization as necessarily having to be adapted to cope with the 'contingencies' which derive from the circumstances of environment, technology, scale, resources, and other factors in the situation in which a unit is operating. This newer approach has grown out of a body of social science research which has reported statistical associations between organizational characteristics and situational variables. It represents, in fact, one of the simplest theoretical models which such results could support, namely that situational characteristics predict dimensions of organization because they present requirements which act as moderately severe constraints upon the choice of an organizational design conducive to high performance. The major difference of this newer approach from earlier organizational theories lies in its acknowledgment that the process of designing organization involves the selection of a configuration that will best suit that particular situation which prevails. 'Contingency theory' has today gained a wide measure of acceptance, at least among those who teach and write on organization, and it may be said to present an important strand of conventional wisdom on the subject.

An excellent exposition of contingency theory has been provided by Lupton (1971: Chapter 4), while the present writer has also summarized its main conclusions (Child 1972). Some of its major implications may briefly be listed. It implies that the requirements for specialization within an organization and for the coordination of specialized activities will vary according to the diversity among the different parts of an organization's environment, particularly with respect to their rates of change and to the speed at which feedback of information can be secured from them (cf. Lawrence and Lorsch 1967). More formalized and centralized methods of integration are seen to be appropriate in less dynamic and diversified environments. Contingency theory also implies that the larger a unit becomes, the more it should take advantage of the opportunities for

237

allocating administrative and advisory activities to staff specialists. The senior management of a larger organization should also recognize the need to delegate decision making of a routine nature, and to rely for maintenance of control and coordination upon standard procedures and formal documentation rather than upon personal surveillance (cf. Pugh *et al.* 1969, Blau and Schoenherr 1971). Thirdly, contingency theory implies that organization and control systems should be designed to suit the prevailing tasks and technology. Thus if the technology exhibits a high degree of stability in the materials or information utilized in tasks, and if routine codifiable techniques can be applied, then a number of organizational features are seen to be appropriate. These include defined and specialized work roles having a low discretionary content, the establishment of coordination within work groups according to plans and procedures, and the separation of technical activities from purely 'line' supervision – in other words, a close approximation to the bureaucratic model (cf. Woodward 1965, Perrow 1970).

This brief summary indicates some of the implications for practical action which are being drawn from recent research into organization, though it does not represent a commentary on the sophistication of the research itself. The new conventional wisdom which has emerged in effect likens the development of organizational structures to a process of 'fine tuning' aimed at striking a balanced response to what may well be conflicting constraints emanating from different elements in the operating situation. These constraints are regarded as given by the situation, and as having effective consequences in that the economic performance achieved is in part a function of how successfully organization is adapted to them. The principal point of reference for contingency theory remains the same as that of earlier approaches, namely a logic of effectiveness. However, the means to attaining this objective are now regarded as being technically far more complex entailing a detailed and sophisticated evaluation of each situation rather than merely an application of *a priori* principles. Contingency theorists would possibly regard their approach when compared to early theories of organization in much the same light as the modern scientist might compare himself with the medieval 'schoolman'. Their work not only appears to remove the question of organizational design from the realm of armchair theorizing but also from the sway of ideological preference. (This latter attribute was also claimed by the pioneering theorists.) Contingency theory in this respect finds its home with the 'end of ideology' movement in social and political thinking, a movement which has, however, attracted charges of sociological naiveté and of an implicit conservative ideological bias. Does a sociological examination of contingency theory lead to similar conclusions?

A SOCIOLOGICAL CRITIQUE OF CONTINGENCY THEORY

The contingency approach unquestionably represents an advance in our appreciation of organization. Lupton (1971) has convincingly argued its practical relevance, pointing out that the newer approach does encourage managers to search for an organizational design to suit their particular operational requirements instead of relying upon a universal precept:

> 'It is of great practical significance whether one kind of managerial style or procedure for arriving at decisions or one kind of organizational structure is suitable for all organizations, or whether the managers in each organization have to find the expedient that will best meet the particular circumstances of size, technology, product, competitive situation and so on. In practice managers do, indeed must, attempt to define the particular circumstances of the unit they manage, and to devise ways of dealing with these circumstances. I have often observed that their success in doing so is limited by their belief that there must be a universal prescription. This belief can obscure some of the possibilities that are open.' (Lupton 1971: p. 125)

The objection to contingency theory lies not so much in what it does say as in its failure to refer adequately to other relevant facets of organizational behaviour. It implies a view of organization which is insufficient from the standpoint of sociological explanation, and this inhibits it from identifying the full extent of opportunities which are likely to exist for variety in organizational design. For managers there is a great deal in contingency theory to recommend, because it does draw attention to certain technical problems of organizing to cope with prevailing circumstances. We may, however, express this

239

in another way: the contingency approach encourages managers to weigh the implications of the operating situation in which they find themselves against their preferred courses of action. The possibility that managers may have preferences for outcomes other than those indicated by an application of contingency theory is an important consideration, and it leads to the first major objection against the theory. This makes the point that decision making about organization is not simply a matter of accommodating to operational contingencies. It is equally a political process into which other considerations, particularly the expression of power holders' values, also enter. A second objection is that contingency theory faces the problems of any explanatory scheme which relies, as it does, upon a notion of functional imperatives. This leads it towards the reification both of postulated exigencies and of the social unit upon which these supposedly bear; in this regard the theory relies upon a sociologically naive mode of explanation and one which is unnecessarily conservative in its implications for the practical possibilities of change. These objections are now examined in turn.

Journalists have been more alert to the political nature of organizational decision making than have many professional social science writers on the subject. Perhaps this has something to do with the fact that the journalist's trade has always led him to probe as to who and what lies behind the formation of policy, while the social scientist has normally found himself able to research only the consequences of policy which has already been established, especially the extent to which the manifest (rather than the latent) objectives of the policy have been achieved. Indeed, many social scientists have been, and still are, employed to advise on the implementation of decisions, but rarely have they been given (or even sought?) access to the policy-making process itself (cf. Baritz 1960). Thus much of the social science literature on organizations makes little or no reference at all to political processes, but implies instead that decisions are made on the basis simply of a more or less informed technical appreciation of the operational situation. An important exception is the work of Barnard (1938), Simon (1960), Cyert and March (1963) and their colleagues on decision making in organizations. Nonetheless, it has in the main been left to correspondents such as Anthony Jay (1967) and John

240

Brooks (1970), or to the sociologist such as Perrow (1970) who is prepared to use their material, to bring out the political nature common to all organizations whether these be the administrative arms of sovereign states, business corporations, or other types of unit. The common element, in Jay's words, is 'the framework they construct within which economic and political necessity interact with the minds and will of men' (1967: p. 22).

Dubin (1962) in his review of available studies of decision making in organizations pointed out the considerable time which often elapses between the recognition of a problem and the decision regarding its solution. One of the reasons for this time-lag is the operation of the political factor. It would appear typical for an attempt to be made to secure some degree of *legitimation* for the proposal in the eyes of interested parties who have power to obstruct the implementation of any decision which they do not accept. During this process there is an effort to accommodate in the decision the disparate, even conflicting, interests held by such individuals or groups. The political process in organizations therefore incorporates an important normative aspect, and it is the means through which the values of various groups impinge to a greater or lesser degree upon organizational decisions. This process operates in regard to the interface between situational factors and the structure of organizations, because political criteria are brought to bear upon the way in which contingencies are interpreted. To refer to an empirical example, Normann (1971) found in thirteen case studies of new product development in Swedish companies that the existing values and power structure in a company played a critical role in predicting reaction to new ideas and information emanating from the environment.

It is also the case, as I have argued elsewhere (Child 1972), that normative considerations may influence the performance standards which are established for an organization. Given that no organizations, in any sphere, operate under conditions of perfect competition, then some degree of choice in perform-ance standards will be available to organizational decision makers without their necessarily incurring any serious threat to the 'survival' of their unit. A well-known historical example is the way in which British Quaker employers early this century operated various policies designed to benefit their employees' welfare at a time when these were widely regarded as being inimical to maintaining a company's economic performance.

In short, the first major objection to contingency theory is that it gives insufficient emphasis to the role of political factors in decisions on organizational policies, including the design of structures. Not only may the response of organizational decision makers to situational factors depend upon their own set of preferences (and to some extent upon those of other groups whose support is needed) concerning the mode of organization to be utilized, but additionally the notion of effectiveness upon which contingency theory relies is meaningful to decision makers only in relation to their own criteria of performance.

A recognition of the part played by the political system in organizations also draws attention to the inadequacy of regarding situational 'contingencies' as functional imperatives for organizational design. This is the second major objection to the contingency approach. Any such view is theoretically questionable because, as we have just argued, it does not adequately describe the orientations which organizational decision makers are themselves likely to hold. Its implication that the relationships between situational variables and organizational variables are in effect 'mechanistic' is also open to qualification, for two reasons. First, some variation appears to be possible in the design of organization for a unit operating within a given situation, without apparently incurring serious consequences for its level of economic performance. Secondly, the type of situation in which a unit is operating may itself be open to some degree of deliberate manipulation and selection on the part of organizational decision makers, and therefore it does not necessarily represent a fixed point of reference for them. There is some evidence available to support these contentions.

An important and well-known example of the choice in organizational design which may exist within given operating situations is provided by the work of the Tavistock Institute, centering around the concept of a 'socio-technical system'. This concept derives from the recognition that a system of work contains distinct yet interrelated technological, socio-psychological, and economic components. Several studies (notably Rice 1958, Trist et al. 1963, Miller and Rice 1967) have recorded experiments which appear to demonstrate that, while the choice

242

of organization at operating levels is limited by technology, the limits do nevertheless allow room for a number of alternatives. In some of the experiments, substantial changes were made in the structure of working groups and in their degree of autonomy within the overall technological rationale of the production process. In most cases these changes had favourable results, both in terms of economic cost and output criteria and in terms of social criteria such as job satisfaction. Many researchers working with the Tavistock approach regard the transference to work groups of some of management's traditional authority for the control and coordination of work as a necessary first step towards any system of more substantial industrial democracy that is to have real meaning for those involved (Thorsrud 1970). The 'job enrichment' approach has similarly entailed deliberate modifications of work roles and of the authority attached to them within an unchanged system of 'tasks' to be accomplished. Again, early results suggest that such changes tend to lead to an increase both in levels of personal satisfaction and of task performance partly because people are now able to use their abilities to a fuller extent (cf. Paul and Roberston 1970, Cotgrove *et al.* 1971).

Experiments such as these only represent marginal adjustments to the structures of organization prevailing in industry today, and in themselves they do not meet the criticism that modern organization is a source of many deprivating and inequitable features in modern society. Indeed, it could be argued that the initiatives described may serve to divert attention away from a recognition of more fundamental sources of inequity, through the effect which they may have of increasing the employee's normative acceptance of managerial definitions of the industrial situation. A similar type of objection has been raised against productivity bargaining by left wing critics such as Cliff (1970). However, the experiments do raise a point of immediate significance, for if relatively limited modifications to prevailing modes of organization can produce a greater level of net social and economic benefit, then there appears to be some reason for supposing that more substantial modifications may also be of merit on social grounds and may possibly incur no significant economic costs. In other words, there seems to be no reason why the availability of choice in organization design should not be explored further.

There is no reason either to suppose that some fixed relationship necessarily prevails between the overall size of the unit and a viable form of organization, or between environmental conditions and a viable form of organization. There are various, quite well-known alternatives for the organization and control of activities within a large unit. These involve various arrangements for the devolution of decision making, alternative rationales for sub-dividing areas of activity, and so on. In effect, these choices of organizational design create in varying measure for the sub-units of a large organization the conditions which might be experienced by a smaller operating unit. This permits some of the freedom of choice which a small independent unit has in deciding how far to utilize bureaucratic modes of administration, with all their possibly constrictive effects upon individual initiative and so on. An example of such adaptation is the use of the profit-centre system which can allow considerable autonomy to a smaller sub-unit in deciding how it should structure its internal organization; it has like the worker in a piece-rate system secured some degree of autonomy through being placed in a sub-contracting relationship to the wider unit. Even in the case of 'service' or 'control' functions such as finance, which operate in relation to the unit as a whole and whose scale of operation is therefore more closely bound to that of the whole unit, there may still be a number of possibilities for changing the nature of their internal organization and definition of roles through the adoption of different techniques, workflow systems or data-processing methods. Shepard's study (1971) of automation and employee 'alienation' suggests that this organizational flexibility does characterize office work in practice.

In regard to environmental conditions, there is a particularly strong measure of agreement between different writers on the broad lines of organizational adaptation which is required for effective performance. The work of Lawrence and Lorsch (1967) does appear to point convincingly towards the necessity of maintaining a balance between the degree of differentiation and integration of functions which is appropriate to the prevailing configuration of environmental circumstances. However, their subsequently reported diagnostic work in industry (1969) suggests that in practice the particular organizational arrangements which may be used to secure this balance do represent quite a range of alternative possibilities. For example, a given degree of integration between specialized areas of activity can be secured via several different combinations of organizational arrangements and the responsibility for operating these may be allocated at different levels in the organizational hierarchy. Such alternatives may well imply very different qualities of experience for the members of an organization who are involved.

The foregoing line of argument does not deny that the relationships between situational and organizational variables reported in comparative studies may reflect pressures to establish organizational arrangements which cope with prevailing circumstances – to a degree. It does, however, call into question any conclusion that these findings imply the presence of situational imperatives for organizational design. Extremely little is known about the nature of cause and effect in this whole area. It is possible that to some extent the relationships discovered are a reflection of the conventional wisdom upon which managers are drawing. This is quite likely in the case of the association between 'bureaucratic' features and large size, probably the most consistent finding so far, for the following reason. What may well be happening in practice, *inter alia*, is that as an organization grows larger it begins to employ 'professional' managers who take some interest in the available management folklore. This still tends to recommend the establishment of routine systems, clear job definitions, the use of delegation, and other bureaucratic features as a basis for orderly and effective operations. Hence as organizations grow larger, such precepts are increasingly applied. So long as we remain unsure about the possibility of this kind of causal process where the currency of ideas is the source of influence rather than situational constraints, we cannot be certain how to interpret much of the research which has provided the basis for contingency theory.

The contingency approach not only specifies that organization should be designed to suit situational circumstances, but it also implies that such circumstances may be taken as given. This latter presumption is not wholly acceptable for two reasons. First, a review of research and discussion on business organizations led the present writer to conclude that if there are limits within which their size, technology, and mode of adjustment to the environment should fall if they are to obtain a high level of economic performance, then these limits do not as yet seem capable of precise definition (Child 1969a: pp. 95–8). Certainly, it is possible to find financially successful business firms operating in a great variety of different circumstances even within the same industry, although it does remain true that the degree of long-term security which they enjoy will probably vary with their size. Economic performance does not appear to be a simple function of an organization's operating circumstances. This helps to explain the second point, which is that the directorates of organizations do in practice over a period of time modify the circumstances in which their organization is operating, and equally that they sometimes refuse to make such changes even when these become possible. The manipulation of situational variables in the light of goals which have been formulated for an organization and in the light of an assessment of its capabilities is, along with adjustments to the goals and capabilities, precisely denoted by the concept of 'corporate strategy'.

We are here reminded again of the way in which a great deal of writing on organization fails to make any adequate reference to the influence of policy formation. For instance, contingency theory postulates environment to be a major constraint upon effective organizational design, but we would argue that this conclusion is inadequate without prior reference to the strategy adopted by organizational decision makers towards the environment. They may well have certain opportunities to select the type of environment in which their organization will operate. Thus business men may have a choice between new markets to enter, educators may exclude certain subjects from their institution's courses, trade union officers may decide on bounds to the types of members recruited. Secondly, larger organizations at least may command sufficient power to enable their policy makers to influence the conditions within environments in which they are already operating. The debate surrounding Galbraith's thesis (1967), that the large business corporation in modern industrial society has a considerable ability to manipulate and even create a demand for its product, centres on this very point. Some degree of environmental selection is open to those in control of most organizations, and some degree of environmental manipulation is open to those in control of most larger organizations.

It has been suggested that such strategies vis-à-vis the environment will reflect the attempts of organizational decision makers to attain their objectives with some degree of certainty (Cyert and March 1963). Stymne made a similar point when he concluded from his detailed studies of three Swedish organizations that 'the problems facing the different organizations can only be explained in connection with simultaneous reference to the environment of the organizations *and* to the established values existing in the organizations' (1970: p. 312). Environmental contingencies cannot therefore be regarded as entirely autonomous from organizational influence. Nor is it adequate to conclude that environmental circumstances determine intra-organizational features in any direct relationship, since important elements of choice are found empirically to intervene. Essentially the same conclusion is reached from a consideration of other situational factors such as size and technology (Child 1972).

In conclusion, the contingency approach does draw attention to certain constraints upon the choice of organization which derive from a need to accommodate to circumstances prevailing in the situation. However, it provides an unduly conservative assessment of the possibilities which probably exist to operate socially preferred forms of organization without incurring significant economic costs because:

1. it overlooks the fact that political and ideological referents already operate in the process of organizational design in addition to the 'technical' referents emphasized in administrative theory;
2. the standards of economic performance against which the consequences of adopting different organizational forms are assessed, are themselves open to some degree of discretion and choice;
3. there is evidence to suggest that within given situations an important degree of choice is available between different modes of organization, without serious diseconomies being incurred;
4. some degree of choice may also be available to organizational decision makers in the long term with regard to situational factors themselves.

These criticisms of the contingency approach suggest that

247

it does not provide an adequate theory of organizational development. In rejecting it as unduly conservative we also have in mind the possibility that the contingency approach may be used for its ideological potential in defence of the *status quo* in contemporary forms of organization. In the light of our argument that there appears to be no overriding objection on the grounds of economic effectiveness to the exploration of new forms of organization, it is appropriate to remind ourselves about the main social consequences of present-day organization and about some of the emergent forces in society which are likely to challenge that mode of organization because of its social consequences. These are the factors which give the question of man and organization its social relevance.

SOCIAL CONSEQUENCES OF ORGANIZATION

Organizations in industry and in other sectors of society have been growing steadily larger. Many of them are now vast aggregations of economic and administrative power. Their elaborate formal structures are the mechanisms designed to translate the hand of the top policy maker upon the levers of power into planned action. Yet, the distance at which organizational structures hold the mass of employees and the general public from the determination of policies that directly affect the conduct of their lives, and the constraining effects of bureaucratic forms upon the meaning and scope permitted to people in their everyday work, are also the very features which have often been described as the root causes of alienation in modern society.

While modern formal organization as we know it is unquestionably a powerful instrument for the provision of desired goods and services on a scale and with an economy previously unknown, it also imposes considerable limitations upon our lives. So far as the public in general is concerned, whether one considers industry, government, or social services, formal organization is the institutionalized means for effecting decisions which establish limits to our freedom as consumers, employees, law-abiding citizens, tax payers, patients, and so on. Most of us work in formal organizations, and the structures of differential power, reward, opportunity, and security which characterize organizations today constitute an important foundation of social stratification within modern society as a whole. In addition, structual arrangements in organizations shape the pervasive environment of what is still the greater part of our waking lives. This environment has a direct bearing upon the quality of experience enjoyed by people at work. Quality of experience at work may, in turn, have profound and largely unresearched long-term consequences for a person's ability to retain the psychological resources necessary for achieving as fully satisfying a life as is potentially open to him (cf. Parker 1971).

The sociological literature suggests that three commonly found structural characteristics of work organization can present socially problematic consequences. Its centralized source of authority tends to create a generalized sense of individual power-lessness and dissatisfaction (cf. Aiken and Hage 1966), which is particularly focused by issues such as redundancy and which has only partly been offset by collective employee organization. Its hierarchical grading of rewards and status is a major basis of inequality in society; it is also an important dimension of conflict both across different levels of management, and between managements and employees (cf. Parker *et al.* 1972). Thirdly, the tendency towards a bureaucratic mode of control which is generally found in all but small organizations often creates a sense of alienation for those who are subjected to it, because of the constraints inherent in its fragmented system of roles narrowly defined by procedure and red tape (cf. Shepard 1971).

Despite the broad sweep of these generalizations and evidence that the deprivations they express are not personally experienced to the same degree by all types of employee, they are sufficiently reflected in the results of the available research to warrant both serious consideration at the present and further study in the future. I would also suggest that considerable care has to be taken with any conclusion that employees have today success-fully accommodated themselves to organizational deprivation, which may be drawn from evidence that certain types of employees have voluntarily chosen to accept alienating jobs which offer relatively high levels of extrinsic reward. For the choice is a 'forced' one as between intrinsic and extrinsic benefits and it does not follow that such employees will not welcome as a positive benefit the reshaping of work roles so as to increase their levels of responsibility and interest, and the quality of workplace social interaction they permit. Thus, Cotgrove *et al.* conclude from their study of 'job enrichment' among nylon spinners: 'We cannot deduce from the fact that workers appeared to be attracted mainly by the money that their involvement in work is purely instrumental. Our evidence shows that there are latent needs which surface when there are opportunities for their satisfaction' (1971: p. 134). Other studies of job enrichment have also concluded that such changes in organization are highly valued by the employees concerned (e.g. Daniel 1970, Paul and Robertson 1970).

Argyris (1958) has employed the concept of a 'psychological work contract' to describe the trading-off by employees of personal costs in deprivating work situations against the largely monetary benefits obtainable from doing the work. The finding of most job satisfaction studies that the majority of employees express satisfaction with their job has to be assessed in the light of this 'contract', that is, in the light of what was expected from work compared to what has been secured, and without reference to any possibility that through experimentation the cost side of the psychological work contract could be reduced. In this regard the expectations of work held by employees may reflect their own adherence to a conventional wisdom that 'things *have* to be done this way here', an attitude which Edwards and Kynaston-Reeves (1971) found among the confectionery workers whom they studied. It has often been said that job satisfaction surveys do not give an accurate picture of the true feelings held by employees about their work, and we would certainly be rash to conclude from evidence that employees express acceptance and even satisfaction with work in modern organization that they would not experience as important benefits changes in the form of that organization.

The results of experiments which have involved modifications, albeit generally limited ones, to a centralized rationale of authority in organization also tend to confirm that such a system imposes unnecessary social and even economic costs. Such developments have entailed, in common with the other changes mentioned, a reduction of restrictions and controls (whether impersonally or personally activated) in favour of greater responsibility and scope for employees. A number of British experiments in the field of industrial participation have produced greater job satisfaction, and often improved rewards to employees and higher levels of economic performance (cf. Butteriss 1971). Indeed, the degree of success so far achieved in producing positive net benefits through such schemes is remarkable when one considers the lack of substantial British experience in implementing and running them, and also in view of the fact that their effective operation requires a shift away from the ingrained attitudes of both managements and employees.

The case for regarding the design of organization not just as a 'technical' problem of securing effective and economic administrative action, but also as a subject for evaluation by reference to broader social criteria, is thus acceptable not only on *a priori* grounds, but also in the light of emerging research findings. Because organization constitutes a system of specified authority relationships having wide ramifications throughout society, it has always in practice been subjected to criteria of social legitimacy as well as to those of economic efficiency. Indeed, if the prevailing forms of organization fail to meet one set of criteria, it is unlikely that they will succeed in completely meeting the other set. A failure to recognize that management faces both a legitimatory and a technical problem (Child 1969b) is perhaps the most serious theoretical deficiency in present-day contingency theories of organization. In the light of a growing challenge to conventional modes of organization, a theory which overlooks the question of legitimacy is likely to prove a poor guide in conditions where there will be a premium for devising radically new forms of collective activity.

ORGANIZATIONAL CHOICE AS AN EMERGENT SOCIAL ISSUE

Much of today's accepted wisdom on organization is fundamentally conservative. Relatively few writers on the subject appear to question the assumption that matters of organizational design represent technical questions which have to be left to appropriately qualified experts. The structure and content of present-day business education reflects the view that access to decision making on such matters depends on surviving a process of rigorous selection and subsequently upon acquiring relevant knowledge and experience. Considerable scepticism is usually expressed about the ability of lower level employees to make a significant contribution to the running of large and complex modern units, and also about their interest in sharing in decision making in the first place. When groups of these self-same employees demonstrate managerial ability, as with the work-in at Upper Clyde Shipbuilders, or in the running of a lengthy unofficial strike as at Pilkingtons, great surprise is expressed, not least by managers themselves (cf. Roberts 1971).

A critical examination of the current trend in writing on organization led us to the view that the 'technicality' of this aspect of management is to some degree mythical. There is probably far more freedom of choice in the design of organization than one would conclude from a reading of this literature. The exercise of choice in practice emerges as a political process in which decisions or organization are influenced by the values of those persons or groups with some power in the decision-making process. Once it is appreciated that a political process is involved, then the question naturally arises as to what range of values, what frame of reference, should be regarded as appropriate for decisions on the design of organization. There would seem to be little *prima facie* reason why this frame of reference should be confined to the values and interests held by directoral groups rather than being extended to encompass those of groups who are affected in one way or another by the operations of the unit in question.

There are, indeed, signs that in the future there will be mounting pressure for decisions on organization (and on other aspects of industrial policy) to be made with prior reference to a much broader framework of costs and benefits than is normally the case today. This requirement for a broader basis of evaluation will be part and parcel of a demand for a greater degree of participation in decision making on the shape and operating rationale of our major institutions in society. We see the approach of this new social outlook in a number of current developments, particularly those concerned with education.

The educational process both shapes and reflects the view of the world held by young people. Educators are themselves being increasingly urged to prepare children to acquire an open-minded, questioning, and adaptive orientation which, it is argued, can alone equip them to cope adequately with exponentially increasing rates of change. Existing institutional structures organized on the basis of the bureaucratic routinization of precedent, and indeed, a reliance upon experience in any form, are now coming to be questioned as useful points of reference in the educative process (e.g. Postman and Weingartner 1971). These views may still be avant garde, but there are many signs that young people have themselves already begun to regard their existing institutional environments in a more critical light, to challenge the conventional, and above all to withhold legitimacy from authority that is not derived from a demonstrable contribution to knowledge or well-being through utilizable competence. The breakdown of authority in schools is now the most common complaint among teachers.

Assuming these changing outlooks are sufficiently deep-rooted to survive, there is some reason to expect that the new generations of entrants to the world of organized work will keenly examine the rationale of organization, both in terms of what is claimed for it and in regard to its external social effects. The first manifestations of this development are already beginning to appear, in the United States at least, as college-educated young people exhibit an apparently growing antipathy towards pursuing careers in large bureaucracies and a generally negative attitude towards authority (Miner 1971). A comparison of studies of American college students from 1958 to 1968 showed that their average scores on the Rokeach Dogmatism Scale (which is an indicator of conservative thinking and of willingness to accept received wisdom) declined significantly over the period. This finding would seem to substantiate the oft-made comparison between the 'silent' student generation of the 1950s and the 'activists' of the 1960s (Ondrack 1971). Ondrack also concludes that organizations which continue to function on traditional authoritarian lines will increasingly fail to attract qualified personnel unless their style is changed. He points out that authoritarianism has been found to vary inversely with level of education, which with the post-Robbins expansion of British higher education and with increasing numbers staying on beyond the school-leaving age, holds out its own prediction of impending challenge to existing modes of organization in Britain.

It is probably a combination of rising educational levels over a higher proportion of the general population and of the revolution in visual mass communications which has already

253

promoted a notable expansion and cohesion of demands that industrial activities be subject to a broader evaluation than merely the profit and loss account. Naderism, a movement which shows every sign of spreading, represents a new activism not only in support of consumer values, but also in support of the rights of the individual within organizations themselves. The 'right to work' and the 'right to participate' have in Britain today gained widespread acceptance at the level of principle, although one still has to look far and wide to find them translated into practice. Nevertheless, the precedents now established by workers' takeovers, the benefits which have accrued to employees from pushing forward the boundaries of workplace control, the experience of industrial particpation and of job enrichment, are all likely to stimulate the demand for more advance along similar lines, particularly if and when the pressing problem of unemployment has eased.

There is today a substantial weight of 'informed opinion' in favour of applying a social cost-benefit philosophy to evaluating the external effects of industrial activity such as pollution. Pollution is, of course, highly visible and its cost can be measured dramatically in terms of the incidence of illness and even life and death. However, there is no reason, at least in principle, why we should not envisage an extension of this perspective to an issue such as the design of organization in its broadest terms. Indeed, one would predict growing pressure for such a development to emanate from the changes in outlook among young educated people which have been mentioned. Knowledge and awareness of the economic and social consequences of alternative modes of organization are still extremely slight and there are as yet only a few clues to the choices that are available. Nevertheless, it should not be forgotten that attempts to apply a wider social evaluation through cost-benefit analysis have themselves, as in the Third London Airport study, created knowledge and awareness. By stimulating research into methods of evaluating costs and benefits previously regarded as entirely intangible, such attempts have generated new knowledge. They have also been vehicles for arousing a wider public awareness of the conflict of values and interests at issue—for example in the Airport study, the conflict between convenience to the air-travelling public and preservation of the countryside.

If, as has been argued in this chapter, it is incorrect to assume that normally very little choice is available between alternative organizational designs, then there would seem to be considerable opportunity for further study to be made of how a social cost-benefit type of perspective may be applied to this area of decision making. The techniques required would involve an extension and considerable refinement of the organizational, behavioural, and perceptual measurements already available. The institutional means for such a development would have to include an extension of participation in the formulation of organizational strategy, a participation which would certainly embrace employees and possibly other interested parties. If such a process were extended through the various sections and levels of organizations so that it was founded upon a framework of opportunities for direct participation, then this development would itself probably represent a substantial longterm social gain in terms of widely held values such as involvement in democratic processes and the opportunity to assume responsibility.

What is being proposed is not a dissolution of order in industry in favour of some form of anarchy, but an active search for new foundations of order. This is, I would suggest, one of the most important subjects to which the social scientist concerned with industrial developments can direct his energies. The field of organizational design remains wide open to an exploration of new methods by which criteria of social wellbeing can be accommodated with the maintenance (and even improvement) of economic performance. Wisdom on this issue does not lie with the conventional.

REFERENCES

AIKEN, M. and HAGE, J. 1966. 'Organizational alienation: a comparative analysis', *American Sociological Review*, 31, 497–507.

ARGYRIS, C. 1958. 'The organization: what makes it healthy?', *Harvard Business Review*, 36, 107–16.

ARGYRIS, C. 1964. *Integrating the individual and the organization*, New York: Wiley.

BARITZ, L. 1960. *The servants of power*, Middletown, Conn.: Wesleyan University Press.

BARNARD, C. I. 1938. *Functions of the executive*, Cambridge, Mass.: Harvard University Press.

BLAU, P. M. and SCHOENHERR, R. A. 1971. *The structure of organizations*, New York: Basic Books.

BROOKS, J. 1971. *Business adventures*, Harmondsworth: Penguin Books.

BUTTERISS, M. 1971. *Job enrichment and employee participation – a study*, London: Institute of Personnel Management.

CHILD, J. 1969a. *The business enterprise in modern industrial society*, London: Collier-Macmillan.

CHILD, J. 1969b. *British management thought*, London: Allen and Unwin.

CHILD, J. 1972. 'Organizational structure, environment and performance – the role of strategic choice', *Sociology*, 6, 1–22.

CLIFF, T. 1970. *The employers' offensive*, London: Pluto Press.

COTGROVE, S., DUNHAM, J., VAMPLEW, C. 1971. *The nylon spinners*, London: Allen and Unwin.

CYERT, R. M. and MARCH, J. G. 1963. *A behavioural theory of the firm*, Englewood Cliffs, N.J.: Prentice-Hall.

DANIEL, W. W. 1970. *Beyond the wage-work bargain*, London: PEP.

DUBIN, R. 1962. 'Businesss behaviour behaviourally viewed', in G. B. Strother (ed.), *Social science approaches to business behaviour*, London: Tavistock.

EDWARDS, C. and KYNASTON-REEVES, T. 1971. 'Explaining attitudes to work: a study of confectionery workers', paper given to the Third Joint Conference on the Behavioural Sciences and Operational Research, London.

GALBRAITH, J. K. 1967. *The new industrial state*, London: Hamilton.

JAY, A. 1967. *Management and Machiavelli*, London: Hodder and Stoughton.

LAWRENCE, P. R. and LORSCH, J. W. 1967. *Organization and environment*, Boston: Harvard Business School.

LAWRENCE, P. R. and LORSCH, J. W. 1969. *Developing organizations: diagnosis and action*, Reading, Mass.: Addison-Welsey.

LUPTON, T. 1971. *Management and the social sciences*, 2nd ed., Harmondsworth: Penguin Books.

MILLER, E. J. and RICE, A. K. 1967. *Systems of organization*, London: Tavistock.

MINER, J. B. 1971. 'Changes in student attitudes toward bureaucratic role prescriptions during the 1960s', *Administrative Science Quarterly*, 16, 351–64.

256

NORMANN, R. 1971. 'Organizational innovativeness: product variation and reorientation', *Administrative Science Quarterly*, 16, 203–15.

ONDRACK, D. A. 1971. 'Examining the generation gap: attitudes towards authority', *Personnel Administration*, May–June, 9–17.

PARKER, S. R. 1971. *The future of work and leisure*, London: MacGibbon and Kee.

PARKER, S. R., BROWN, R. K., CHILD, J., SMITH, M. A. 1972. *The sociology of industry*, 2nd ed., London: Allen and Unwin.

PAUL, W. J. and ROBERTSON, K. B. 1970. *Job enrichment and employee motivation*, London: Gower Press.

PERROW, C. 1970. *Organizational analysis: a sociological view*, London: Tavistock.

POSTMAN, N. and WEINGARTNER, C. 1971. *Teaching as a subversive activity*, Harmondsworth: Penguin Books.

PUGH, D. S., HICKSON, D. J., HININGS, C. R., TURNER, C. 1969. 'The context of organization structures', *Administrative Science Quarterly*, 14, 91–114.

RICE, A. K. 1958. *Productivity and social organization*, London: Tavistock.

ROBERTS, K. 1971. 'Militancy and conflict: some dimensions of the Pilkington case', paper given to the Third Joint Conference on the Behavioural Sciences and Operational Research, London.

SHEPARD, J. M. 1971. *Automation and alienation*, London: MIT Press.

SILVERMAN, D. 1970. *The theory of organizations*, London: Heinemann.

SIMON, H. A. 1960. *The new science of management decision*, New York: Harper.

STYMNE, B. 1970. *Values and processes*, Lund: SIAR.

THORSRUD, E. 1970. 'A strategy for research and social change in industry', *Social Science Information*, 9, 65–90.

TRIST, E. L., HIGGIN, G. W., MURRAY, H., POLLOCK, A. B. 1963. *Organizational choice*, London: Tavistock.

URWICK, L. 1933. 'Organization as a technical problem', reprinted in L. Gulick and L. Urwick (eds.), *Papers on the science of administration*, New York: Columbia University Press, 1937.

WOODWARD, J. 1965. *Industrial organization – theory and practice*, London: Oxford University Press.

R

Index

258